Torque 3D Game Development Cookbook

Over 80 practical recipes and hidden gems for getting the most out of the Torque 3D game engine

David Wyand

[PACKT]
PUBLISHING

BIRMINGHAM - MUMBAI

Torque 3D Game Development Cookbook

First published: January 2013

Production Reference: 1180113

Published by Packt Publishing Ltd.
Livery Place
35 Livery Street
Birmingham B3 2PB, UK.

ISBN 978-1-84969-354-7

www.packtpub.com

Cover Image by Valentina D'silva

Credits

Author

David Wyand

Reviewers

Logan Foster

Ahmad Iftikhar

Konrad Kiss

Chip Lambert

Acquisition Editor

Kartikey Pandey

Lead Technical Editor

Arun Nadar

Technical Editors

Prasanna Joglekar

Merin Jose

Dominic Pereira

Copy Editor

Ruta Waghmare

Project Coordinator

Anurag Banerjee

Proofreaders

Clyde Jenkins

Dirk Manuel

Indexer

Monica Ajmera Mehta

Graphics

Valentina D'silva

Production Coordinator

Pooja Chiplunkar

Cover Work

Pooja Chiplunkar

About the Author

David Wyand grew up in Toronto, Canada, and graduated in Chemical Engineering from the University of Toronto in 1994. Following graduation, he went to run the network management system at a major telecommunications company; did freelance 2D compositing and 3D animation work for the Toronto entertainment industry; and started his own consulting firm to set up network management systems at various telecommunications and power companies in Canada and the U.S. He then left that behind to work in the video game industry.

Starting with the successful 2005 launch of a tool for game artists to visualize their work in real time, he moved on to game engine development. In 2006, he joined GarageGames as a full-time contractor and has been working with them ever since. During this time he has had his hands in nearly every game engine the company has released. Today he is the Head of Torque 3D Development at GarageGames.

In 2009 he started Gnometech Inc. (`http://www.gnometech.com`) to begin developing his own commercial games. In 2010 he released Greenwood Faire, a web-based 3D world in a medieval setting. Since then he has created other online 3D worlds under the `Zworldo.com` banner, and is looking to the future of virtual reality and unique input devices.

Big thanks to Julie, Matthew, Malcolm, and Melanie for their love and support. Especially Julie, who took the kids away many a day so I could write. I also want to thank my mom and dad for all the usual reasons.

About the Reviewers

Logan Foster is the Art Director for Fluik Entertainment Inc., a mobile game development studio based in Edmonton, Alberta.

As a 13-year veteran of 3D and 2D art development and production design and development for games and digital media, he has contributed to over a dozen original IP and contract PC/ Mac, console, mobile, social, serious, and web-based games during his career.

Outside of his normal work duties, he also contributes as a private beta tester for Autodesk, has spoken at several independent game development festivals on the topic of art production for games, and in 2009 helped co-found and continues to help run GameCamp Edmonton, an industry organization whose goal is to help further advocate and network the game development industry in Alberta.

> I would like to thank my wife Erin and kids Nathan and Seraphina for putting up with all the long hours and craziness that comes with working in the game industry.

Ahmad Iftikhar, 25, is the CEO of a cutting edge design and development company, Creativebugs Pvt. Ltd.

He received his B.Sc. Honors degree in Multimedia with majors in game designing from the University of South Asia, Lahore, Pakistan.

He has over 6 years of experience in design and development, and has expertise on in various tools including Autodesk 3DS Max, Maya, Zbrush, Adobe Photoshop, illustrator, After effects Premiere, Unreal Engine, Cry Engine, Crytek, Unity3D, and Torque.

He has worked on a number of projects for renowned organizations including iWin, Digital Chocolate, Game View Studios, Tintash, Sandlot Games, Bramerz, Hands-on, and several Google-affiliated products. He has also rendered his services for National Guard Services, on the Pennsylvania Project.

He has a number of projects to his credit including Coconut Queen, Tap Fish, Tap Ranch, and several other 3D game projects based on game engines.

Konrad Kiss is a programmer by profession with over 16 years of field experience. He is a co-founder and acting CTO of the Hungary, Europe based independent game developer studio, Bitgap. His field of expertise primarily includes massively multiplayer architectures and strategic game design. He received a honorary associate status from GarageGames in 2009.

In his free time he enjoys exploring new possibilities in cloud computing through Amazon Web Services. He is currently working on an HTML5 game framework focusing on multiplayer 2D action games supported by Amazon DyamoDB and a scalable Node.js based server architecture.

First of all, I'd like to thank my wife, Ildiko, for putting up with my crazy work schedules and my kids, Lia and David, who would always help me rediscover true fun in playing games.

I'd like to thank the Torque community for being friendly and professional. They kept me going even when it was overwhelmingly hard. I also owe a great deal to David Wyand, the author of this magnificent book, along with Steve Acaster, Daniel Buckmaster, Rene Damm, Ben Garney, Michael Hall, Manoel Neto, Phillip O'Shea, Chris Robertson, Tom Spilman, and of course the entire team at GarageGames—past and present. You guys are the best!

Chip Lambert has been a member of the GarageGames community since early 2002 and has followed each iteration of the Torque engine since then. He owns Crusader Games, a small independent company in southern West Virginia that uses the Torque engine family and publishes tabletop RPG supplements. When not trying to change the world with his products, he works as an Applications Developer for Bluefield College.

I would like to thank my beautiful wife Kelley who is my moon and star, my true sunshine Kaitlyn, my mom, and of course dad, I still miss you. Thank you all for the love and encouragement. And of course everyone at GarageGames for their hard work over the years.

www.PacktPub.com

Support files, eBooks, discount offers and more

You might want to visit www.PacktPub.com for support files and downloads related to your book.

Did you know that Packt offers eBook versions of every book published, with PDF and ePub files available? You can upgrade to the eBook version at www.PacktPub.com and as a print book customer, you are entitled to a discount on the eBook copy. Get in touch with us at service@packtpub.com for more details.

At www.PacktPub.com, you can also read a collection of free technical articles, sign up for a range of free newsletters and receive exclusive discounts and offers on Packt books and eBooks.

http://PacktLib.PacktPub.com

Do you need instant solutions to your IT questions? PacktLib is Packt's online digital book library. Here, you can access, read and search across Packt's entire library of books.

Why Subscribe?

- Fully searchable across every book published by Packt
- Copy and paste, print and bookmark content
- On demand and accessible via web browser

Free Access for Packt account holders

If you have an account with Packt at www.PacktPub.com, you can use this to access PacktLib today and view nine entirely free books. Simply use your login credentials for immediate access.

Table of Contents

Preface

Torque 3D is a low cost, fully featured game engine that provides a time-tested foundation in multiplayer networking and a next generation graphics engine. This game engine provides the TorqueScript scripting language to allow users to start building their games, and also full source code to the engine when users are serious about making the game engine their own. Torque 3D comes with a suite of tools that allows the user to craft their game worlds, and supports industry standard file formats for graphics and sound. Torque 3D also supports using Physics third-party libraries, such as PhysX and Bullet, and the FMOD sound library when the user wants to take advantage of what these libraries have to offer.

Out-of-the-box Torque 3D allows the user to create a wide variety of games without needing to look to other sources to fill in the gaps, other than the usual graphics and sound editing tools, of course. This plus access to source code is the reason, a number of educational institutions are using Torque 3D in their courses.

Torque 3D Game Engine Cookbook is a practical reference guide to the latest version of the Torque 3D game engine, and takes the reader beyond the basics provided by the GarageGames *FPS Tutorial*. Each chapter covers a common topic of game development, and exposes the reader to some less understood and hidden gems that developers may not come across through other material. By the end of the book, readers should come away with a better understanding of the internals of the Torque 3D game engine, and be inspired to try new things that they may not have thought of before.

What this book covers

Chapter 1, TorqueScript: The Only Script You Need to Know, covers the scripting language of Torque 3D. TorqueScript is used to define game objects and to create the rules of play. This chapter teaches some important— and often lesser known – TorqueScript concepts and shortcuts.

Chapter 2, Working with Your Editors, looks at using the various editors that are part of Torque 3D that are used to build your game. Many of these recipes will help you work faster, or help add that extra bit of polish and performance to your game.

Chapter 3, Graphical User Interface, discusses some important graphical user interface concepts that often come up while working on a game, but whose information can be hard to come by. The recipes in this chapter make use of Torque 3D's built-in GUI editor to arrange controls, as well as TorqueScript to define how the controls operate.

Chapter 4, Camera and Mouse Controls, explores the various camera types available in Torque 3D, and their control by the user and the game. Beyond controlling the in-game camera, this chapter also covers using the mouse to manipulate objects within a game.

Chapter 5, Your Graphics Evolved, introduces Torque 3D's graphics pipeline through the creation of custom-coded materials and postFx. This includes taking advantage of Torque 3D's advanced lighting model. This chapter also covers using the built-in video recording features of Torque 3D.

Chapter 6, Make That Sound Happen, is where we discover the various methods of playing sound effects in Torque 3D and when to use them. This chapter also touches on how to modify a game's music or other sound according to the current gameplay mood.

Chapter 7, Game Objects, takes us into the details of some of the objects that make up a game's atmosphere. This includes background animation, precipitation, lightning, and triggering events throughout an in-game day.

Chapter 8, Multiplayer Servers, shows us how to start up and allow others to connect to our game, as well as how to administer it. In addition, we discover how to access the player's connections on a client or server, and how to broadcast a message to all connected players.

Chapter 9, Importance of Networking, provides several examples of connecting Torque 3D to various external network services, and how to make Torque 3D respond to network requests. This chapter also covers how to send event messages between a game's clients and server.

Chapter 10, Miscellaneous Gameplay Features, looks at the various parts of Torque 3D that help you expand on the gameplay rules that are already available, as well as how to build your own. This includes modifying how player and weapon objects function, finding any objects within a given range, and making use of Torque 3D's message producer/consumer system.

What you need for this book

Torque 3D Game Development Cookbook is useful for the majority of Torque 3D developers. Each chapter covers a common topic of game development, starting with TorqueScript, the scripting language of Torque 3D used to define game objects and build gameplay rules. It is expected that the reader has completed the *FPS Tutorial* available on the GarageGames site (www.garagegames.com/products/torque-3d) or the equivalent. A basic understanding of TorqueScript and using Torque 3D's built-in editors is required.

Torque 3D is now an open source product under the MIT license, and is available for free to everyone. Links to the latest version and other useful information is available from the Torque 3D product page on the GarageGames site at `www.garagegames.com/products/torque-3d`. The source code and example templates are also available directly from the GitHub repository at `www.github.com/GarageGames/Torque3D`. In order to compile the game engine from the source code you will need to have access to Visual Studio. You may also download a precompiled package by following the instructions on the Torque 3D GitHub repository.

Any text editor may be used to create and edit TorqueScript files. Torsion, a commercial TorqueScript editor, may be used as an alternative. It is available for purchase from the GarageGames web store.

Who this book is for

Torque 3D Game Development Cookbook is aimed at developers that are interested is working with the latest version of the Torque 3D game engine. This book will be helpful for developers that have already gone through the *FPS Tutorial* on the GarageGames site and are looking for more information on getting the most out of Torque 3D.

Conventions

In this book, you will find a number of styles of text that distinguish between different kinds of information. Here are some examples of these styles, and an explanation of their meaning.

Code words in text are shown as follows: Change its `noCursor` property from a value of `1` to a value of `0`.

A block of code is set as follows:

```
%val1 = "1 2 3";
%val2 = setWord( %val1, 5, "4" );
echo( getWordCount( %val2 ) );
```

When we wish to draw your attention to a particular part of a code block, the relevant lines or items are set in bold:

```
// Load up the Game GUIs
    exec("art/gui/defaultGameProfiles.cs");
    exec("art/gui/PlayGui.gui");
    exec("art/gui/ChatHud.gui");
    exec("art/gui/playerList.gui");
    exec("art/gui/hudlessGui.gui");
    exec("art/gui/controlsHelpDlg.gui");
    exec("art/gui/mainmenulevel.gui");
    exec("art/gui/mainmenulevelsplash.gui");
```

Any command-line input or output is written as follows:

```
operateOnFields1();
```

New terms and **important words** are shown in bold. Words that you see on the screen, in menus or dialog boxes for example, appear in the text like this: " Drag-and-drop the **GuiTextEditCtrl** control on to Canvas of the editor to the left-hand side.".

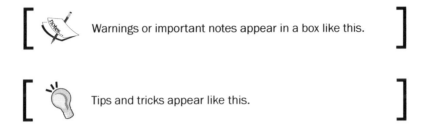

Warnings or important notes appear in a box like this.

Tips and tricks appear like this.

Reader feedback

Feedback from our readers is always welcome. Let us know what you think about this book—what you liked or may have disliked. Reader feedback is important for us to develop titles that you really get the most out of.

To send us general feedback, simply send an e-mail to feedback@packtpub.com, and mention the book title via the subject of your message.

If there is a topic that you have expertise in and you are interested in either writing or contributing to a book, see our author guide on www.packtpub.com/authors.

Customer support

Now that you are the proud owner of a Packt book, we have a number of things to help you to get the most from your purchase.

Downloading the color images of this book

We also provide you a PDF file that has color images of the screenshots used in this book. The color images will help you better understand the changes in the output. You can download this file from http://www.packtpub.com/sites/default/files/downloads/3547OT_Images.pdf.

Downloading the example code

You can download the example code files for all Packt books you have purchased from your account at `http://www.PacktPub.com`. If you purchased this book elsewhere, you can visit `http://www.PacktPub.com/support` and register to have the files e-mailed directly to you.

Errata

Although we have taken every care to ensure the accuracy of our content, mistakes do happen. If you find a mistake in one of our books—maybe a mistake in the text or the code—we would be grateful if you would report this to us. By doing so, you can save other readers from frustration and help us improve subsequent versions of this book. If you find any errata, please report them by visiting `http://www.packtpub.com/support`, selecting your book, clicking on the **errata submission form** link, and entering the details of your errata. Once your errata are verified, your submission will be accepted and the errata will be uploaded on our website, or added to any list of existing errata, under the Errata section of that title. Any existing errata can be viewed by selecting your title from `http://www.packtpub.com/support`.

Piracy

Piracy of copyright material on the Internet is an ongoing problem across all media. At Packt, we take the protection of our copyright and licenses very seriously. If you come across any illegal copies of our works, in any form, on the Internet, please provide us with the location address or website name immediately so that we can pursue a remedy.

Please contact us at `copyright@packtpub.com` with a link to the suspected pirated material.

We appreciate your help in protecting our authors, and our ability to bring you valuable content.

Questions

You can contact us at `questions@packtpub.com` if you are having a problem with any aspect of the book, and we will do our best to address it.

1

TorqueScript: The Only Script You Need to Know

In this chapter we will cover the following topics:

- ▸ Accessing delimited fields within a string
- ▸ Iterating on words in a string list
- ▸ Retrieving components of a variable using accessors
- ▸ Iterating on objects in a SimSet or SimGroup collection
- ▸ Getting a random object from a SimSet or SimGroup collection
- ▸ Finding an object in a SimSet or SimGroup collection using its internal name
- ▸ Executing a method on a SimSet or SimGroup collection
- ▸ Creating a new SimObject instance
- ▸ Creating a new internal name only SimObject instance
- ▸ Creating a new Datablock object
- ▸ Creating a new singleton
- ▸ Extending a SimObject instance using the class property
- ▸ Using a variable to access methods or properties of a SimObject instance
- ▸ Using call() to call a variable method on a SimObject instance with arguments
- ▸ Using call() to call a variable function with arguments
- ▸ Using script arrays as dictionaries

- ▶ Using `ArrayObject` and custom script sorting callbacks
- ▶ Scheduling `SimObject` methods
- ▶ Scheduling functions
- ▶ Activating and deactivating a package

Introduction

TorqueScript is the scripting language of the Torque 3D game engine. It is used to define game objects and to create the rules of play. It also forms the basis for manipulating the GUI system of Torque 3D.

All TorqueScript files have a `.cs` extension. These files may be edited with a standard text editor, or a program such as Torsion, which was made for working with TorqueScript. TorqueScript files may also be precompiled into `.dso` files. This is a binary representation of the TorqueScript code, and prevents others from modifying it. Very often a game will ship with only the precompiled `.dso` files.

In this chapter we will learn about some important–and often lesser known–TorqueScript concepts and shortcuts. Let's jump right in!

Accessing delimited fields within a string

When working with lists in TorqueScript, be it a list of scene object IDs or a set of Cartesian coordinates, we will invariably come across space-delimited strings. For example, calling the `getPosition()` method on a scene object will return a three-field string such as `13.4 -2.1 96.35` that represents the world distance along the x, y, and z axes, respectively.

TorqueScript provides a number of functions that allows us to access and manipulate the fields within space-delimited strings. In this recipe we will learn how to use these functions when working with string variables.

Getting ready

We will be adding a new TorqueScript function to a project based on the Torque 3D `Full` template and try it out using the `Empty Terrain` level. If you haven't already, use the Torque Project Manager (`Project Manager.exe`) to create a new project from the `Full` template. It will be found under the `My Projects` directory. Then start up your favorite script editor, such as Torsion, and let's get going!

How to do it...

We are going to write a TorqueScript function that will parse a space-delimited string and
output the results to the console. This is done as follows:

1. Open the game/scripts/client/client.cs script file and add the following
    code to the bottom:

```
function operateOnFields1()
{
    // Get the player's position in the world.
    // Will be a string in the form of "x y z".
    %position =
        ServerConnection.getControlObject().getPosition();

    // Print out the player's position to the
    // console in its raw format
    echo("Raw player position: " @ %position);

    // Get the number of fields in the returned
    // position string
    %count = getWordCount(%position);

    // Print the value of each field to the console
    echo("Player position by field index:");
    for (%i=0; %i<%count; %i++)
    {
        echo("   " @ %i @ ": " @ getWord(%position, %i));
    }

    // Print out only the x and y fields
    echo("Player x and y position only: "
            @ getWords(%position, 0, 1));

    // Set the 3rd field (the z value) to 0
    %position = setWord(%position, 2, "0");
    echo("Position variable with new z value: " @ %position);
```

```
      // Remove the z value (3rd field) to only be
      // left with "x y"
      %position = removeWord(%position, 2);
      echo("Position variable with no z value: " @ %position);
   }
```

2. Start up our game under the `My Projects` directory and load the `Empty Terrain` level. Open the console using the tilde (~) key and enter the following at the bottom of the screen:

   ```
   operateOnFields1();
   ```

   In the console we will see the following output:

   ```
   ==>operateOnFields1();
   Raw player position: 0.121759 1.13497 240.67
   Player position by field index:
      0: 0.121759
      1: 1.13497
      2: 240.67
   Player x and y position only: 0.121759 1.13497
   Position variable with new z value: 0.121759 1.13497 0
   Position variable with no z value: 0.121759 1.13497
   ```

How it works...

The previous code walks us through all of the functions used to access and manipulate the variables that contain space-delimited fields. We will now examine each of these functions and learn how to make use of them.

After obtaining the player's world position, our first action in the previous example is to get the number of fields within the space-delimited string (the `%position` variable). This is done using the `getWordCount()` function that has the following form:

```
amount = getWordCount( string );
```

In this form, `string` is the space-delimited string that contains the number of fields we want to eventually parse. The `getWordCount()` function returns the number of fields counted. The previous code stores this value into the `%count` variable. If there are no fields in the string, then `0` is returned.

With the number of fields now known, we can retrieve the individual x, y, and z values of the `%position` variable based on an index. To do this we use the `getWord()` function that has the following form:

```
field = getWord( string, index );
```

Here, the `string` parameter is the space-delimited string to parse, and the `index` parameter is the field number to retrieve. The `getWord()` function returns a string containing the single requested field. If the field index does not exist within the passed-in string, an empty string is returned.

The next action performed in the example code is to retrieve more than one field at a time. Specifically, the code extracts the x and y values from the player's position (the first and second field). We use the `getWords()` function to retrieve more than one field, which has the following form:

```
fields = getWords( string, startIndex, [endIndex] );
```

Here, the `string` parameter is the space-delimited string to parse, the `startIndex` parameter is the start of the range to retrieve, and the optional `endIndex` parameter is the end of the field range. If `endIndex` is not provided or has a value of `-1`, then all of the fields at the end of the string are returned.

The `getWords()` function returns a string containing all of the requested fields. If none of the requested fields exist within the passed-in string, an empty string is returned.

The example code then goes on to manipulate the `%position` variable by changing its z value (the third field). This is done with the `setWord()` function that has the following form:

```
result = setWord( string, index, replacement );
```

Here, the `string` parameter is the space-delimited string to modify, the `index` parameter is the field index in the string to modify, and the `replacement` parameter is the string used to replace the current value of the field. The `setWord()` function returns a new string with the modifications and doesn't change the passed-in string. If we wanted to modify the original variable, we would just use the same variable name for the return value as we did for the passed-in string. For example, consider the following code:

```
%position = setWord(%position, 2, "0");
```

The new string will essentially replace the previous string stored in `%position`.

If the index passed-in to `setWord()` is larger than the number of fields in the given string, the returned string is padded with empty fields to make up the difference, essentially appending the replacement string on to the end. For example, the following code would print a count of six to the console (the fifth index accesses the sixth field):

```
%val1 = "1 2 3";
%val2 = setWord( %val1, 5, "4");
echo( getWordCount( %val2 ) );
```

The final action in the example code removes a field from the string variable. This is done using the `removeWord()` function that has the following form:

```
result = removeWord( string, index );
```

Here, the `string` parameter is the space-delimited string to modify, and the `index` parameter is the field index in the string to remove. The `removeWord()` function returns a new string with the modifications and doesn't change the passed-in string. If the given field index does not exist within the string, the original string is returned unchanged.

As with the `setWord()` function, if we want to modify the original variable, we would need to pass it in as the `string` parameter as well as use it to store the result. This is done in the example code with the `%position` variable.

There's more...

While space-delimited strings are the most common type of list we will come across in TorqueScript, spaces are not the only way to delimit a string. Tabs and new lines may also be used. We could use tab delimiters when we want the fields to contain spaces, and new line delimiters when we want the fields to contain spaces or tabs.

The whole *Word* family of functions we just explored (`getWord()` and so on) actually works with more than just spaces. They treat all the spaces, tabs, and new lines as valid delimiters. But what if we don't want to count spaces as a delimiter, such as with a list of peoples' combined first and last names ("John Smith")? There are two other families of functions that narrow the scope of what is a valid delimiter: *Field* and *Record*.

Skipping spaces (only tab and new line delimiters)

The *Field* family of functions performs all of the same operations as the *Word* family of functions, except they only use tabs and new lines as field delimiters. For example, put the following function at the end of the `game/scripts/client/client.cs` script file:

```
function operateOnFields2()
{
    // Build up a list of tab delimited name
    %list = "John Smith" TAB "Mary Contrary" TAB "Fido";

    // Get the number of tab delimited fields
    %count = getFieldCount(%list);

    // Print out a list of fields by index
    for (%i=0; %i<%count; %i++)
    {
        echo("Field " @ %i @ ": " @ getField(%list, %i));
    }
}
```

Start up our game under the `My Projects` directory and load the `Empty Terrain` level. Open the console using the tilde (~) key and enter the following at the bottom of the screen:

```
operateOnFields2();
```

The following will be output to the console:

```
==>operateOnFields2();
Field 0: John Smith
Field 1: Mary Contrary
Field 2: Fido
```

With the *Field* family of functions, any field that contains spaces is treated as a single field.

Skipping spaces and tabs (only new line delimiters)

The *Record* family of functions performs all of the same operations as the *Word* family of functions, except they only use new lines as field delimiters. For example, put the following function at the end of the `game/scripts/client/client.cs` script file:

```
function operateOnFields3()
{
    // Build up a list of new line delimited items
    %list = "0" TAB "First item" NL
            "1" TAB "Second item" NL
            "2" TAB "Third item";

    // Get the number of tab delimited fields
    %count = getRecordCount(%list);

    // Print out a list of fields by index
    for (%i=0; %i<%count; %i++)
    {
        echo("Field " @ %i @ ": '"
            @ getRecord(%list, %i) @ "'");
    }
}
```

Start up our game under the `My Projects` directory and load the `Empty Terrain` level. Open the console using the tilde (~) key and enter the following at the bottom of the screen:

```
operateOnFields3();
```

The following will be output to the console:

```
==>operateOnFields3();
Field 0: '0^First item'
Field 1: '1^Second item'
Field 2: '2^Third item'
```

In the console, the output above the caret (^) symbol represents a tab. With the *Record* family of functions, any field that contains spaces and tabs is treated as a single field.

See also

► *Iterating on words in a string list*

► *Retrieving components of a variable using accessors*

Iterating on words in a string list

While creating a game there are times that we need to step through a string list, one item at a time, and do some work on that item. An example could be a collection of object IDs produced by a volumetric search of the scene. We then want to do something with these found objects, such as possibly applying damage. In this recipe, we will learn a quick way to retrieve each item in a string list and do something with that item.

Getting ready

We will be adding some new TorqueScript functions to a project based on the Torque 3D `Full` template and try it out using the `Empty Terrain` level. If you haven't already, use the Torque Project Manager (`Project Manager.exe`) to create a new project from the `Full` template. It will be found under the `My Projects` directory. Then start up your favorite script editor, such as Torsion, and let's get going!

How to do it...

We are going to write a TorqueScript function that will retrieve each item from a string list and do some work on it as follows:

1. Open the `game/scripts/server/game.cs` script file and add the following code to the bottom:

```
function parseStringList1()
{
    // Populate a variable with some sample object ID's.
    //This could have come from an axis aligned bounding box
    //search in the scene.
    %objects = "1121 1122 1438 1643 2025 1118 1564";

    // Step through each object in the string list.
    // This string list could contain any valid
    // string characters and doesn't need to be
    // limited to object ID's.
    echo("-- Starting string list iteration");
    foreach$ (%id in %objects)
    {
        // Perform some action on the object
```

```
        doSomething(%id);
    }
    echo("-- Finished string list iteration");
}

function doSomething(%objID)
{
    // Print out the object ID to the console.
    echo("Processing object ID: " @ %objID);
}
```

2. Start up our game under the `My Projects` directory and load the `Empty Terrain` level. Open the console using the tilde (~) key and enter the following at the bottom of the screen:

   parseStringList1();

   In the console we will see the following output:

   ==>parseStringList1();
   -- Starting string list iteration
   Processing object ID: 1121
   Processing object ID: 1122
   Processing object ID: 1438
   Processing object ID: 1643
   Processing object ID: 2025
   Processing object ID: 1118
   Processing object ID: 1564
   -- Finished string list iteration

How it works...

The previous code uses the `foreach$()` function to retrieve each item in the string list and does some work on it. In this example, the item is passed on to another function.

The `foreach$()` function is different than most of the looping TorqueScript functions (such as `for()`) in that it takes two parameters that are separated by the `in` word rather than a semicolon. It is also unusual in that it creates a new variable to hold a string of the item. The `foreach$()` function has the following form:

```
foreach$( item in stringList)
{
    ... Do something with item ...
}
```

Here, the `stringList` parameter is the list of items to be processed, and the `item` parameter is a new variable that is created to hold a string of the item. It is the `item` variable that we work on. In our previous example this is the `%id` variable.

There's more...

There is another way to step through the items in a string by using the `getWordCount()` and `getWord()` functions. For example, put the following function at the end of the `game/scripts/server/game.cs` script file after the code we entered in the `foreach$()` example:

```
function parseStringList2()
{
    // Populate a variable with some sample object ID's.
    %objects = "1121 1122 1438 1643 2025 1118 1564";

    // Get the number of items in the string list
    %count = getWordCount(%objects);

    // Step through each object in the string list.
    // This string list could contain any valid string
    // characters and doesn't need to be limited to
    // object ID's.
    echo("-- Starting string list processing");
    for (%i=0; %i<%count; %i++)
    {
        // Get the object ID from the string list
        %id = getWord(%objects, %i);

        // Perform some action on the object
        doSomething(%id);
    }
    echo("-- Finished string list processing");
}
```

Start up our game under the `My Projects` directory and load the `Empty Terrain` level. Open the console using the tilde (~) key and enter the following at the bottom of the screen:

parseStringList2();

In the console we will see the following output:

==>parseStringList2();

-- Starting string list processing

Processing object ID: 1121

```
Processing object ID: 1122
Processing object ID: 1438
Processing object ID: 1643
Processing object ID: 2025
Processing object ID: 1118
Processing object ID: 1564
-- Finished string list processing
```

The results end up being the same as when we used the `foreach$()` function. So why would we use this method over the `foreach$()` method? Well, for one thing, we will see this pattern in a number of stock Torque 3D scripts that were written prior to `foreach$()` being added to the TorqueScript language. We will also see this pattern in a lot of game developers' script code, just because they are not aware of the newer `foreach$()` function (now you are one of the special ones that do know!).

One advantage of `foreach$()` over using the `getWordCount()` and `getWord()` patterns to step through a list–other than a lot less script code–is that you don't have to perform two calls into the engine (`getWordCount()` and `getWord()`); every call we don't have to make back to the engine is a performance increase.

But then why would we actively use this alternative pattern at all? It is the only way to work with the other types of delimiters, such as tab and a new line. By replacing `getWordCount()` and `getWord()` with `getFieldCount()` and `getField()` respectively, not spaces but only tabs and new lines are treated as delimiters, and by replacing them with `getRecordCount()` and `getRecord()`, neither spaces nor tabs, but only new lines are treated as delimiters. This allows us to work with different types of data.

See also

▸ *Accessing delimited fields within a string*

Retrieving components of a variable using accessors

Under TorqueScript position, vector, matrix, and color variables are all very similar. They are made up of a string with space-delimited components (or fields). For example, a position variable may be defined as follows:

```
// A position is of the form "x y z"
%position = "1.2 0.34 13.22";
```

TorqueScript provides a set of special accessors to work with these common types of variables. This allows us to access each individual component and manipulate it.

Getting ready

We will be adding a new TorqueScript function to a project based on the Torque 3D `Full` template and try it out using the `Empty Terrain` level. If you haven't already, use the Torque Project Manager (`Project Manager.exe`) to create a new project from the `Full` template. It will be found under the `My Projects` directory. Then start up your favorite script editor, such as Torsion, and let's get going!

How to do it...

We are going to write a TorqueScript function that will demonstrate how to retrieve components of a variable using the special accessors as follows:

1. Open the `game/scripts/server/game.cs` script file and add the following code to the bottom:

```
function variableAccessors1()
{
    // A position is of the form "x y z"
    %position = "23.0 2.35 9.78";

    // Print out each component to the console
    echo("Position X: " @ %position.x);
    echo("          Y: " @ %position.y);
    echo("          Z: " @ %position.z);
    echo("\n");

    // Add one to the position's y component
    %position.y += 1;

    // Print out each component to the console
    echo("New Position X: " @ %position.x);
    echo("             Y: " @ %position.y);
    echo("             Z: " @ %position.z);
    echo("\n");

    // Define a vector in the form of "x y z w"
    %vector = "1 0 0 1";

    // Print out each component to the console
    echo("Vector X: " @ %vector.x);
    echo("        Y: " @ %vector.y);
    echo("        Z: " @ %vector.z);
    echo("        W: " @ %vector.w);
    echo("\n");
```

```
    // A color is of the form "r g b a"
    %color = "128 0 128 255";

    // Print out each color component to the console
    echo("Color R: " @ %color.r);
    echo("       G: " @ %color.g);
    echo("       B: " @ %color.b);
    echo("       A: " @ %color.a);
    echo("\n");

    // Modify the color components
    %color.r += 64;
    %color.g += 64;
    %color.b = 0;

    // Print out each color component to the console
    echo("New Color R: " @ %color.r);
    echo("           G: " @ %color.g);
    echo("           B: " @ %color.b);
    echo("           A: " @ %color.a);
}
```

2. Start up our game under the `My Projects` directory and load the `Empty Terrain` level. Open the console using the tilde (~)key and enter the following at the bottom of the screen:

   variableAccessors1();

   In the console we will see the following output:

   ==>variableAccessors1();

   Position X: 23.0

   **   Y: 2.35**

   **   Z: 9.78**

   New Position X: 23.0

   **   Y: 3.35**

   **   Z: 9.78**

```
Vector X: 1
       Y: 0
       Z: 0
       W: 1


Color R: 128
      G: 0
      B: 128
      A: 255


New Color R: 192
          G: 64
          B: 0
          A: 255
```

How it works...

TorqueScript provides two sets of convenience accessors to help work with components of a variable. The first set is **x, y, z,** and **w**. This set is most often used with the x, y, and z components of position and vector variables; and we will nearly always use the first three accessors, ignoring the **w** accessor. The second set is **r, g, b,** and **a**, which correspond to the red, green, blue, and alpha components of a variable containing color information.

There's more...

Behind the scenes, whenever we use one of these special accessors, TorqueScript is retrieving the corresponding space-delimited field within the variable. So the **x** and **r** accessors refer to the first field, the **y** and **g** accessors refer to the second field, and so on.

This also means that the positional/vector accessors and color accessors can be freely mixed together. For example, the red component of a color variable may just as easily be retrieved using the **x** accessor, and the alpha component may be retrieved with the **w** accessor. This also works the other way round with the components of a vector retrieved using the color accessors. We can see this in action by copying the following function at the end of the `game/scripts/server/game.cs` script file:

```
function variableAccessors2()
{
    // Define a vector in the form of "x y z w"
    %vector = "1 0 0 1";
```

```
// Print out each xyzw component to the console
echo("Vector X: " @ %vector.x);
echo("       Y: " @ %vector.y);
echo("       Z: " @ %vector.z);
echo("       W: " @ %vector.w);
echo("\n");

// Print out each rgba component to the console
echo("Vector R: " @ %vector.r);
echo("       G: " @ %vector.g);
echo("       B: " @ %vector.b);
echo("       A: " @ %vector.a);
}
```

Start up our game under the `My Projects` directory and load the `Empty Terrain` level. Open the console using the tilde (~) key and enter the following at the bottom of the screen:

```
variableAccessors2();
```

In the console we will see the following output:

```
==>variableAccessors2();
Vector X: 1
       Y: 0
       Z: 0
       W: 1


Vector R: 1
       G: 0
       B: 0
       A: 1
```

The results demonstrate that we can retrieve components of a variable using either set of accessors.

See also

▸ *Accessing delimited fields within a string*

Iterating on objects in a SimSet or SimGroup collection

The `SimSet` and `SimGroup` classes hold collections of game objects, also known as **SimObject** (the base class of nearly every object in Torque 3D). In this recipe we will iterate through a collection of objects in order to perform some operation on them.

Getting ready

We will be adding a new TorqueScript function to a project based on the Torque 3D `Full` template and try it out using the `Empty Terrain` level. If you haven't already, use the Torque Project Manager (`Project Manager.exe`) to create a new project from the `Full` template. It will be found under the `My Projects` directory. Then start up your favorite script editor, such as Torsion, and let's get going!

How to do it...

We are going to write a TorqueScript function that will iterate through the objects of a `SimSet` or `SimGroup` collection as follows:

1. Open the `game/scripts/server/game.cs` script file and add the following code to the bottom:

```
function iterateSimGroup1()
{
    // Iterate through the MissionGroup SimGroup to retrieve
    // each SimObject.  This holds the top level objects from
    // the loaded level.
    foreach (%obj in MissionGroup)
    {
        // Print some information about the object in the group
        echo(%obj.getId() SPC %obj.getClassName());
    }
}
```

2. Start up our game under the `My Projects` directory and load the `Empty Terrain` level. Open the console using the tilde (~) key and enter the following at the bottom of the screen:

```
iterateSimGroup1();
```

In the console we will see the following output:

```
==>iterateSimGroup1();
4275 LevelInfo
4276 ScatterSky
```

```
4277 TerrainBlock
4278 SimGroup
```

How it works...

The `foreach()` function (which is different than the `foreach$()` function that is used to parse space-delimited strings) is used to iterate through a `SimSet` or `SimGroup` collection in order to retrieve one `SimObject` instance at a time and perform some operation on it. In this example, the ID and class name of object are output to the console.

The `foreach()` function is different than most of the looping TorqueScript functions (such as `for()`), in that it takes two parameters that are separated by the word `in` rather than a semicolon. It is also unusual in that it creates a new variable to hold the current `SimObject` instance (the `%obj` variable in our previous example). The `foreach()` function has the following form:

```
foreach( object in simgroup)
{
    ... Do something with object ...
}
```

Here, the `simgroup` parameter is the collection of objects to be processed (could also be a `SimSet` parameter), and the `object` parameter is a new variable that is created to hold the current `SimObject` instance. It is the `object` variable that we do work on.

There's more...

An alternative method to access a object collection of a `SimSet` or `SimGroup` parameter is to use a standard `for()` loop and `getObject()` method of the collection. For example, put the following function at the end of the `game/scripts/server/game.cs` script file, following the code we entered in the `foreach()` example:

```
function iterateSimGroup2()
{
    // Get the number of objects in the SimGroup
    %count = MissionGroup.getCount();

    // Iterate through the MissionGroup
    for (%i=0; %i<%count; %i++)
    {
        // Retrieve the object
        %obj = MissionGroup.getObject(%i);

        // Print some information about the object in the group
        echo(%obj.getId() SPC %obj.getClassName());
    }
}
```

Start up our game under the `My Projects` directory and load the `Empty Terrain` level. Open the console using the tilde (~) key and enter the following at the bottom of the screen:

```
iterateSimGroup2();
```

In the console we will see the following output:

```
==>iterateSimGroup2();
4275 LevelInfo
4276 ScatterSky
4277 TerrainBlock
4278 SimGroup
```

The results end up being the same as when we used the `foreach()` function. There is no real advantage of using this method over the `foreach()` method. We do often see this pattern in a number of stock Torque 3D scripts that were written prior to `foreach()` being added to the TorqueScript language. We will also see this pattern in a lot of game developers' script code just because they are not aware of the newer `foreach()` function (now you are one of the special ones that do know!).

See also

▸ *Getting a random object from a SimSet or SimGroup collection*

▸ *Finding an object in a SimSet or SimGroup collection using its internal name*

▸ *Executing a method on a SimSet or SimGroup collection*

Getting a random object from a SimSet or SimGroup collection

Sometimes we have a collection of `SimObject` instances in a `SimSet` or `SimGroup` collection and we would like to retrieve a single, random object from this collection. In this recipe we will discover a quick and easy method to do just that.

Getting ready

We will be adding a new TorqueScript function to a project based on the Torque 3D `Full` template and try it out using the `Empty Terrain` level. If you haven't already, use the Torque Project Manager (`Project Manager.exe`) to create a new project from the `Full` template. It will be found under the `My Projects` directory. Then start up your favorite script editor, such as Torsion, and let's get going!

How to do it...

We are going to write a TorqueScript function that will demonstrate how to retrieve a random `SimObject` instance from a `SimSet` or `SimGroup` collection as follows:

1. Open the `game/scripts/server/game.cs` script file and add the following code to the bottom:

```
function getRandomObject1()
{
    // Retrieve a random object from the MissionGroup.  This holds
    // the top level objects from the loaded level.
    %object = MissionGroup.getRandom();

    // Print some information about the object to the console
    echo(%object.getId() SPC %object.getClassName());
}
```

2. Start up our game under the `My Projects` directory and load the `Empty Terrain` level. Open the console using the tilde (~) key and enter the following at the bottom of the screen:

    getRandomObject1();

    In the console, we will see the following output (you may have a different object chosen):

    ==>getRandomObject1();

    4276 ScatterSky

How it works...

The `getRandom()` method of a `SimSet` and `SimGroup` collection returns a randomly selected `SimObject` ID from the collection. If the collection is empty, a value of `-1` is returned.

See also

▶ *Iterating on objects in a SimSet or SimGroup collection*

▶ *Finding an object in a SimSet or SimGroup collection using its internal name*

▶ *Executing a method on a SimSet or SimGroup collection.*

Finding an object in a SimSet or SimGroup collection using its internal name

`SimObject` instances may optionally have a globally unique name. This makes it easy to work with a `SimObject` instance from any script function or method. However, this can clutter up the global namespace and there is the possibility of naming collisions. `SimObject` instances may also have an internal name that need only be unique within its direct parent `SimSet` or `SimGroup` collection. We most often find internal names being used in Torque 3D's GUI system where all `GuiControl` objects are also the `SimGroup` collections, and they are always organized in a hierarchy. In this recipe we will retrieve a `SimObject` instance from its collection based on its internal name.

Getting ready

We will be adding a new TorqueScript function to a project based on the Torque 3D `Full` template and try it out using the `Empty Terrain` level. If you haven't already, use the Torque Project Manager (`Project Manager.exe`) to create a new project from the `Full` template. It will be found under the `My Projects` directory. Then start up your favorite script editor, such as Torsion, and let's get going!

How to do it...

We are going to write a TorqueScript function that will demonstrate how to find a `SimObject` instance using its internal name as follows:

1. Open the `game/scripts/server/game.cs` script file and add the following code to the bottom:

```
function getByInternalName1()
{
   // Create a SimGroup
   new SimGroup(MyGroup);

   // Create some script objects with unique internal
   // names and add each one to our SimGroup.
   // The ScriptObject class is just a generic SimObject that
   // we can create in TorqueScript.
   %so = new ScriptObject()
           {
               internalName = "name1";
           };
   MyGroup.add(%so);

   %so = new ScriptObject()
           {
```

```
                internalName = "name2";
            };
    MyGroup.add(%so);

    %so = new ScriptObject()
            {
                internalName = "name3";
            };
    MyGroup.add(%so);

    // Find an object in the SimGroup using its internal name
    %object = MyGroup.findObjectByInternalName("name2");

    // Print some information about the object to the console
    echo("Found object " @ %object.getId()
        @ " with internal name: " @ %object.internalName);

    // Clean up the SimGroup and all of the script objects
    MyGroup.delete();
}
```

2. Start up our game under the My Projects directory and load the Empty Terrain level. Open the console using the tilde (~) key and enter the following at the bottom of the screen:

    getByInternalName1();

    In the console we will see the following output:

    ==>getByInternalName1();

    Found object 4154 with internal name: name2

How it works...

So that we may see the internal name search in action, we first create some SimObject instances and add them to a SimGroup collection. In our previous example we use the ScriptObject class for our SimObject instance. The ScriptObject class is the most basic SimObject derived class we can build from script, and can come in handy when we want an object that can hold arbitrary data. We give a unique value to the internalName property of each ScriptObject class.

With all of the objects and a group collection set up, we use the findObjectByInternalName() method of a SimGroup collection. This method is also available in a SimSet collection and has the following form:

```
foundObject = SimGroup.findObjectByInternalName( name,
[searchChildren] );
```

Here, the `name` parameter is the internal name we wish to search for in the `SimGroup` collection, and the optional `searchChildren` parameter indicates the child collections should be searched when set to `true` (it is `false` by default). If a `SimObject` instance with its `internalName` property matches the requested `name`, it is returned. If no `SimObject` instance matches or there are none yet in the collection, `0` is returned.

There's more...

Let's look at some additional ways to search for a `SimObject` class in a `SimSet` or `SimGroup` collection.

Including children SimSet and SimGroup collections in the search

The `SimSet` and `SimGroup` classes are derived from the `SimObject` class, and therefore may also be children of a `SimSet` or `SimGroup` collection. One place we come across this is with a Torque 3D level file. At the top is a `SimGroup` collection named `MissionGroup`. Under this group are a number of different objects, and usually a number of different `SimGroup` objects in order to better organize objects of the level. The `Empty Terrain` level that we have been using in our examples has a child `SimGroup` collection named `PlayerDropPoints` that holds all the locations that a player may spawn at.

Another place we come across a hierarchy of `SimGroup` objects is when working with Torque 3D's GUI system. All GUI objects are derived from the `GuiControl` class, which itself is a `SimGroup` collection. This means that any `GuiControl` class can be a child of another `GuiControl` class. So as to not clutter up the global namespace with the names of `GuiControl` objects, we often use the `internalName` property as much as possible.

When we want to find a `GuiControl` class to work with (such as one of many radio buttons in a group), we perform an internal name search at some parent or grandparent `GuiControl`. If you keep the `internalName` property unique among `GuiControl` instances in a dialog window for example, we can start the search with the `GuiControl` class of the window and need not worry about name collisions with other dialog windows.

To perform a search starting from a `SimGroup` or `SimSet` collection and include all of its children, we will set optional `searchChildren` parameter of the `findObjectByInternalName()` method to `true`. For example, consider the following line of code:

```
%object = MyGroup.findObjectByInternalName("name3", true);
```

Starting with `MyGroup` this will search through all children `SimGroup` and `SimSet` objects until it comes across the first `SimObject` instance with its `internalName` property set to `name3`. If no `SimObject` instance matches or there are no objects in the collection, a value of `0` is returned.

Using the special -> operator

Using `findObjectByInternalName()` is very useful, especially if we pass-in a computed variable to its `name` parameter. But if we know the exact name to search for, there is a much less verbose shortcut. We can use the special `->` operator. For example, look at the following code:

```
%object = MyGroup->name2;
```

The new code is equivalent to the following code:

```
%object = MyGroup.findObjectByInternalName("name2");
```

Just like this usage of `findObjectByInternalName()` the `->` operator will not search in child `SimGroup` or `SimSet` objects.

Another handy usage of the `->` operator occurs when we want to immediately call a method on the found object. In this case we can just append the method to the search call as follows:

```
MyGroup->name2.doSomething(true);
```

What happens here is, first a `SimObject` instance with the internal name of `name2` is found, and then the `doSomething()` method is called on that `SimObject` instance.

Using the special --> operator

As with the `->` operator discussed in the previous section, the `-->` operator is also a shortcut for using `findObjectByInternalName()`. The only difference is that the `-->` operator will also search in child `SimGroup` and `SimSet` instances when looking for a matching internal name on a `SimObject` instance. For example, consider the following line of code:

```
%object = MyGroup-->name2;
```

This is equivalent to the following code, with the `searchChildren` parameter set to `true`:

```
%object = MyGroup.findObjectByInternalName("name2", true);
```

Another handy usage of the `-->` operator occurs when we want to immediately call a method on the found object. In this case we can just append the method to the search call as follows:

```
MyGroup-->name2.doSomething(true);
```

What happens here is first a `SimObject` instance with the internal name of `name2` is found in all the children `SimGroup` and `SimSet` objects, and then the `doSomething()` method is called on that `SimObject` instance. We often find this pattern when working with the `GuiControl` objects.

See also

▸ *Iterating on objects in a SimSet or SimGroup collection*

▸ *Getting a random object from a SimSet or SimGroup collection*

▸ *Executing a method on a SimSet or SimGroup collection*

Executing a method on a SimSet or SimGroup collection

During game play we may want to call the same method on all the `SimObject` instances that belong to a `SimSet` or `SimGroup` collection. Rather than iterate through each `SimObject` instance in the collection and execute its method, TorqueScript has a handy one-line shortcut that we'll make use of in this recipe.

Getting ready

We will be adding a new TorqueScript function to a project based on the Torque 3D `Full` template and try it out using the `Empty Terrain` level. If you haven't already, use the Torque Project Manager (`Project Manager.exe`) to create a new project from the `Full` template. It will be found under the `My Projects` directory. Then start up your favorite script editor, such as Torsion, and let's get going!

How to do it...

We are going to write a TorqueScript function that will demonstrate how to execute a method on all the `SimObject` instances in a `SimGroup` collection as follows:

1. Open the `game/scripts/server/game.cs` script file and add the following code to the bottom:

```
function executeMethodOnGroup1()
{
    // Create a SimGroup
    new SimGroup(MyGroup);

    // Create some script objects with some properties and
    // add each one to our SimGroup.  Give each a class
    // property so they belong to the same subclass and have
    // access to the same method.
    // The ScriptObject class is just a generic SimObject that
    // we can create in TorqueScript.
    %so = new ScriptObject()
            {
                class = "MyClass1";
```

```
                internalName = "name1";
                myValue1 = "abc";
            };
    MyGroup.add(%so);

    %so = new ScriptObject()
            {
                class = "MyClass1";
                internalName = "name2";
                myValue1 = "123";
            };
    MyGroup.add(%so);

    %so = new ScriptObject()
            {
                class = "MyClass1";
                internalName = "name3";
                myValue1 = "a1b2";
            };
    MyGroup.add(%so);

    // Execute our method on all SimObjects in the group.
    // This is the same as iterating through the group
    // and calling object.method() on each of them.
    echo("-- Starting callOnChildren()");
    MyGroup.callOnChildren(outputProperties, "myValue1");
    echo("-- Finished callOnChildren()");

    // Clean up the SimGroup and all of the script obejcts
    MyGroup.delete();
}

// A method for our custom script class
function MyClass1::outputProperties(%this, %propertyName)
{
    // Get the script object's SimObject ID
    %id = %this.getId();

    // Get the script object's internal name
    %name = %this.internalName;

    // Get the value of the passed-in property name
    %value = %this.getFieldValue(%propertyName);

    // Print out to the console
    echo("ScriptObject ID:" @ %id
        @ "  Name:" @ %name @ "  Value:" @ %value);
}
```

2. Start up our game under the `My Projects` directory and load the `Empty Terrain` level. Open the console using the tilde (~) key and enter the following at the bottom of the screen:

`executeMethodOnGroup1();`

In the console we will see the following output:

`==>executeFunctionOnGroup1();`

`-- Starting callOnChildren()`

`ScriptObject ID:4153  Name:name1  Value:abc`

`ScriptObject ID:4154  Name:name2  Value:123`

`ScriptObject ID:4155  Name:name3  Value:a1b2`

`-- Finished callOnChildren()`

How it works...

The `SimGroup` and `SimSet` `callOnChildren()` methods automatically step through each child `SimObject` instance and if the requested method is valid on the object, it is called with the passed-in arguments. The `callOnChildren()` method has the following form:

```
SimGroup.callOnChildren( method, args... );
```

Here, the `method` parameter is the method to be called on each of the `SimObject` objects in the collection, and the `args...` parameter is actually a variable number of arguments that will be passed-in to the method. In our previous example we pass-in one argument, which is the name of the property we wish our method to process.

The `callOnChildren()` method doesn't just process the child `SimObject` instances that are part of a `SimGroup` or `SimSet` collection, it also traverses any child `SimGroup` or `SimSet` collection, and executes the method on their `SimObject` instances.

There's more...

If we want to call a method only on all the `SimObject` objects that are the immediate children of a `SimGroup` or `SimSet` collection and not traverse through the hierarchy of the collection, we can use the `callOnChildrenNoRecurse()` method. It has the same form as `callOnChildren()` as follows:

```
SimGroup.callOnChildrenNoRecurse( method, args... );
```

We could modify the method call of the `SimGroup` collection from our previous example and replace it with `callOnchildrenNoRecurse()` as follows:

```
MyGroup.callOnChildrenNoRecurse(outputProperties, "myValue1");
```

With our particular example, we end up with the same output to the console, as there are no child `SimGroup` or `SimSet` objects that would be skipped by using `callOnChildrenNoRecurse()`.

See also

▶ *Iterating on objects in a SimSet or SimGroup collection*

▶ *Getting a random object from a SimSet or SimGroup collection*

▶ *Finding an object in a SimSet or SimGroup collection using its internal name*

Creating a new SimObject instance

A `SimObject` instance is the base class from which all the other classes that can be accessed using TorqueScript are derived. We don't work with the `SimObject` class directly, but rather work with one of the derived classes. In this recipe we will see the various ways to construct a new `SimObject`-based class.

How to do it...

Creating a `SimObject`-based class is straightforward and there are a number of options available that we will look into later. Here we will create a `ScriptObject` instance, the simplest `SimObject` derived class, and assign it to a variable as follows:

```
%object = new ScriptObject();
```

How it works...

We use the `new` keyword to create a new `SimObject`-based class, which returns the new object so it may be stored into a variable for future use.

There's more...

There are a number of different options when it comes to creating a `SimObject` derived class. Let's take a look at them.

Creating a new SimObject instance with a globally unique name

If we want a `SimObject` instance to be accessible from anywhere in the script ,we can assign a global name to it. Then when we want to work with the `SimObject` instance we can just use its name. As an example, we will create a `Player` class object and assign a globally unique name to it as follows:

```
new Player(MyPlayer);
```

Here we create a new `Player` class object and give it a globally unique name of `MyPlayer`. Making use of the return value of the `new` keyword in a local variable is optional as we can now access this new object with its unique name. For example, this is how we obtain the player's position using the name of the object:

```
%pos = MyPlayer.getPosition();
```

What happens if there is already another object that has the same global name as the one we wish to create? Normally Torque 3D will output an error to the console stating **Cannot re-declare object** and the new object will not be created (the `new` keyword will return a value of `0`). However, this behavior may be modified through the use of the `$Con::redefineBehavior` global variable. The following table lists the accepted values for this variable:

String value	Impact on object creation
replaceExisting	This deletes the current object with the same name and replaces it with the new object.
renameNew	This adds a number to the end of the name of the new object. This number starts at one and is incremented until a unique name combination is found.
unnamedNew	This removes the global name from the new object.
postfixNew	This appends a string to the end of the name of the new object. This string is defined in the global variable `$Con::redefineBehaviorPostfix` and is set to an empty string by default.
oldRedefineBehavior	This indicates the default condition of not creating the new object. This is also the behavior when `$Con::redefineBehavior` is set to an empty string.

Modifying `$Con::redefineBehavior` must be done with care as it affects how the object creation system of Torque 3D operates. It can also have a non-intuitive impact on the global name of a new object.

Creating a new SimObject instance with defined properties

We can set up properties of a new `SimObject` instance at the same time the object is created. This is done by writing a list of properties and their values within curly braces as part of the object creation. Setting properties at the time of object creation saves a lot of typing later on. It also provides immediate values for the properties of an object rather than first having them set to some default value. For example, we can set the properties for a new `Player` object as follows:

```
new Player(MyPlayer)
    {
        datablock = SoldierDatablock;
        position = "0 0 10";
        size = "1 1 1";
        squad = "Bravo";
    };
```

In this example we are setting the standard `datablock`, `position`, and `size` properties for the `Player` class. We are also setting a script-specific property called `squad`. This is known as a **dynamic** property and only means something to our game play code and not the core Torque 3D engine.

Creating a new SimObject instance based on another SimObject instance

Sometimes we want to create a new `SimObject` instance whose properties are based on another, previously created `SimObject` instance. This previously created `SimObject` instance is known as the **copy source** and is passed-in as part of the creation process of a `SimObject` instance. For example, we will create a new `SimObject` instance based on the `Player` class object that we created in the previous example as follows:

```
new Player(MyPlayer2 : MyPlayer)
    {
        position = "2 0 10";
    };
```

In this example, the `MyPlayer2` object will have all of the same properties (including the dynamic ones) as the `MyPlayer` object, except for the `position` property that we've explicitly set. This full-copying of properties only occurs if the copy source object is of the same class as the new `SimObject` instance. If the copy source is of a different class, only the dynamic properties (if any) will be copied over and not the class-specific ones.

It should also be noted that this is only a copy of properties at the time of object creation. There is no parent/child relationship occurring. In our previous example, modifying a property on the `MyPlayer` object later on will have no impact on the properties of `MyPlayer2`.

See also

- ▶ *Creating a new internal name only SimObject instance*
- ▶ *Creating a new Datablock object*
- ▶ *Creating a new singleton*
- ▶ *Extending a SimObject instance using the class property*

Creating a new internal name only SimObject instance

The internal name of a `SimObject` instance is not exposed to the world in the same way that its optional globally unique name is. We may access it using the `internalName` property of the `SimObject` instance and it is useful when searching for `SimObject` instances within a `SimGroup` or `SimSet` collection. When working with the `GuiControl` objects we will often make use of the internal name. Creating a new internal name only `SimObject` instance is a rarely used feature of TorqueScript, but we will learn to create it in this recipe.

How to do it...

Creating an internal name only `SimObject` instance is almost the same as creating an ordinary `SimObject` instance. The difference comes down to how we decorate the name we use. Here we will create a `ScriptObject` instance with an internal name, the simplest `SimObject` derived class, and assign it to a variable:

```
%object = new ScriptObject([MyScriptObject]);
```

How it works...

By surrounding the name of the `SimObject` instance with square brackets, Torque 3D automatically sets the `internalName` property of object rather than its globally unique name. If we call the `getName()` method on our new `ScriptObject` instance, it will return an empty string. But if we call the `getInternalName()` method, `MyScriptObject` will be returned.

There's more...

This shortcut to setting the internal name of a `SimObject` instance can be handy when working with `GuiControl` instances. The normal pattern works like the following:

```
new GuiWindowCtrl(MyDialog) {
    ... some properties here ...

    new GuiControl() {
        internalName = "control1";
        ... some properties here ...
    };
    new GuiControl() {
        internalName = "control2";
        ... some properties here ...
    };
};
```

With this pattern we have to set the `internalName` property of each `GuiControl` class manually. Using the special name decorators, the `internalName` property will be set automatically as follows:

```
new GuiWindowCtrl(MyDialog) {
    ... some properties here ...

    new GuiControl([control1]) {
        ... some properties here ...
    };
    new GuiControl([control2]) {
        ... some properties here ...
    };
```

See also

▶   *Creating a new SimObject instance*

▶   *Creating a new Datablock object*

▶   *Creating a new singleton*

▶   *Extending a SimObject instance using the class property*

Creating a new Datablock object

Datablock objects have static properties and are used as a common data store between game objects that derive from the `GameBase` class. They are defined on the server and are passed to clients (by `SimObject` ID only) during the initial transmission of a game level. In this recipe we'll see how to build a new `Datablock` object.

How to do it...

Creating a `Datablock` instance is straight forward. Here we will create a `StaticShapeData` `Datablock`, one of many possible `Datablock` classes as follows:

```
datablock StaticShapeData(MyShapeData)
{
    category = "Scenic";
    shapeFile = "art/shapes/rocks/rock1.dts";
    computeCRC = true;
    isInvincible = true;
};
```

How it works...

We use the `datablock` keyword when creating a new `Datablock` class object and always give it a unique global name. This name is used by other objects to reference this `Datablock` through the use of `datablock` property of the `GameBase` class.

If we happen to create two `Datablock` instances with the same global name but of different classes, then a **Cannot Re-declare data block with a different class** error is output to the console and nothing is done with the second `Datablock` instance. However, if the two global names and classes match, then all of the properties from the second `Datablock` instance are copied into the first.

There's more...

There are a number of different things to keep in mind when it comes to creating a `Datablock` instance. Let's take a look at them.

Creating a new Datablock object based on another Datablock object

We can base the properties of one `Datablock` instance on a previously created `Datablock` instance through the use of a copy source during the creation of the `Datablock` object. The process is the same as when using the `new` keyword. See the *Creating a new SimObject instance* recipe for more information on using a copy source.

Limited total number of Datablocks

The `SimObject` ID of a `Datablock` instance comes from a special pool that is reserved for the `Datablock` class. This ID pool only allows 1024 `Datablock` instances to be defined per game level. This number may be increased by changing the source code of Torque 3D. It is this special `SimObject` ID that is transferred between the server and client in a multiplayer game, and is used by the `GameBase` derived classes to reference their `Datablock` object on the client.

The datablock keyword should only be used on the server

Use of the `datablock` keyword should be limited to the server script files. Only the server keeps a track of the special `Datablock` ID pool, and all the `Datablock` objects on the client are deleted just prior to a game level being loaded.

Datablock properties should be considered static

Once a `Datablock` object has been created, its properties should be considered static. It is possible to modify the properties of a `Datablock` object at any time, just as with any other `SimObject`, but this should be avoided. The modified `Datablock` properties are not retransmitted between the server and client and will result in strange errors during game play.

See also

- ▸ *Creating a new SimObject instance*
- ▸ *Creating a new internal name only SimObject instance*
- ▸ *Creating a new singleton recipes*

Creating a new singleton

A **singleton** is a `SimObject` instance that we only ever want one instance of. Typically we use singletons for shader objects, materials, and some audio objects. In this recipe we will learn how to create an object as a singleton.

How to do it...

Creating a singleton is straight forward. Here we will create a `Material` singleton, one of a number of `SimObject` classes that may be created as a singleton, as follows:

```
singleton Material(DECAL_scorch)
{
    baseTex[0] = "./scorch_decal.png";
    translucent = true;
    translucentBlendOp = None;
    translucentZWrite = true;
    alphaTest = true;
    alphaRef = 84;
};
```

How it works...

We use the `singleton` keyword when creating a new `SimObject` class object that we want only one instance of, and always give a unique global name to it. Other than ensuring that only one instance of this object will exist, the creation process is exactly the same as when the `new` keyword was used.

See also

- ▸ *Creating a new SimObject instance*
- ▸ *Creating a new internal name only SimObject instance*
- ▸ *Creating a new Datablock object*

Extending a SimObject instance using the class property

TorqueScript allows us to extend the script methods of a `SimObject` derived class through the use of the `class` property. This is a very powerful feature as we can modify the behavior of a `SimObject` instance without the need to change its source code. In this recipe, we will learn how to make use of the `class` property to extend the methods available to a `SimObject` instance.

Getting ready

We will be adding a new TorqueScript function to a project based on the Torque 3D `Full` template and try it out using the `Empty Terrain` level. If you haven't already, use the Torque Project Manager (`Project Manager.exe`) to create a new project from the `Full` template. It will be found under the `My Projects` directory. Then start up your favorite script editor, such as Torsion, and let's get going!

How to do it...

We are going to write a TorqueScript function that will demonstrate how to extend a `SimObject` instance using its `class` property as follows:

1. Open the `game/scripts/server/game.cs` script file and add the following code to the bottom:

```
function useClassProperty1()
{
    // Create a ScriptObject and define its class property.
    // The ScriptObject class is just a generic SimObject that
    // we can create in TorqueScript.
    new ScriptObject(MyScriptObj)
        {
            class = MyExtensionClass1;
        };

    // Call the first method defined by the new class
    %result = MyScriptObj.addValues(2, 3);

    // Output the result to the console
    echo("addValues(2, 3) returned: " @ %result);

    // Call the second method defined by the new class
    MyScriptObj.newMethod();
```

```
    // Clean up our object
    MyScriptObj.delete();
}

// First method defined by our new class
function MyExtensionClass1::addValues(%this, %param1, %param2)
{
    return %param1 + %param2;
}

// Second method defined by our new class
function MyExtensionClass1::newMethod(%this)
{
    // Get the top level C++ class this object derives from.
    %objClass = %this.getClassName();

    // Output to the console
    echo(%objClass SPC %this.getId()
        @ " is using the MyExtensionClass1 class");
}
```

2. Start up our game under the `My Projects` directory and load the `Empty Terrain` level. Open the console using the tilde (~) key and enter the following at the bottom of the screen:

   useClassProperty1();

   In the console we will see the following output:

   ==>useClassProperty1();

   addValues(2, 3) returned: 5

   ScriptObject 4152 is using the MyExtensionClass1 class

How it works...

In the example code we create a `ScriptObject` instance and set its `class` property to `MyExtensionClass1`. This extends the namespace of the `ScriptObject` instances to include all the methods that are defined by this new class. We then create two methods for this new class: `addValues()` and `newMethod()`. The first method takes two parameters, adds them together, and returns the result. The second method takes no parameters and just outputs some information to the console.

Making use of these new methods is straight forward. We just call them on the object like any other method. The Torque 3D engine takes care of everything for us.

There's more...

There is a lot more to know about working with the `class` property and extending the namespace of a `SimObject` instance. Let's take a look at these points.

Working with a class namespace after object creation

Object creation is not the only time we can extend the methods of a `SimObject` instance. We can either set the `class` property of the object directly or use the `setClassNamespace()` method to extend a `SimObject` instance at any time. The `setClassNamespace()` method has the following form:

```
SimObject.setClassNamespace( name );
```

Here the `name` parameter is the equivalent value passed-in to the `class` property. This also allows us to modify the class namespace hierarchy of a `SimObject` instance after having already set the `class` property to a different value. We can even clear the class namespace of a `SimObject` instance by passing-in an empty string.

If we want to know whether a `SimObject` instance is making use of a particular class namespace, we can use the `isInNamespaceHierarchy()` method. This method searches through the entire namespace tree of the object and has the following form:

```
result = SimObject.isInNamespaceHierarchy( name );
```

Here the `name` parameter is the namespace to search for, and the `result` is either `true` or `false` depending on whether the `SimObject` instance is making use of the given namespace or not. This is different from the `isMemberOfClass()` method, which only tests if the object is an instance of the given C++ class.

Extending even further with the superClass property

We can add a second layer of new methods through setting the **superClass** property of a `SimObject` instance. By using this property, we insert another set of methods between the C++ class of the object and the class namespace set with the `class` property.

It is not very common to make use of the `superClass` property, and sometimes it can be confusing understanding where each method call is routed to. But this extra namespace layer is available to those advanced users if they need it.

As with the **class** property, we can set the `superClass` instance either at the time of object creation or any time afterwards. To set the `superClass` namespace after object creation, we can set the `superClass` property directly or use the `setSuperClassNamespace()` method. The `setSuperClassNamespace()` method has the following form:

```
SimObject.setSuperClassNamespace( name );
```

Here the `name` parameter is the equivalent value passed-in to the `superClass` property.

Understanding the namespace hierarchy

The `class` and `superClass` properties of the `SimObject` instance are powerful features that allow us to extend the functionality of Torque 3D through script. However, it can be confusing to figure out where a method call will be handled. Let's walk through how this works behind the scene.

Unfortunately, the `class` and `superClass` properties have misleading names. They are not used to extend the class of a `SimObject` instance in a C++ sense. What they do is allow us to add new namespaces to an object when it comes to method lookup. We can insert new functionality into the namespace hierarchy of an object and intercept a method call before it is passed on to the C++ engine layer.

The namespace hierarchy of an object derived from a `SimObject` instance looks like the following list, with the numbers exhibiting the actual order:

1. Optional globally unique name is used as a namespace
2. Optional `class` property namespace
3. Optional `superClass` property namespace
4. Direct C++ class
5. Parent C++ class
6. Grandparent C++ class and so on...

So when we call a method on a `SimObject` instance, it is first sent to the globally unique name of the object as a namespace, if any. This allows us to write the methods that are specific to that object instance. If it is not handled at this level, the method call is passed on to the `class` property namespace, if any. If the method call is not handled there, it is passed on to the `superClass` property namespace if it has been defined. If the method call has still not been handled at this point, it then moves on to the C++ class hierarchy, where it is passed along until it reaches the `SimObject` class.

When a method call is handled at the previous hierarchy levels 1, 2, or 3, we can decide to continue to pass the method call along the call chain. This allows us to intercept a method call but still allows for the original functionality. To do this we use the special `Parent` namespace to call the method again.

It's time for an example. Add the following code to the end of the `game/scripts/server/game.cs` script file:

```
function useClassProperty2()
{
    // Create a ScriptObject and define its class property.
    // The ScriptObject class is just a generic SimObject that
    // we can create in TorqueScript.
    new ScriptObject(MyScriptObj)
        {
```

```
            class = MyExtensionClass2;
        };

    // Get the name of our ScriptObject.  Normally this
    // would just return our globally unique name, but
    // our class namespace will change how this method
    // works.
    %result = MyScriptObj.getName();

    // Output the result the console
    echo("getName() returned: '" @ %result @ "'");

    // Clean up our object
    MyScriptObj.delete();
}

function MyExtensionClass2::getName(%this)
{
    // Call the parent method and obtain its result
    %result = Parent::getName(%this);

    // Return our modified result
    return "Our name is: " @ %result;
}
```

Now start up our game under the My Projects directory and load the Empty Terrain level. Open the console using the tilde (~) key and enter the following at the bottom of the screen:

```
    useClassProperty2();
```

In the console we will see the following output:

```
    ==>useClassProperty2();

    getName() returned: 'Our name is: MyScriptObj'
```

The MyExtensionClass2 namespace defines the getName() method and the ScriptObject instance is making use of this namespace by setting its class property. When we call the getName() method of the object, as expected the MyExtensionClass2 intercepts it.

Within MyExtensionClass2::getName() the original getName() method is called with the static Parent namespace. This is done with the following code:

```
    // Call the parent method and obtain its result
    %result = Parent::getName(%this);
```

As this is a static call we need to manually include our object with the method call. Here this is done by passing in the `%this` variable as the first parameter to `getName()`. This `Parent` call eventually makes its way to the C++ `SimObject` class, where the globally unique name of the object is retrieved and passed into the `%result` variable. `MyExtensionClass2::getName()` uses this result for its own work and passes everything back to the caller.

Limitations of the class property

A limitation of using the `class` property is that once a class namespace has been assigned to a particular C++ class, it may only be used by that C++ class from then on.

For example, we had assigned the `MyExtensionClass1` class namespace to the `class` property of a `ScriptObject` instance at the beginning of this recipe. From that point onwards, we can only use the `MyExtensionClass1` class namespace with another `ScriptObject` instance. If we were to try to assign the same class namespace to a `Player` class instance, we would get an error in the console and the assignment would not occur.

The `superClass` property does not have this limitation. You may reuse a namespace between different C++ classes, so long as you limit its use to the `superClass` property.

See also

▸ *Creating a new SimObject instance*

▸ *Creating a new internal name only SimObject instance*

Using a variable to access methods or properties of a SimObject instance

Sometimes we don't know the global unique name of a `SimObject` instance or its ID when writing our script code. We may need to look up the name or ID, or even compute it. In these cases, we need to be able to reference a `SimObject` instance using a variable and in this recipe, we will learn how to do just that.

Getting ready

We will be adding a new TorqueScript function to a project based on the Torque 3D `Full` template and try it out using the `Empty Terrain` level. If you haven't already, use the Torque Project Manager (`Project Manager.exe`) to create a new project from the `Full` template. It will be found under the `My Projects` directory. Then start up your favorite script editor, such as Torsion, and let's get going!

How to do it...

We are going to write a TorqueScript function that will demonstrate how to retrieve the properties and methods of a `SimObject` instance using a variable as follows:

1. Open the `game/scripts/server/game.cs` script file and add the following code to the bottom:

```
function variableObjectAccess1()
{
    // Build some ScriptObjects to work with.
    // The ScriptObject class is just a generic SimObject that
    // we can create in TorqueScript.
    new ScriptObject(MyScriptObj1)
        {
            MyValue1 = "obj1";
        };

    new ScriptObject(MyScriptObj2)
        {
            MyValue1 = "obj2";
        };

    new ScriptObject(MyScriptObj3)
        {
            MyValue1 = "obj3";
        };

    // Access each ScriptObject using a computed variable
    for (%i=0; %i<3; %i++)
    {
        // We will reference the object using its globally
        // unqiue name.  Build out that name here.
        %name = "MyScriptObj" @ (%i + 1);

        // Get a property's value from the ScriptObject.
        %value = %name.MyValue1;

        // Print out to the console
        echo("ScriptObject " @ %name
            @ " has a value of: " @ %value);
    }

    // Clean up our ScriptObejcts also using a computed
    // variable
    for (%i=0; %i<3; %i++)
    {
        // Build the name of the object
        %object = "MyScriptObj" @ (%i + 1);
```

```
        // Delete the ScriptObject using its delete() method.
        %object.delete();
    }
}
```

2. Start up our game under the My Projects directory and load the Empty Terrain level. Open the console using the tilde (~) key and enter the following at the bottom of the screen:

   variableObjectAccess1();

   In the console we will see the following output:

   ```
   ==>variableObjectAccess1();
   ScriptObject MyScriptObj1 has a value of: obj1
   ScriptObject MyScriptObj2 has a value of: obj2
   ScriptObject MyScriptObj3 has a value of: obj3
   ```

How it works...

In the example code we first set up some ScriptObject objects to work with. We give each ScriptObject instance a global unique name and some data to hold. We then move on to step through each object and retrieve its data using a for() loop. We want to focus on this part as shown in the following code:

```
        // We will reference the object using its globally
        // unqiue name.  Build out that name here.
        %name = "MyScriptObj" @ (%i + 1);
```

Here we build up a string variable named %name using a constant string that is appended with a computed value. When put together, these give us a string that matches the global unique name of each ScriptObject instance. We then use this string variable to retrieve the data from the ScriptObject instance as follows:

```
        // Get a property's value from the ScriptObject.
        %value = %name.MyValue1;
```

Within the Torque 3D engine, any time we attempt to access a property or method using the dot (.) operator, the engine performs a search in the SimObject name dictionary based on the preceding variable. If the name is found in the dictionary, the property is retrieved or the method is executed. If the name is not found in the dictionary, an error is output to the console. Our previous example code performs the same lookup when executing the delete() method as follows:

```
        // Build the name of the object
        %object = "MyScriptObj" @ (%i + 1);

        // Delete the ScriptObject using its delete() method.
        %object.delete();
```

See also

▶ *Using call() to call a variable method on a SimObject instance with arguments*

Using call() to call a variable method on a SimObject instance with arguments

There are times when we don't know the name of the method of a `SimObject` instance while writing a script code. In these circumstances, we need to be able to call the method of a `SimObject` instance based on a variable. This recipe will show us how to use the `SimObject` `call()` method to execute another method, with possible passed-in arguments.

Getting ready

We will be adding a new TorqueScript function to a project based on the Torque 3D `Full` template and try it out using the `Empty Terrain` level. If you haven't already, use the Torque Project Manager (`Project Manager.exe`) to create a new project from the `Full` template. It will be found under the `My Projects` directory. Then start up your favorite script editor, such as Torsion, and let's get going!

How to do it...

We are going to write a TorqueScript function that will demonstrate how to programmatically call a `SimObject` method as follows:

1. Open the `game/scripts/server/game.cs` script file and add the following code to the bottom:

```
function callSimObjectMethod1()
{
   // Set up an array to hold the methods we
   // will call.
   %methods[0] = "getPosition";
   %methods[1] = "getEulerRotation";
   %methods[2] = "getScale";

   // Iterate through the MissionCleanup SimGroup to retrieve
   // each SimObject.  This holds the top level objects that
   // have been created since the game level has started.
   foreach (%obj in MissionCleanup)
   {
      // Print some information about the object in the group
      echo(%obj.getId() SPC %obj.getClassName());
```

```
      // If the object derives from a SceneObject then call
      // our methods
      if (%obj.isMemberOfClass(SceneObject))
      {
          for (%i=0; %i<3; %i++)
          {
              // Call the method and obtain its result.
              // Note: none of our methods require passing
              // an argument.
              %result = %obj.call(%methods[%i]);

              // Output the result to the console
              echo("   " @ %methods[%i] @ "(): " @ %result);
          }
      }
   }
}
```

2. Start up our game under the My Projects directory and load the Empty Terrain level. Open the console using the tilde (~) key and enter the following at the bottom of the screen:

callSimObjectMethod1();

In the console we will see the following output:

```
==>callSimObjectMethod1();
4281 ScriptObject
4289 Camera
  getPosition(): -0.277961 -0.851682 243.342
  getEulerRotation(): 0 -0 -0
  getScale(): 1 1 1
4290 Player
  getPosition(): 0.595642 1.25134 240.748
  getEulerRotation(): 0 -0 67.1649
  getScale(): 1 1 1
4291 SimGroup
```

How it works...

Our example code first fills up an array with the methods we will call on the objects. It then loops though all the dynamically created objects in the scene and if an object derives from the `SceneObject` class, call our methods on it using the `SimObejct call()` method.

The `SimObject call()` method has the following form:

```
result = SimObject.call( method, args... );
```

Here, the `method` parameter is the method we want to call on the `SimObject` instance, and the `args...` parameter is actually an optional set of arguments to pass into `method`. The `call()` method returns the output as denoted by `result` of the method call, if any.

If the given method does not exist on the `SimObject` instance, an empty string is returned. No error will be output to the console.

There's more...

If we are unsure whether a particular method exists on a `SimObject` instance, we can use the `isMethod()` method. It has the following form:

```
result = SimObject.isMethod( method );
```

Here the `method` parameter is the method name to search for, and `result` is either `true` or `false` depending on whether the method exists on the `SimObject` instance or not.

See also

- ▶ *Using a variable to access methods or properties of a SimObject instance*
- ▶ *Using call() to call a variable function with arguments*

Using call() to call a variable function with arguments

There are times when we don't know the name of a script function while writing a script code. In these circumstances, we need to be able to call a function based on a variable. This recipe will show how to use the `call()` method to execute a function, with possible passed-in arguments.

Getting ready

We will be adding a new TorqueScript function to a project based on the Torque 3D `Full` template and try it out using the `Empty Terrain` level. If you haven't already, use the Torque Project Manager (`Project Manager.exe`) to create a new project from the `Full` template. It will be found under the `My Projects` directory. Then start up your favorite script editor, such as Torsion, and let's get going!

How to do it...

We are going to write a TorqueScript function that will demonstrate how to programmatically call a function as follows:

1. Open the `game/scripts/server/game.cs` script file and add the following code to the bottom:

```
function getUniqueID1(%idType)
{
    // Determine the function to use based on the
    // passed-in ID type
    switch$ (%idType)
    {
        case 0:
            %function = "generateUUID";

        case 1:
            %function = "getRealTime";

        case 2:
            %function = "getSimTime";

        default:
            %function = "generateUUID";
    }

    // Call the function
    %result = call(%function);

    // Return the result
    return "Your unique ID is: " @ %result;
}
```

2. Start up our game under the `My Projects` directory and load the `Empty Terrain` level. Open the console using the tilde (~)key and enter the following at the bottom of the screen:

    `getUniqueID1(0);`

    In the console we will see the following output:

    `==>getUniqueID1(0);`

    `Your unique ID is: 7be5014c-7d5a-11e1-b801-e57f4eda779f`

3. We can try another run by entering a new command at the bottom of the screen:

    `getUniqueID1(1);`

    In the console we will see the following output:

    `==>getUniqueID1(1);`

    `Your unique ID is: 294298553`

How it works...

Our example code chooses a particular function name to use based on a parameter passed into our function. It then uses the standard `call()` function to call the function by name, do something with the result, and return the result to the caller. The `call()` function has the following form:

```
result = call( function, args... );
```

Here the `function` parameter is the console function we want to call, and the `args...` parameter is actually an optional set of arguments to pass into `function`. The `call()` function returns the result denoted by the `result` parameter of the function call, if any.

If the given function does not exist, an empty string is returned. No error will be output to the console.

There's more...

If we are unsure whether a particular function exists, we can use the `isFunction()` method. It has the following form:

```
result = isFunction( functionName );
```

Here the `functionName` parameter is the function name to search for, and `result` is either `true` or `false`, depending on whether the function exists or not.

See also

▸ *Using call() to call a variable method on a SimObject instance with arguments*

Using script arrays as dictionaries

Arrays are a common form of data structure found in nearly all programming languages. When working with an array, you start at a zero-based index and keep incrementing the index until the array is full. TorqueScript arrays are a little different, in that their index need not be consecutive, nor do they even need to be a number. In this recipe, we will learn how to use TorqueScript arrays to store and retrieve arbitrarily indexed data, sometimes referred to as **dictionaries**.

Getting ready

We will be adding a new TorqueScript function to a project based on the Torque 3D `Full` template and try it out using the `Empty Terrain` level. If you haven't already, use the Torque Project Manager (`Project Manager.exe`) to create a new project from the `Full` template. It will be found under the `My Projects` directory. Then start up your favorite script editor, such as Torsion, and let's get going!

How to do it...

We are to write a TorqueScript function that will demonstrate how to use arrays as dictionaries as follows:

1. Open the `game/scripts/server/game.cs` script file and add the following code to the bottom:

```
function getWeaponDamage(%weaponName)
{
   // Begin by defining some damage amounts for
   // various weapons.  Normally we would set this
   // up at the beginning of the game rather than
   // every time this function is called.
   $WeaponDamage["pistol"] = 2;
   $WeaponDamage["rifle"] = 6;
   $WeaponDamage["rocket"] = 12;

   // Look up the damage amount
   %damage = $WeaponDamage[%weaponName];

   // Check if the damage amount was found.  If not
   // then set it to some default value.
   if (%damage $= "")
```

```
        {
            // The damage was an empty string and was
            // therefore not found in our array.  Set it
            // to a default value.
            %damage = 1;
        }

        return %damage;
    }
```

2. Start up our game under the `My Projects` directory and load the `Empty Terrain` level. Open the console using the tilde (~) key and enter the following at the bottom of the screen:

    getWeaponDamage("pistol");

    In the console we will see the following output:

    ==>getWeaponDamage("pistol");

    2

3. We can try another run with a different weapon by entering the following new command at the bottom of the screen:

    getWeaponDamage("rocket");

    In the console we will see the following output:

    ==>getWeaponDamage("rocket");

    12

4. We will also try a weapon that is not in the array as follows:

    getWeaponDamage("knife");

    In the console we will see the following output:

    ==>getWeaponDamage("knife");

    1

How it works...

The code example first sets up a global array so we have some data to play with. Normally this sort of set up would be outside of the function we're using. Our global array is special in that each index is actually a string.

The `getWeaponDamage()` function then attempts to retrieve the given weapon from the array as follows:

```
// Look up the damage amount
%damage = $WeaponDamage[%weaponName];
```

If an empty string is returned, we know that the weapon name was not found in the array. We then provide some default damage value. If the weapon name was found in the array, we use its damage value.

Behind the scenes, TorqueScript is not actually creating any sort of traditional array to hold these values. When you use square brackets ([,]) to denote an array index, what actually happens is TorqueScript appends the index to the name of an array. So using our previous example, the definition for weapon damage of the rifle looks like the following:

```
$WeaponDamage["rifle"] = 6;
```

But what TorqueScript is doing behind the scenes looks like the following:

```
$WeaponDamagerifle = 6;
```

You can test this out yourself by typing the following line into the console after running our `getWeaponDamage()` function at least once:

```
echo($WeaponDamagerifle);
```

If you do this you will see **6** printed to the console as expected.

So in the end, accessing the index of an array is just a string lookup into the TorqueScript variable table.

See also

▶ *Using ArrayObject and custom script sorting callbacks*

Using ArrayObject and custom script sorting callbacks

The `ArrayObject` class provides a true key/value pair dictionary in TorqueScript. It allows for easy searching and counting of key/value pairs and can optionally remove duplicates by either key or value. An `ArrayObject` class may also sort by key or value using standard algorithms, but it also supports custom sorting using script callbacks. In this recipe, we will see how to set up a custom sort callback that will be used by an `ArrayObject` instance.

Getting ready

We will be adding a new TorqueScript function to a project based on the Torque 3D `Full` template and try it out using the `Empty Terrain` level. If you haven't already, use the Torque Project Manager (`Project Manager.exe`) to create a new project from the `Full` template. It will be found under the `My Projects` directory. Then start up your favorite script editor, such as Torsion, and let's get going!

How to do it...

We are going to write a TorqueScript function that will demonstrate how to custom sort an `ArrayObject` as follows:

1. Open the `game/scripts/server/game.cs` script file and add the following code to the bottom:

```
function sortArrayObject1()
{
   // Create a new ArrayObject
   %array = new ArrayObject();

   // Fill the array with any SceneObject in the
   // MissionGroup SimGroup.
   foreach (%obj in MissionGroup)
   {
      if (%obj.isInNamespaceHierarchy("SceneObject"))
      {
         // This is a SceneObject so add it to the array
         %array.add(%obj.getId(), %obj.getClassName());
      }
   }

   // Fill the array with any SceneObject in the
   // MissionCleanup SimGroup.
   foreach (%obj in MissionCleanup)
   {
      if (%obj.isInNamespaceHierarchy("SceneObject"))
      {
         // This is a SceneObject so add it to the array
         %array.add(%obj.getId(), %obj.getClassName());
      }
   }

   // Sort the array's keys in ascending order using our
   // custom sort function.  This function will sort
   // all objects according to their world y position.
   %array.sortfk(arraySortFunction1);
```

```
    // Now output the list of objects to the console
    %count = %array.count();
    for (%i=0; %i<%count; %i++)
    {
        // The key holds the SimObject ID
        %key = %array.getKey(%i);

        // The value hold the class name
        %value = %array.getValue(%i);

        // Get the object's position
        %pos = %key.getPosition();

        // Print to the console
        echo(%value @ " [" @ %key @ "] Y Position: " @ %pos.y);
    }
}

// Our array sort function.  %a and %b hold the
// SimObject ID's of the objects to sort (the keys).
function arraySortFunction1(%a, %b)
{
    %posA = %a.getPosition();
    %posB = %b.getPosition();

    if (%posA.y < %posB.y)
        return -1;
    else if (%posA.y > %posB.y)
        return 1;
    else
        return 0;
}
```

2. Start up our game under the `My Projects` directory and load the `Empty Terrain` level. Open the console using the tilde (~) key and enter the following at the bottom of the screen:

sortArrayObject1();

In the console we will see the following output:

==>sortArrayObject1();

TerrainBlock [4277] Y Position: -1024

ScatterSky [4276] Y Position: 0

Camera [4289] Y Position: 0.250583

Player [4290] Y Position: 5.14696

How it works...

The example code begins by creating the `ArrayObject` instance that will be used to store some objects. It then steps through all the `MissionGroup` and `MissionCleanup` objects and stores any `SceneObject` instances it finds onto the array. The `SimObject` ID of the object is used as the key, and the class name of the object is used as the value.

With the array populated, we do an ascending sort using our custom sorting function, `arraySortFunction1()` as follows:

```
// Sort the array's keys in ascending order using our
// custom sort function.  This function will sort
// all objects according to their world y position.
%array.sortfk(arraySortFunction1);
```

The code then steps through the sorted array and prints the results to the console.

The critical component here is our custom sorting function, `arraySortFunction1()`. Each time the function is called, it passes two items to compare. As we're doing a key-based sort, the key of each item is passed to our sort function. When we created the array we placed `SimObject` ID of each `SceneObject` instance into the key, so we may now use the key to retrieve information about the `SceneObject` instance. In our case we get the world position of each object as follows:

```
%posA = %a.getPosition();
%posB = %b.getPosition();
```

The rule for the sorting function is that if item A is less than item B then return a value of `-1`. If item A is greater than B then return a value of `1`. And if items A and B are equal, return a value of `0`. It is up to our sorting function to determine what makes item A lesser than or greater than item B. In our example we're using world Y position of each object as follows:

```
if (%posA.y < %posB.y)
    return -1;
else if (%posA.y > %posB.y)
    return 1;
else
    return 0;
```

We then end up with a nicely sorted list from the lowest Y position to highest Y position that we output to the console.

See also

> ▸ *Using script arrays as dictionaries*

Scheduling SimObject methods

Scheduling allows for an action to occur sometime in the future. In TorqueScript we may have a schedule to trigger a method of an object after a specified amount of time has passed. In this recipe, we will learn how to schedule method of a `SimObject` instance.

Getting ready

We will be adding a new TorqueScript function to a project based on the Torque 3D `Full` template and try it out using the `Empty Terrain` level. If you haven't already, use the Torque Project Manager (`Project Manager.exe`) to create a new project from the `Full` template. It will be found under the `My Projects` directory. Then start up your favorite script editor, such as Torsion, and let's get going!

How to do it...

We are going to write a TorqueScript function that will demonstrate how to schedule a method of a `SimObject` instance as follows:

1. Open the `game/scripts/server/game.cs` script file and add the following code to the bottom:

```
function scheduleObjectMethod1()
{
    // Create a new ScriptObject that will have a
    // method scheduled
    new ScriptObject(MyScheduleObject);

    // Schedule a method to execute 250ms from now.  This
    // method is found in the MyScheduleObject namespace and
    // takes one parameter: the time the schedule was started.
    // We store the returned event ID in case we want to cancel
    // the schedule before it calls the method.
    MyScheduleObject.eventId =
        MyScheduleObject.schedule(250, myMethod, getRealTime());
}

// Our function that will be executed by the object's
// schedule.
function MyScheduleObject::myMethod(%this, %startTime)
{
    // Get the current time
    %currentTime = getRealTime();
```

```
        // Calculate the time delta
        %delta = %currentTime - %startTime;

        // Output to the console
        echo("Event ID " @ %this.eventId @ " sat for "
            @ %delta @ "ms before it was called");
    }
```

2. Start up our game under the `My Projects` directory and load the `Empty Terrain` level. Open the console using the tilde (~) key and enter the following at the bottom of the screen:

   scheduleObjectMethod1();

   In the console we will see the following output:

   ==>scheduleObjectMethod1();

   Event ID 1 sat for 256ms before it was called

How it works...

The example code begins by creating a `ScriptObject` instance with a globally unique name of `MyScheduleObject`. This name is later used as the namespace for the method that will be scheduled. The example code then schedules the method using the `SimObject` `schedule()` method as follows:

```
        MyScheduleObject.eventId =
            MyScheduleObject.schedule(250, myMethod, getRealTime());
```

The `schedule()` method has the following form:

```
    eventID = SimObject.schedule( time, method, args... );
```

Here the `time` parameter is the delay in milliseconds before the method is executed, the `method` parameter is the name of the method on the `SimObject` instance to execute, and the `args...` parameter is actually a variable number of optional arguments that are passed to given `method`. The `eventID` value of the scheduled event is returned by `schedule()`, so that we may cancel the schedule before it is invoked.

The actual time it takes for the scheduled method to execute may be greater than the delay time requested. This can be due to a number of factors, such as current engine load. However, the delay will never be less than the requested time.

There's more...

If the `SimObject` instance is deleted before the schedule has fired, the schedule will automatically be canceled. It is also possible to manually cancel a schedule by using the `cancel()` function. This function has the following form:

```
cancel( eventID );
```

Here the `eventID` parameter is the value returned by the `schedule()` method of the `SimObject` instance.

See also

▸ *Scheduling functions*

Scheduling functions

Scheduling allows for an action to occur sometime in the future. In TorqueScript we may have a schedule invoke a function after a specified amount of time has passed. In this recipe we will learn how to schedule a function.

Getting ready

We will be adding a new TorqueScript function to a project based on the Torque 3D `Full` template and try it out using the `Empty Terrain` level. If you haven't already, use the Torque Project Manager (`Project Manager.exe`) to create a new project from the `Full` template. It will be found under the `My Projects` directory. Then start up your favorite script editor, such as Torsion, and let's get going!

How to do it...

We are going to write a TorqueScript function that will demonstrate how to schedule a function as follows:

1. Open the `game/scripts/server/game.cs` script file and add the following code to the bottom:

```
function scheduleFunction1()
{
    // Schedule a function to execute 250ms from now.  This
    // function takes one parameter: the time the schedule
    // was started.  We store the returned event ID in case
    // we want to cancel the scedule before it calls the
    // function.
```

```
    $MyEventID =
        schedule(250, 0, myScheduledFunction, getRealTime());
}

// Our function that will be executed by the schedule.
function myScheduledFunction(%startTime)
{
    // Get the current time
    %currentTime = getRealTime();

    // Calculate the time delta
    %delta = %currentTime - %startTime;

    // Output to the console
    echo("Event ID " @ $MyEventID @ " sat for "
        @ %delta @ "ms before it was called");
}
```

2. Start up our game under the `My Projects` directory and load the `Empty Terrain` level. Open the console using the tilde (~) key and enter the following at the bottom of the screen:

   scheduleFunction1();

   In the console we will see the following output:

   ==>scheduleFunction1();

   Event ID 1 sat for 256ms before it was called

How it works...

The example code schedules our `MyScheduleFunction` using the `schedule()` function that has the following form:

```
    eventID = schedule( time, SimObjectID, function args... );
```

Here, the `time` parameter is the delay in milliseconds before the function is executed. The `SimObjectID` parameter is an optional object to invoke this function on (or `0` if no object), the `function` parameter is the name of the function to execute, and the `args...` parameter is actually a variable number of optional arguments that are passed to the given `function`. The `eventID` parameter of the scheduled event is returned by `schedule()` so that we may cancel the schedule before it is invoked.

If a `SimObject` ID is provided to the `schedule()` function, the schedule essentially operates as if we used the `SimObject schedule()` method. If the `SimObject` ID is left as `0` then the function is invoked on its own.

The actual time taken for the scheduled method to execute may be greater than the delay time requested. This can be due to a number of factors, such as current engine load. However, the delay will never be less than the requested time.

There's more...

It is possible to manually cancel a schedule by using the `cancel()` function. This function has the following form:

```
cancel( eventID );
```

Here the `eventID` parameter is the value returned by the `schedule()` function.

See also

 ▶   *Scheduling SimObject methods*

Activating and deactivating a package

TorqueScript packages allow us to encapsulate functions and `SimObject` methods into chunks that may be turned on and off. Packages are often used to modify the behavior of standard code, such as for a particular game play type. In this recipe, we will learn how to create a package and then how to activate and deactivate it.

Getting ready

We will be adding a new TorqueScript function to a project based on the Torque 3D `Full` template and try it out using the `Empty Terrain` level. If you haven't already, use the Torque Project Manager (`Project Manager.exe`) to create a new project from the `Full` template. It will be found under the `My Projects` directory. Then start up your favorite script editor, such as Torsion, and let's get going!

How to do it...

We are going to write a TorqueScript function that will demonstrate how to work with packages as follows:

1. Open the `game/scripts/server/game.cs` script file and add the following code to the bottom:

```
function printStuff1()
{
    echo("Non-packaged printStuff1()");

    // Print out four random numbers to the console
    for (%i=0; %i<4; %i++)
    {
        echo("Number " @ %i @ ": " @ getRandom());
    }
}

//Start the definition of our package
package ChangeItUp
{
    function printStuff1()
    {
        echo("Packaged printStuff1()");

        // This version of the function just counts to 10
        %counter = "";
        for (%i=1; %i<=10; %i++)
        {
            %counter = %counter SPC %i;
        }

        echo(%counter);
    }
};

// This function will test everything out
function unitTest1()
{
    // Invoke the non-packaged function
    printStuff1();

    // Activate the package
    activatePackage(ChangeItUp);

    // Invoke what should be the packaged function
    printStuff1();

    // Deactivate the package
```

```
        deactivatePackage(ChangeItUp);

        // Now we should be back to the non-packaged
        // function
        printStuff1();
    }
```

2. Start up our game under the `My Projects` directory and load the `Empty Terrain` level. Open the console using the tilde (~) key and enter the following at the bottom of the screen:

   `unitTest1();`

   In the console we will see the following output:

   ```
   ==>unitTest1();
   Non-packaged printStuff1()
   Number 0: 0.265364
   Number 1: 0.96804
   Number 2: 0.855327
   Number 3: 0.473076
   Packaged printStuff1()
    1 2 3 4 5 6 7 8 9 10
   Non-packaged printStuff1()
   Number 0: 0.982307
   Number 1: 0.639691
   Number 2: 0.278508
   Number 3: 0.888561
   ```

How it works...

The example code first defines an ordinary function, `printStuff1()`. It just prints out four random numbers to the console. Then the code defines a package named `ChangeItUP`. A **package** is defined by using the `package` keyword followed by the name of the package. Any function or method that is defined within the curly braces of the package will override the same regular function or method when the package is activated. When a package is deactivated, the overridden functions and methods go back to their regular versions.

The `unitTest1()` function demonstrates this in action. It first invokes the regular `printStuff1()` function. Then the `ChangeItUp` package is activated. Now when `printStuff1()` is called, it is the one defined within the package that is used. Finally, the package is deactivated and the regular `printStuff1()` function is called.

There's more...

The order in which the packages are activated and deactivated is important. When multiple packages are activated we have what is called the **package stack**. If the same function or method is defined across multiple packages and all of those packages are activated, the last package that was activated will be where the function or method is called.

If a package in the middle of the stack is deactivated, then all packages that were activated later in the stack (following the one we are about to deactivate) will also be deactivated.

To get a view of the current package stack use the `getPackageList()` function. This function returns a space-delimited list of all of the currently active packages, and in the order in which they were activated.

2
Working with Your Editors

In this chapter we will cover the following topics:

- ▸ Setting up fogging of the level
- ▸ How to cover seams and texture changes using decals placed in the *World Editor*
- ▸ Copying the transform of an object to another object in the *World Editor*
- ▸ How to change the material of an object in the *World Editor*
- ▸ Setting up a glow mask using the *Material Editor*
- ▸ Using a convex shape as a zone
- ▸ Setting zone-specific ambient lighting
- ▸ Grouping adjacent zones together

Introduction

Torque 3D includes a lot of built-in tools to help us create and refine a game and all that goes into it. The **World Editor** window is the gateway to all of the various editors that are available, and may be accessed by pressing *F11* during game play. The following table lists all of the different editors available from the *World Editor*:

Editor	Description
Object Editor	This helps you add and delete objects, and position, rotate, and scale them. It also allows you to modify the properties of an object.
Terrain Editor	You can raise and lower the terrain or create holes in the terrain.
Terrain Painter	This helps you to apply materials to the surface of the terrain.
Material Editor	This allows you to create and manipulate materials that are used by all 3D objects in the level.
Sketch Tool	You can create convex shapes to be used as placeholders, or as textured game objects themselves.
Datablock Editor	You can create and manipulate the static properties used by various game objects.
Decal Editor	This helps you to place decals around the level on the terrain and static objects.
Forest Editor	You can place high performance rendered foliage within the level of the game.
Mesh Road Editor	You can create 3D roads in the level by drawing splines.
Mission Area Editor	This allows you to define the bounds for the level.
Particle Editor	You can create and modify particle systems.
River Editor	You can create 3D rivers in the level by drawing splines.
Road and Path Editor	You can create decal-based roads or paths that conform to the terrain within the level by drawing splines.
Shape Editor	This helps you to edit the setup of a 3D shape, including materials used, collision shapes, and levels of detail.

The *Object Editor* is where we spend most of our time when working on a level of our game. Within this editor we can add and move 3D objects, as well as change their properties. This is also the default editor that comes up when we press *F11*. Because of this, many people use the terms *World Editor* and *Object Editor* to mean the same thing.

In this chapter we will touch on some of the lesser-discussed, although no less important, aspects of the various editors. Many of these recipes will help us work faster, or help add that extra bit of polish and performance to our game.

For an overview of all the editors of Torque 3D, please see the Torque Art Primer on the official documentation page at `http://www.garagegames.com/documentation/torque-3d`.

Setting up fogging of the level

Using fog is a very common method of adding depth to a scene. Fog can help separate distant objects from those up-close, and can even be used to separate the hills from the valleys. Having fog in a scene also allows us to reduce the render distance to help increase a game's performance. In this recipe, we will set up fog parameters in a level.

Getting ready

Start up Torque 3D and launch a level of your game, then press *F11* to open the *World Editor*. As we want to manipulate the scene objects, the *Object Editor* should be selected (*F1* or by using the **Editors** menu). A level based on the `Empty Terrain` level of `Full` *template* could be used as a good example.

How to do it...

The following steps add fog to a level that did not have it applied originally:

1. Select `theLevelInfo` class object in the **Scene Tree** window. By default it is named **theLevelInfo** class object.

2. In the property inspector (the window named as **Inspector**), scroll until you locate the **Fog** section.

3. Click on the colored box to the right-hand side of the **fogColor** property to open the **Color Picker** dialog box. Choose a light color, such as white, and click on the **Select** button in the dialog.

4. Set the **fogDensity** property to `0.04`.

5. Set the **fogDensityOffset** property to `0`.

6. Set the **fogAtmosphereHeight** property to `0`.

We now have fog in the level as the following screenshot demonstrates:

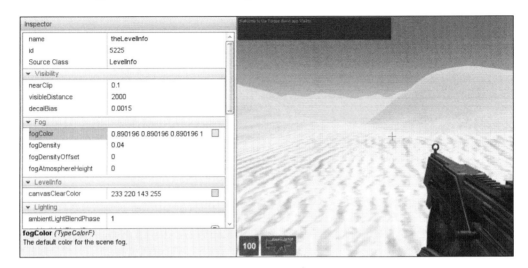

How it works...

The `fogColor` property of `theLevelInfo` class is blended with the scene based on the distance of a pixel from the camera. It is a blend between the actual color of the pixel and the color added by the `fogColor` property. The further away a pixel is from the camera, the more it tends towards the value of `fogColor` than towards the color of the pixel, until finally only the color of the fog (as defined by the `fogColor` property) is drawn. Choosing a value of the `fogColor` property that closely matches our background horizon color enhances the effect.

The `fogDensity` property determines how fast the `fogColor` property is applied to a pixel. As you would expect, the higher the value of `fogDensity`, the less distance there is until the full `fogColor` value is rendered. This value is used exponentially rather than linearly, so some experimentation is required to find the best fit for your level.

The `fogDensityOffset` property sets the radius at which the fog begins. This allows us to push out the fog away from the camera, providing a fog-free volume around the camera. Setting the `fogDensityOffset` property to `0` causes the fog to begin immediately in front of the camera. By pushing out the start of the fog we can keep the details of the scene up-close, while washing out the more distant objects, adding to the apparent depth of a level.

The `fogAtmosphereHeight` property is unique in that it is an absolute height value. When set to a value other than `0`, it defines the maximum absolute height at which the fog is applied. This causes a blend from the `fogColor` property at lower elevations to normal coloring of the scene at a `fogAtmosphereHeight` elevation. This helps provide a greater distinction between the hills and valleys of a level, with it appearing that fog is collecting in the valleys.

The following image on the left-hand side has `fogAtmosphereHeight` set to 0, while the image on the right-hand side has it set to 300. Using the `fogAtmosphereHeight` property makes the fog look like it is collecting in the valleys.

There's more...

Let's take a look at what else can affect fog rendering of a level.

Fog and the ScatterSky class

When we are using the `ScatterSky` class in a game level, it takes over control of the fog color of the level. The fog color is calculated internally, based on how the sky is currently colored (determined by the location of the sun in the sky and the other `ScatterSky` properties), rather than relying on `fogColor` parameter of `theLevelInfo` class. This algorithmic control of the color of the fog is to provide a better transition between fogged elements and the sky based on real world observations.

The `ScatterSky` class does provide the `fogScale` property to allow us some control over coloring of the fog. The `fogScale` property is multiplied with the calculated fog color to provide the final coloring. This allows us to tint the final fog color based on our artistic preferences.

Unfortunately, there is a minor issue with fog rendering and using the `ScatterSky` class. Fortunately however, this issue only comes up when changing the values in the *World Editor* and does not affect normal game play. If we have a `ScatterSky` class instance in our scene, and if we ever change the properties of `theLevelInfo` class, the rendered fog color will switch from the calculated `ScatterSky` one and revert to the `fogColor` property of `theLevelInfo` class.

To get back to the proper fog color, we just need to save our level and reload it. This is a minor annoyance as we don't often modify `theLevelInfo` class. But it can be quite disconcerting when the fog color suddenly changes and we're not prepared for it!

How to cover seams and texture changes using decals placed in the World Editor

When placing 3D objects within a game level sometimes there is a hard, visible transition when two or more objects intersect with each other. An example would be a rock outcrop object and the terrain. We may want to soften this transition between objects for better visual appeal. In this recipe we will add decals to the level to help cover up these seams between objects.

Getting ready

Start up `FPS Example` in Torque 3D and launch the `Deathball Desert` level. Press *Alt + C* to switch to the third-person camera, and then press *F11* to open the *World Editor*. As we want to manipulate the manually-placed decals, open the *Decal Editor* window by pressing *F7*, or using the **Editors** menu.

How to do it...

In the following steps we are going to place a decal to cover up a seam between a 3D shape and the terrain:

1. Fly the camera to where we will place the decals. For our `Deathball Desert` example, we will fly to one of the many rock towers that are placed on top of the terrain.

2. Go to the **Library** tab of the *Decal Editor* window.

3. Choose the `RockyCliffDecal` template.

4. Make sure the **Add Decal** tool is chosen from the toolbar of the *Decal Editor* window on the left-hand side of the screen, or press *5*.

5. Navigate the mouse and click near the bottom of the rock tower where it meets the terrain. This will place a decal instance, and it may have some texture stretching either along the rock tower or the terrain.

6. Click on the **Rotate Decal** tool (or press *3*) from the toolbar of the *Decal Editor* window.

7. Click-and-drag the rotation axis gizmo until the texture stretching has disappeared. You may need to rotate the decal along multiple axes to get it to look just right.

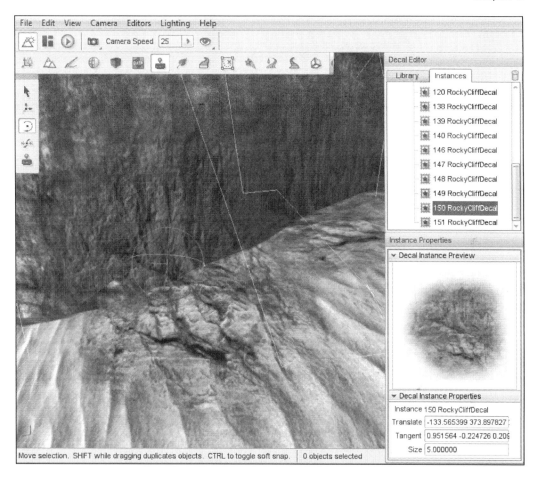

8. Click on the **Scale Decal** tool (or press *4*) from the toolbar of the *Decal Editor* window.

9. Shrink the decal instance by clicking and dragging the scale axis gizmo. Decals may only be scaled uniformly along all axes.

10. Click on the **Move Decal** tool (or press *2*) from the toolbar of the *Decal Editor* window.

11. Move the decal instance vertically until it is centered on the seam between the rock tower and the terrain.

How it works...

Decals are often used to add details to a level. Scorch marks, cracks, manhole covers, and puddles are all good examples of decals being used. They may also be used to bridge a visible seam or texture discontinuity where two objects touch. In our previous example from the `Deathball Desert` level, we're using decals to cover up the seam between a rock tower and the sandy terrain.

The trick to these types of decals is we want them to blend smoothly between the two objects. This requires a texture with an alpha channel that makes the edges of the decal transparent.

The other trick is getting the texture projection angle just right for the decal. If it is too steep relative to the surface of either object, the texture will appear stretched, and often we will lose the nice alpha transparency and end up with a hard edge. By tweaking the projection angle of the decal using the **Rotate Decal** tool of the *Decal Editor* window, we can get rid of (or at least minimize) the stretching and end up with a good-looking decal.

There's more...

Let's continue our discussion about decals.

Working with decal instances

Once we have placed a few decals in the level we need to be able to manage them. The **Instances** tab of the *Decal Editor* window is where we will find a list of all the manually placed decals. The list is sorted by decal `Datablock` name. We can expand each `Datablock` entry to obtain a list of all the decal instances that use that `Datablock` entry. Clicking on an instance will select it in the scene, ready to be modified.

To delete a decal instance we select it from the list, and then press the *Delete* key.

TSStatic shapes and decalType property

`TSStatic` class objects have a `decalType` property found under the `Collision` group of the property inspector, that is the window named **Inspector**. This property determines the elements of geometry of a shape that decals will wrap around, with the choices of: `Bounds`, `Collision Mesh`, `None`, and `Visible Mesh`.

Unfortunately, with Torque 3D 2.0 this property is ignored. Decals instead look to the `collisionType` property to determine the geometry they will project onto. The future version of Torque 3D will correct this issue.

Copying the transform of an object to another in the World Editor window

When working with objects in the *World Editor* there are times when we want one object to have the same transform as another. This includes the world position of that object, its rotation, and its scale. For example, we may want to stack one crate on top of another. To facilitate this, we could give both crates the same transform and then move one crate on top of the other using the axis gizmo. To copy and paste the transform of an object we use the **Transform Selection** dialog.

Getting ready

Start up Torque 3D and launch a level of your game, then press *F11* to open the *World Editor*. As we want to manipulate the scene objects, the *Object Editor* should be selected (*F1* or by using the **Editors** menu). Make sure there are at least two objects in the level: the object that will be the source of the transform, and the destination object.

How to do it...

In the following steps we will copy the transform from one scene object and paste it onto another:

1. Select the scene object that we will copy the transform from by either clicking on it using the mouse, or choosing it from the **Scene Tree** window.

2. Open the **Transform Selection** dialog found under the **Object** menu. Click on the **Get** button found within the **Position**, **Rotation**, and **Scale** sections of the dialog. The various text edit fields will populate themselves with the values of the object. This is shown in the next screenshot:

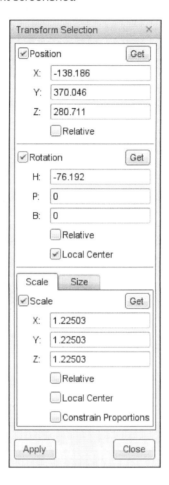

3. Select the scene object that we want to paste the transform information to. Either click on it using the mouse, or choose it from the **Scene Tree** window.

4. Click on the **Apply** button at the bottom of the **Transform Selection** dialog. The selected object will now have the same position, rotation, and scale as the source object.

How it works...

The **Transform Selection** dialog makes it easy to copy all of the transform information of an object and paste it into another object's transform information. We select an object and get all of its transform attributes, then select another object, and apply those attributes.

There's more...

The **Transform Selection** dialog lets us do more than just copy all the transform information from one object and paste it to another. Let's take a look.

Copying only position (or rotation, or scale) of an object

Each section of the **Transform Selection** dialog has a checkbox. When we click on the **Apply** button of the dialog, only those sections that have the checkbox checked will be applied to the selected object. So if we only want to modify the position of an object we will make sure that only the **Position** checkbox has a checkmark.

Please note that when we click on the **Get** button of a section, that section is automatically marked to apply its values.

Nudging the selected object

The **Transform Selection** dialog can be used to slightly nudge the position, rotation, or scale of an object in a desired direction. For example, if we wanted to move the selected object 1 cm along the x axis, it can be done as follows:

1. Enter `0.01`, `0`, `0` into the **X**, **Y**, and **Z** position of the **Transform Selection** dialog.
2. Make sure that the **Position** section is the only one that has its checkbox marked.
3. Click on the **Relative** checkbox of the **Position** section so it has a checkmark.
4. Click on the **Apply** button of **Transform Selection** dialog.

Now each time the **Apply** button is clicked on, the object will move 1 cm along the x axis. By having the **Relative** checkbox set, the selected object will move by the given amount rather than jump to that world position. If we find that the object has moved too far by clicking on the **Apply** button too many times, we can just undo the operation with *Ctrl + Z*. Using this method allows us to easily nudge objects around a level in discrete amounts.

Rotating an object using degrees

The *Object Editor* in the property inspector (the **Inspector** window) only allows us to modify the rotation of an object using an axis and angle notation, which represent the exact rotation of an object. This internal format can be difficult for us to work with compared to working in the standard Euler angles, even if the Euler angles can suffer from gimbal lock.

The **Transform Selection** dialog can be used to rotate an object using the standard Euler angles. Its **H**, **P**, and **B** fields are **Heading**, **Pitch**, and **Roll** angles of an object in degrees. Normally these values are the absolute angles of the object. However, when the **Relative** checkbox of the dialog is set, it is possible to nudge an object along each of the axes independently.

Manipulating more than one object

The **Transform Selection** dialog may be used to modify more than one object at a time. We just need to select all of the objects we wish to manipulate, and then clicking on the **Apply** button will change all of them at once. When working with multiple objects there are a few things to be aware of.

Changing the absolute world position of multiple objects at once (without the **Relative** checkbox set) uses the calculated center of all of the objects, rather than the origin of the objects themselves. This keeps all positions of the objects relative to each other constant while moving them all as a group to the specified world position.

When modifying the rotation of multiple objects at once, the behavior of the **Transform Selection** dialog is dependent on the **Local Center** checkbox. Without it set (which is the default option) then all the objects will rotate about a calculated center of the group. Unless the origin of an object happens to line up with the calculated center, an object will both move and rotate as if it is orbiting about this center. When this checkbox is set, each object will rotate about its own origin.

Changing the scale of multiple objects at once also depends on the **Local Center** checkbox. As with rotation, this checkbox determines if the scale occurs at a calculated center, or based at the origin of each individual object.

It is important to note that Torque 3D does not support skewing objects. A **skew** is a scale in a direction other than along the local X, Y, or Z axis of an object. Rather than perform a skew, Torque 3D will always scale a rotated object along its local axis.

How to change the material of an object in the World Editor

When we add a 3D object to a level using the *World Editor*, it always has the same set of materials as defined by the artist (using the *Material Editor* window or through scripts). Sometimes we want to keep the same object geometry and just change the materials used. An example would be two soccer nets with distinct coloring while having the same shape. This process of changing the materials of an object in Torque 3D is called **skinning**. In this recipe, we will change the materials of an object to be different than the default materials by modifying the properties of an object using the *World Editor* window.

Getting ready

Before we can skin a 3D object, we need to prepare it and its materials or surfaces in a 3D modeling application. We will then have to set up the new skinned `Material` instances using a text editor, such as Torsion, to have their `mapTo` properties set correctly. Afterwards we can tweak the `Material` instances using the *Material Editor* window. Here we'll provide an example of a soccer net object, but the steps will be similar for your own objects:

1. In your 3D modeling application, give each material that you wish to skin a prefix of `base_`. Any material that doesn't start with `base_` will not change when the shape is skinned. Depending upon your modeling application, you may also need to add this prefix to the texture filenames as well.

2. Export your 3D model for use in Torque 3D as you normally would.

3. Set up the `Material` class instances of your 3D model in Torque 3D for the base material. Usually these are placed in a `materials.cs` TorqueScript file along with the 3D shape file. These will be used for all the objects that are not skinned. For example, the base `material` for the net and posts of a soccer goal could look like the following code:

```
Singleton Material(Mat_Base_Goal_Net)
{
    // Map this Material instance to the named
    // material or surface on the 3D shape.   Include
    // the "base_" prefix.
    mapTo = "base_goalnet";

    // The diffuse texture to use for this material.
    // The texture's name could be anything and doesn't
    // need to include the base_ prefix.
    diffuseMap[0] = "base_goal_net_d.dds";

    // The normal map to use for this material
    // The texture's name could be anything and doesn't
    // need to include the base_ prefix.
    normalMap[0] = "base_goal_net_n.dds";

    // Use the alpha channel to make the 'holes' in
    // the net.
    translucent = true;
    translucentBlendOp = "None";
    alphaTest = true;
    alphaRef = 127;
};

Singleton Material(Mat_Base_Goal_Post)
```

```
{
   // Map this Material instance to the named
   // material or surface on the 3D shape.   Include
   // the "base_" prefix.
   mapTo = "base_goalpost";

   // The diffuse texture to use for this material
   diffuseMap[0] = "base_goal_post_d.dds";

   // The normal map to use for this material
   normalMap[0] = "base_goal_post_n.dds";
};
```

4. Create a set of the `Material` class instances that will be used to skin the object. Continuing our example, we will set up the net and post materials of the soccer goal for the first team. The `Material` instances of another team would be set up in the same way but would reference different textures as follows:

```
Singleton Material(Mat_Team1_Goal_Net)
{
   // We will use a team1 prefix for this skin
   mapTo = "team1_goalnet";

   // New texture for this skin
   diffuseMap[0] = "team1_goal_net_d.dds";

   // We will use the same normal map
   normalMap[0] = "base_goal_net_n.dds";

   // Use the alpha channel to make the 'holes' in
   // the net.
   translucent = true;
   translucentBlendOp = "None";
   alphaTest = true;
   alphaRef = 127;
};

Singleton Material(Mat_Team1_Goal_Post)
{
   // We will use a team1 prefix for this skin
   mapTo = "team1_goalpost";

   // New texture for this skin
   diffuseMap[0] = "team1_goal_post_d.dds";

   // We will use the same normal map
   normalMap[0] = "base_goal_post_n.dds";
};
```

With the 3D object and its `Material` class instances ready to go, start up Torque 3D and launch a level of your game, then press *F11* to open the *World Editor*. As we want to manipulate the scene objects, the *Object Editor* should be selected (*F1* or by using the **Editors** menu). Add the object we want to skin to the level.

How to do it...

In the following steps, we will modify the materials used by an object in the scene:

1. Select the 3D object that is to be skinned in the scene.
2. Using the property inspector, scroll until you find the `skin` property of the object.
3. Type the skin prefix you would like to use, minus the trailing underscore. Using the previous soccer net example, we would enter `team1` as the skin prefix.
4. Press the *Enter* key or *Tab* key to set the skin value.

How it works...

When the `skin` property of a 3D object is set, the `Material` instances of the object whose `mapTo` property has a prefix of `base_` will automatically be remapped to make use of the new `Material` class instances. Any of the `Material` instances of the object that do not start with `base_` will not be touched.

The following picture is an example of material skinning in action. On the left-hand side, the example shows the soccer goal using the `base` materials. On the right-hand side, the soccer goal, using the `team1` materials, shows the color of the team as red stripes on the posts and a red oval on the back of the net:

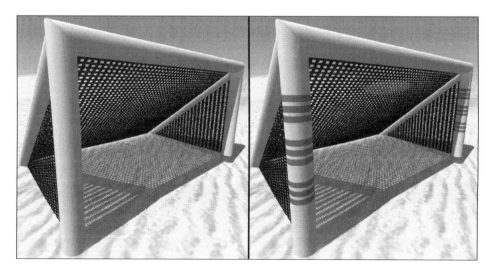

There's more...

The `skin` property supports more options than were covered in this section. Let's take a look at them now.

Modifying materials that do not start with base_

Even though the `mapTo` property of a `Material` instance doesn't start with `base_`, it is still possible to skin it with only a little more work. With the following format, the `skin` property of a 3D object allows us to directly skin any material:

```
Original mapTo text = new mapTo text
```

For example, if our soccer net simply had its `Material mapTo` property defined as `net`, we could skin it to use a red-colored `net Material` instance with the following entered into the `skin` property of the object:

```
net=red_net
```

This will skin a single material of an object, without touching any others.

Skinning multiple materials at once

It is possible to change multiple materials on a single 3D object at once by separating each skin change with a semicolon. If our soccer net has two materials named `net` and `posts` that we wish to change to a red-colored `Material` instance, we could do this with the following:

```
net=red_net;posts=red_posts;
```

Something to watch for is when we want to modify all the materials that start with `base_` as well as those that do not use the `base_` prefix. In this case, we need to explicitly state that we want to modify the `base_` materials. For example, consider the following line of code:

```
base=team1;net=red_net
```

This will skin all the materials that start with `base_` as well as the `net` material. As mentioned previously, you do not want to include the underscore at the end of the base text.

Setting up a glow mask using the Material Editor window

Torque 3D makes it easy to make a material emissive (not affected by lighting) and glow using the *Material Editor* window. However, activating these `Material` class properties makes the entire material emissive and glow. In this recipe, we will learn how to mask out the glow region of a material to limit its effect.

Getting ready

This recipe requires some work to be done in the Paint program of your choice, as well as in Torque 3D. We will describe the Paint program steps in general terms as each application is different. However, most Paint programs that are in-depth enough for game development, support the same general operations.

In Torque 3D we will be using the *Materials Editor* window to modify the material properties of a 2D object.

How to do it...

In the following steps, we will create a new glow texture and apply it to an object:

1. Start up your Paint program and load in the texture file we'll use as a base. This could be the texture used for the body of your game character, for example.

2. Create a new layer on the texture.

3. Select, copy, and paste the parts from the base texture that are to glow on to the new layer. Or draw the glowing bits of the texture on the new layer by hand.

4. After the new layer is complete with only the glow parts in place, delete the base texture layer. This should leave the parts of the texture that will glow, while the rest of the texture will be considered transparent.

   The following screenshot from the **GNU Image Manipulator Program (GIMP)** Paint program shows a glow texture for only the badge part of a backpack texture:

5. Save our texture as a PNG file with a new name. We will end up with a texture file that contains an alpha channel to mask out the areas that will not glow.

6. Now start up Torque 3D and load the level your game. Open the *World Editor* window by pressing *F11*.

7. Add the shape you want to have glow to the level using the *Object Editor* (press *F1* or use the **Editors** menu) or fly the camera to an existing shape.

8. Switch to the *Material Editor* window by pressing *F4* or use the **Editors** menu.

9. Click on the **Open Existing Material** button (the button with a folder icon) to open the **Material Selector** menu. Choose the material we want to add a glow to and click on the **Select** button.

10. At the top of the **Material Properties** section of the *Material Editor* window, there is a drop-down control that reads as **Layer 0**. Click on this drop-down control and choose **Layer 1**.

11. Click on the **Edit** button for the **Diffuse Map** option. Choose the glow texture with the alpha map that we built previously.

12. Scroll down to the **Lighting Properties** section of **Layer 1**. Click on the **Emissive** and **Glow** checkboxes. Your object will now glow only in the areas drawn on the texture used in **Layer 1**.

13. Click on the **Save Material** button at the top of the **Material Properties** section to save our changes.

How it works...

Torque 3D supports `Material` instances with up to four textures layered on top of each other. Layer 0 is the base, and layers 1 through 3 are placed on top. Using a texture with an alpha channel for each layer beyond the first allows the layers to blend with each other.

By placing a specific glow texture on layer 1 of the `Material` instance, the glow effect for the layer will only render where the texture is drawn. This is not limited to just the glow and emissive properties. Any of the **Lighting Properties** and **Animation Properties** for the `Material` instance are applied only to the currently chosen layer.

The following screenshot is a comparison of the glow settings of a material. On the left-hand side, the **Emissive** and **Glow** lighting properties have been turned on for `Layer 0` in the *Material Editor* window. This makes the entire `Material` instance glow. On the right-hand side, a `Diffuse Map` parameter has been added to `Layer 1` that includes an alpha channel to mask out the areas that should not glow. The **Emissive** and **Glow** lighting properties have been turned on for only this layer:

There's more...

Let's discuss some possible issues with this recipe and look at another approach that we can take.

Effect of alpha threshold on glow

If a `Material` property is set to be transparent and an alpha threshold other than zero is set (under the **Advanced** section of the *Material Editor* window), the alpha threshold will be applied to all layers. This means that the alpha channel for the glow texture on layer 1 will be cut into, reducing its size. If this becomes an issue, we may need to use more than one `Material` instance for the glow effect, as is discussed in the following section.

Using more than one material

Another way we can limit the regions of a glow effect on a 3D object is to have two or more `Material` instances defined for the object. The first `Material` instance would be applied to all of the triangles of an object that should not glow, while the second `Material` instance would be set to glow on layer 0. This setup requires that we define these separate materials or surfaces within our 3D modeling application.

The advantage of taking this route is we can safely apply an alpha threshold to either `Material` instance without it affecting the glow. The disadvantage is that the glowing regions must be on triangle boundaries within the 3D model. You can have only a portion of a triangle glow by having a glow mask on layer 1 of the `Material` instance.

The soldier character included in Torque 3D is a good example of using one `Material` instance (called `Mat_Soldier_Main`) to define most of the soldier's surface, and a second `Material` instance (called `Mat_Soldier_Dazzle`) to define the surfaces to glow. You can check out the soldier in the *Shape Editor* window.

Using a convex shape as a zone

In Torque 3D, zones are used to control which 3D objects will be rendered within a level, based on the current camera position and rotation. If the camera cannot see into a zone, such as through a connected `Portal` object (this acts like a window); or is not within the zone itself, the objects inside the zone are not rendered. This allows us to have far more objects within the level than could normally be rendered all at once due to performance concerns. Normally, a `Zone` object is box-shaped. In this recipe, we will learn how to create a new convex shape and use it as a `Zone` object.

Getting ready

Start up Torque 3D and launch a level of your game, then press *F11* to open the *World Editor*. As we want to create and manipulate special convex objects, the Sketch Tool should be selected (*F5* or by using the **Editors** menu).

How to do it...

In the following steps, we will create a `ConvexShape` object and turn it into a custom-shaped `Zone` object:

1. We will start by creating a new `ConvexShape` object. Hold down the *Alt* key, then click-and-drag out the base of the convex shape somewhere in the level. With the base now in place, let go of the mouse button, and move upwards. This gives the convex shape its height. Finally, click once to fix the size of the convex shape in place.

2. We can now click on any of the faces of convex shape and perform the standard axis gizmo operations on them. Click on one of the vertical faces and use the **Move** tool to make the convex shape bigger.

3. Now let's split one of the faces and rotate it. Click on the top face and activate the **Rotate** tool. Hold down the *Ctrl* key and use the axis gizmo to rotate about either the x or y axis. This will split the face in half, and we can rotate the face to give it some slope.

We are now done creating our convex shape, so let's switch to the *Object Editor* by pressing *F1* or using the **Editors** menu. Our newly-created convex shape will automatically be selected in the **Scene Tree** window.

4. To convert the convex shape into a `Zone` object, right-click on the `ConvexShape` instance in the **Scene Tree** window to bring up a menu. From this menu choose **Convert to Zone**.

5. Our convex shape will now be changed into a `Zone` object while maintaining its form. We can now use this new zone just like any other `Zone` object.

How it works...

The most common type of `Zone` object is a simple box. However, there are times when the space we wish to put into a zone does not easily fit a box.

In these cases, we can use the Sketch Tool to first build up a convex shape. Then we can convert this shape into a `Zone` object by right-clicking on the context menu on the **Scene Tree** window. We can also go back the other way by bringing up the context menu in the **Scene Tree** window for a `Zone` object, and converting it back to a `ConvexShape` object. This allows us to easily test out the object culling of a zone, and then go back and adjust the shape of the zone.

There's more...

Let's continue with some tips about building and using zones.

Quickly zoning a level

When roughing out the zones for a level, it may be easiest to start with the standard, box-shaped `Zone` objects. We can quickly add those to the scene, move them into place, and resize them using the axis gizmo.

Once all of the zones are in place, we can convert those `Zone` objects that need to better fit their environment by converting them to `ConvexShape` objects. For example, a cylindrical room, or a twisty cave system could both make use of non-box shaped zones. We then use the Sketch Tool to adjust the convex shapes as appropriate, and then convert them back into zones again.

Game engine performance considerations

The standard box-shaped `Zone` objects are the least taxing on the game engine when it is determining which objects in the level to cull, and which objects to render. Because of this performance concern, it is best to use the standard `Zone` objects whenever possible. Usually it does not matter that the zones exactly match the level geometry.

It is also a good idea to use as few `Zone` objects as possible. It is always a trade-off between having tight, perfectly fitting zones versus allowing some objects to render even if the player may not actually see them.

The concept of fewer zones also carries over to the `Portal` object we use to join zones together. Rather than have one portal per window for a bank of windows along the same wall, it is better to have a single portal that covers all of the windows and not worry about the small bit of wall between them.

The following picture is a comparison of two different `Portal` setups (the green boxes) for a store front. The top image demonstrates building a `Portal` object per opening: one `Portal` object for the entrance and one `Portal` object per window. The bottom image demonstrates using a single `Portal` object to cover all the three openings at once, providing better engine performance:

Finally, while it is also possible to convert a convex shape to a `Portal` object using the context menu of the **Scene Tree** window, this should only be done under extreme circumstances. Each extra edge that exists on a `Portal` object incurs a penalty when calculating the culling frustum (the volume seen through the portal by a camera). So it is best to stick with box-shaped portals as much as possible.

See also

▸ *Setting zone-specific ambient lighting*

▸ *Grouping adjacent zones together*

Setting zone-specific ambient lighting

Zones are mainly used to determine which objects in a level should render and which shouldn't, based on the current camera position and rotation. In addition, Zone objects may also control the ambient lighting (the lighting that appears to come from all directions) for the region within the Zone. A good example of this is a cave system where the sun should not reach all the way in. In this recipe, we will look at how to set up custom ambient lighting for a Zone object that is different from the rest of the level.

Getting ready

Start up Torque 3D and launch a level of your game, then press *F11* to open the *World Editor*. As we want to manipulate the scene objects, the *Object Editor* should be selected (*F1* or by using the **Editors** menu). Make sure there is at least one Zone object already in the level.

How to do it...

In the following steps we will modify ambient lighting properties of a Zone object:

1. Select the Zone object that will have the custom ambient lighting set.

2. Scroll to the **Lighting** section in the property inspector for the Zone object.

3. Click on the **useAmbientLightColor** checkbox to mark this zone as having a custom ambient light level and color.

4. Click on the **ambientLightColor** color edit button to open the **Color Picker** dialog box.

5. Choose the color to use for ambient lighting of the Zone objects. For no ambient lighting, change the color to black.

6. Click on the **Select** button of **Color Picker** to set the ambient light color of the zone.

How it works...

When the player or camera enters a `Zone` object, the ambient lighting normally comes from the settings of the level. However, there are times when we want the ambient light color to be different, such as when we're in a cave. By setting up the `Zone` instance to have a custom ambient light color, when the camera enters or leaves the `Zone` object, the ambient lighting will smoothly transition between the values of the level, and the values of the `Zone` object.

The speed at which the ambient lighting transitions between values is determined by the **ambientLightBlendPhase** setting on the `LevelInfo` object of the level. Its value is the number of seconds to take to perform the transition, with a default value of one second.

See also

- ▸ *Using a convex shape as a zone*
- ▸ *Grouping adjacent zones together*

Grouping adjacent zones together

Normally we use a `Portal` object to join the `Zone` objects together. This acts as a window, or doorway between the zones. However, there are times when adding portals is counterproductive, and we just want to have a number of zones treated as one unit. An example of this is when using convex-shaped zone objects to fill up an oddly-shaped room, and we want the whole room to be treated as one big zone.

In this recipe, we will look at how to have two or more `Zone` objects considered a single zone, without the use of `Portal` objects.

Getting ready

Start up Torque 3D and launch a level of your game, then press *F11* to open the *World Editor*. As we want to manipulate the scene objects, the *Object Editor* should be selected (*F1* or by using the **Editors** menu). Make sure there are at least two `zone` objects already in the level, and that they are next to each other.

How to do it...

In the following steps, we will group a number of Zone objects together so that they are treated as a single zone:

1. We start by making sure that all the Zone objects we want to be grouped together are slightly overlapping each other. If this is not the case, use the object **Move** tool to shift the zones around.

2. Select the first Zone object to group.

3. Using the property inspector, scroll down to the **Zoning** section. In the **zoneGroup** text edit field, enter a non-zero value. If this is the first zone group for the level, enter a value of 1.

4. Go to each of the Zone objects that are to be grouped and make their **zoneGroup** setting match the one we set up in the third step.

How it works...

When the zoneGroup property of a Zone object is set to zero, the zone is not considered to be grouped with any other zones. By setting the zoneGroup property to any non-zero value, the Zone object is automatically grouped with the other zones that have the same zoneGroup value.

When zones are grouped together, it is as if there is a portal joining them together. The camera can see all objects in all grouped zones with the same zoneGroup value. We need to make sure there is some overlap between the grouped zones, otherwise when the camera moves between zones, there will be a space where the objects of the grouped zones are not visible. The grouped zones need to continuously flow into each other.

The following picture is looking down inside a tower towards its floor. There are four Zone objects, each with a custom shape to fit the interior of the tower. The Zone objects all have their zoneGroup property set to the same number, so the object culling system treats them all as one zone:

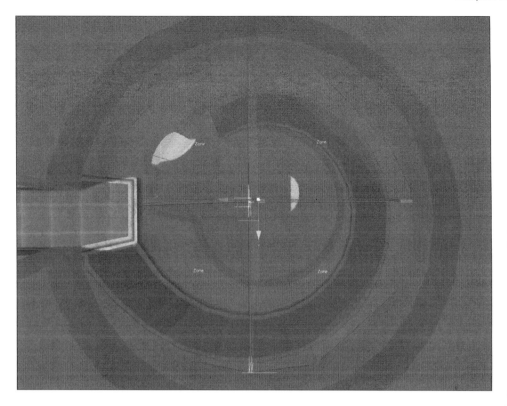

See also

▸ *Using a convex shape as a zone*

▸ *Setting zone-specific ambient lighting*

3
Graphical User Interface

In this chapter, we will cover the following topics:

▶ Creating a password text edit box

▶ Using `pushDialog()` and `popDialog()` and setting up the UI file to work with them

▶ Displaying metrics (such as FPS) from the console

▶ Displaying a list of all the game objects

▶ Displaying a level at the main menu

▶ Dragging and dropping between two windows

Introduction

Torque 3D includes an extensive **graphical user interface** (**GUI**) system. It is relied upon by the in-game systems, as well as by all of the editors. The primary method of creating and manipulating GUI controls (for the main menu of a game, **head-up display** (**HUD**), and so on) is through the *GUI Editor*. The *GUI Editor* is always accessible and may be opened by pressing the *F10* key. When it comes to making the UI functional, we usually need to turn to TorqueScript methods and functions to get the job done.

In this chapter, we will discuss some important GUI concepts that often come up while working on a game, but whose information can be hard to come by. For an introduction to the *GUI Editor*, please see the GUI Editor Overview on the official documentation page at `http://www.garagegames.com/documentation/torque-3d`.

Creating a password text edit box

There are times when we don't want to display the characters being entered into a text edit GUI control, for example, when entering a password. In this recipe, we will learn how to set up properties of a text edit control to mask the characters being typed by the user.

Getting ready

For this recipe, we will be working with the *GUI Editor*. We begin by starting up our game (such as the one built using the `Full` template), and at the main menu pressing *F10* to launch the *GUI Editor*. We can then either choose the **New Gui** option from the **File** menu to start with a blank Canvas, or click on **Open** to open an existing `.gui` file from the **File** menu.

How to do it...

In the following steps we will add a new text control and set it up for password entry:

1. Select the **Library** tab from the top-right corner of the *GUI Editor*. This will display a list of all possible GUI controls that may be placed on the Canvas of the editor.

2. Expand the **Text** rollout section for a list of all text-based GUI controls, as shown in the next screenshot:

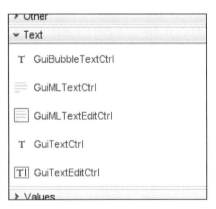

3. Drag-and-drop the **GuiTextEditCtrl** control on to the Canvas of the editor to the left-hand side.

4. Select the **GUI** tab from the top-right corner of the *GUI Editor*. This will display a tree list of all GUI control instances, as well as the properties for our `GuiTextEditCtrl`.

5. Scroll the properties list to the **Text Input** section.

6. Find the **password** property of the GUI control and select its checkbox, as shown in the next screenshot:

How it works...

When the `password` property of a `GuiTextEditCtrl` instance is set to true, the control will display an asterisk for each user-entered character. This masks out what the user is typing to prevent others from being able to read the entered text.

There's more...

The `passwordMask` property of the `GuiTextEditCtrl` class defines the character that will be used to mask the user's input. By default, it is set to an asterisk.

Using pushDialog() and popDialog() and setting up the UI file to work with them

There are times when we want to present to the user additional information that is overlaid on the current screen. This could take, for example, the form of a window with a *Yes* or *No* question that the user needs to answer for the game. In this recipe, we will create a new `GuiWindowCtrl` control that we will present to the user over the top of the current screen content, and have this window dismissed when the user clicks on a button.

Getting ready

For this recipe we will be working with the *GUI Editor*. We begin by starting up our game (such as the one built using the `Full` template) and at the **Main Menu** section, pressing *F10* to launch the *GUI Editor*.

How to do it...

In the following steps we will create a new dialog window and display it to the user:

1. From the **File** menu, choose **New Gui**. This will open the **Create new GUI** dialog box.

2. Within the **GUI Name** field enter a name as `DialogTest`.

3. Make sure that the **GUI Class** drop-down menu is set to **GuiControl**. Look at the next screenshot:

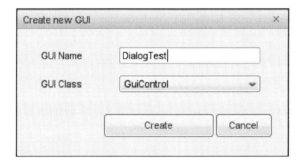

4. Click on the **Create** button of the dialog box. This will create a new empty GUI in the *GUI Editor* with a checkerboard background.

5. Select the **Library** tab from the top-right corner of the *GUI Editor*. This will display a list of all possible GUI controls that may be placed on the Canvas of the editor.

6. Expand the **Containers** rollout. Drag-and-drop the **GuiWindowCtrl** control onto the Canvas of the editor to the left-hand side.

7. Adjust the width of the new control window using one of the sizing handles. We want the window to be large enough to hold a button control.

8. Expand the **Buttons** rollout under the **Library** tab. Drag-and-drop a **GuiButtonCtrl** control onto the middle of our new **GuiWindowCtrl**.

9. Select the **GUI** tab from the top-right corner of the *GUI Editor*. This will display a tree list of all GUI control instances, as well as the properties for our `GuiButtonCtrl`.

10. Find the `text` property of the button and give it a value of `Close` as shown in the next screenshot:

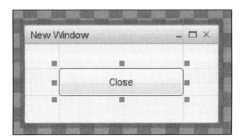

11. Find the `command` property of the button and give it a value of `Canvas.` `popDialog(DialogTest).`

12. From the **File** menu, choose **Save As**. This will open the *file-saving* dialog box. Go to the **art/gui** directory and click on the **Save** button of the dialog box.

13. From the drop-down menu at the top-left corner of the *GUI Editor* (it should contain the name of our control, **DialogTest**), choose **MainMenuGui**. Doing this takes us back to the main menu GUI.

14. Press *F10* to exit the *GUI Editor* and return to the main menu.

15. Open the console using the tilde (~) key and enter the following code at the bottom of the screen:

```
Canvas.pushDialog(DialogTest);
```

16. Press the tilde (~) key again to close the console. The `DialogTest` window is now sitting there waiting for an input.

17. Click on the **Close** button of the dialog box to dismiss it and return to the main menu.

How it works...

The `Canvas` represents the area that Torque 3D draws into. It is made up of a number of layers, with the bottommost layer as the currently displayed screen, for example, the main menu or 3D play field of the game as rendered using the `PlayGui` control. The `pushDialog()` method of `Canvas` places the given GUI onto the layer over the top of the main content, or optionally on the user-supplied layer. This method has the following form:

```
Canvas.pushDialog( control, [layer], [center] );
```

Here, the `control` parameter is the name (or the `SimObject` ID) of a `GuiControl` class to place on to the next layer.

The optional `layer` parameter can be used to force the given dialog onto a specific `Canvas` layer, and defaults to `0` if not supplied (the standard location for all dialog boxes). It is possible to have more than one dialog box in the same layer, so it is rare that we will need to touch this parameter. (A dialog box that is on a layer other than `0` will survive the `Canvas` content change).

The optional `center` parameter indicates that the dialog box should be centered on the `Canvas`, and defaults to `false`. However, this parameter may not operate as you would expect. Setting this parameter to `true` will center the root GUI control of the dialog box, which, in our previous example, is an actual `GuiControl` option and not our `GuiWindowCtrl`. If we want our `GuiWindowCtrl` to be automatically centered on the screen, we will have to set its `horizSizing` and `vertSizing` properties just as with any other GUI control.

For most dialog boxes, it is important that the root control be a `GuiControl` class and not `GuiWindowCtrl` of the dialog box (or whatever is being used for the dialog box as it doesn't have to be a `GuiWindowCtrl` control). When a dialog box is pushed to the `Canvas`, its root control is automatically resized to the same size as the `Canvas`. Therefore, if we were to make the `GuiWindowCtrl` control as the root control of the dialog box, the window will be stretched to take up the entire screen.

To remove a dialog box, we use the `popDialog()` method of `Canvas`, which has the following form:

```
Canvas.popDialog( [control] );
```

Here the `control` parameter is an optional parameter that provides the name (or the `SimObject` ID) of the dialog box to remove. If no control is given, then the last dialog box that was pushed to layer 0 of the `Canvas` (the layer all dialog boxes are placed on by default) will be removed. More often than not, we do provide the name of the dialog box just to make sure we don't accidentally pop the wrong dialog box.

There's more...

Let's continue the discussion about dialog boxes.

Executing the .gui file of the dialog box

Whenever a new GUI is created using the *GUI Editor*, the new `.gui` file will need to be executed using an `exec()` command somewhere in the TorqueScript files. In our previous example, we saved the dialog box to `art/gui/DialogTest.gui`. We need to execute this file so that the dialog box will be available the next time we run the game.

One convenient place to do this is in the `initClient()` function, which can be found in `scripts/init.cs` along with the other game GUIs. Open that script file in a text editor, or Torsion, and find the `initClient()` function. Enter the following code just below the `controlsHelpDlg.gui` line:

```
exec("art/gui/DialogTest.gui");
```

This will ensure that the dialog box is available when we need it.

Standard dialog box callbacks

There are two callbacks that are used to inform a root `GuiControl` control of the dialog box about its current state on the Canvas:

- ▶ `onDialogPush()`: This is called on the root control when `Canvas.pushDialog()` is used
- ▶ `onDialogPop()`: This is called on the root control when `Canvas.popDialog()` is used

While not often defined, these two callbacks can be used to set up or gracefully exit a dialog box as needed. Internally, the **PostFXManager** dialog box uses `onDialogPush()` to build all of the required settings just before being presented to the user.

Making a non-modal dialog box

By default, when we create a new dialog box using the *GUI Editor*, it is a modal dialog box. This means that the user may not interact with any GUI controls that are underneath the dialog box. However, sometimes we want to push a dialog box onto the `Canvas` but still allow the user to interact with other controls. This could be an inventory window for an RPG, for example. To change our previously-created dialog box into a non-modal one, do the following:

1. Press *F10* to open the *GUI Editor*.
2. Choose our **DialogTest** GUI from the drop-down control at the top of the screen.
3. Make sure that the **GUI** tab at the top-right corner of the editor is selected.
4. Select the **DialogTest** control from the tree list.
5. Find the **profile** property of the control. Click on the drop-down control and choose the **GuiModelessDialogProfile** option from the list.
6. From the **File** menu select **Save** to save the changes.

Now, when we push the dialog box to the `Canvas` it will operate in a non-modal way and not block the user's input to other controls (that are not part of the dialog box) on the `Canvas`.

Difference between pushDialog() and setContent()

The `Canvas` object has two methods for changing what GUI controls are displayed. We've already discussed the `pushDialog()` method in this recipe. This method is used to display individual GUI elements to the user, such as a window filled with other GUI controls, without disturbing the main content of the `Canvas`. Very often a dialog box is modal, meaning it doesn't allow the user to access GUI controls outside of the dialog box, but it doesn't have to be modal.

The other method available for changing the set of displayed GUI controls is `setContent()`, which has the following form:

```
Canvas.setContent( control );
```

Here, the `control` parameter is the name (or the `SimObject` ID) of a `GuiControl` object. Using this method will automatically remove all layer 0 dialog boxes from the screen, and set the overall `Canvas` content to the given GUI control. For example, this method is used to go from the main menu content to the `PlayGui` content (the usual control used to display the 3D world of the game).

When using `setContent()`, Torque 3D will issue a couple of callbacks to inform the controls of their change in status. `onUnsetContent()` is called on the previous GUI control that made up the content of the `Canvas`. Its only parameter is the `SimObject` ID of the GUI control that will become the new content for the `Canvas`. `onSetContent()` is called on the GUI control that has just been made the new `Canvas` content. Its only parameter is the `SimObject` ID of the GUI control that used to be the content of the `Canvas`, or 0 if this is the first time the content of the `Canvas` has been set up.

Using a different root control for the dialog box

While it is common to use a `GuiControl` class as the root control for a dialog box, it is not required. Any other GUI control class may be substituted so long as we take into account that it will automatically be resized to fill the entire `Canvas` when the dialog box is pushed.

For example, we could use a `GuiBitmapCtrl` option instead of a `GuiControl` option as the root of the dialog box. We could then assign a black image with a 50 percent alpha channel to the bitmap control. Now when the dialog box is displayed with `pushDialog()`, it will appear that the entire screen is darkened and slightly faded. This informs the user that they no longer have access to any GUI controls outside of the dialog box, and also makes the dialog box itself stand out.

Displaying metrics (such as FPS) from the console

While building a game, it can be useful to see various performance statistics from Torque 3D. Examples include **frames per second (FPS)** and **milliseconds per frame (mspf)** counters, as well as the number of polygons rendered. In this recipe, we will learn how to display these performance statistics as a heads-up display by entering commands into the console.

Getting ready

For this recipe, we will be working with the console while a game is running. Start up your own game or launch the `FPS Tutorial` game that comes with Torque 3D, and load a level to run your character through.

How to do it...

In the following steps we will display various metrics on the screen:

1. Open the console using the tilde (~) key.

2. Enter the following at the bottom of the screen:

   ```
   metrics("fps gfx");
   ```

A white box containing a number of **FPS** and **GFX** counters appears at the top of the screen. The following screenshot shows the **FPS** and **GFX** metrics displayed over the top of the FPS Tutorial game.

How it works...

The metrics() function is used to enable and disable the display of various performance statistics. This function has the following form:

```
metrics( [expression] );
```

Here, the `expression` parameter is a space-delimited text string containing a list of all collections of statistics to display. If the expression parameter is left blank then the metrics HUD is turned off.

In the previous example, the `fps gfx` string is passed in to the `metrics()` function. This space-delimited list indicates that we want to see the statistics from two Torque 3D systems: frame rendering counters and graphics subsystem counters. If we only wanted to see the frame rendering counters we would pass in a string of `fps` and the graphics statistics would no longer be presented.

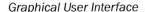

Let's take a look at all of the various metrics we can display, as well as how to build our own game-specific metrics.

A list of all standard metrics

The following table lists all of the standard available metrics and what they describe:

Metric	Description
`basicShadow`	This gives information on shadowing while using basic lighting with the following status:
	▸ **Active**: This indicates the number of `SceneObjectLightingPlugin` objects in this frame.
	▸ **Updated**: This indicates that the number of shadows are updated in this frame.
	▸ **Elapsed Ms**: This indicates the number of milliseconds spent in this frame while updating shadows.
`decal`	This gives information about rendered decals (only available in debug builds) with the following status:
	▸ **Batches**: This indicates the number of batches of decals that are rendered in this frame.
	▸ **Buffers**: This indicates the *total* number of primitive buffers allocated in the decal pool.
	▸ **DecalsRendered**: This indicates the number of individual decals rendered in this frame.

Metric	Description
forest	This gives information about forest objects with the following status: ▸ **Cells**: This is the number of top-level forest cells (not currently used). ▸ **Cells Meshed**: This is the number of top-level forest cells rendered with at least one mesh. ▸ **Cells Billboarded**: This is the number of forest cells that render with all billboarded imposters. ▸ **Meshes**: This is the total number of meshes rendered in this frame. ▸ **Billboards**: This is the total number of billboards rendered in this frame.
fps	This gives the per-frame timing information with the following status: ▸ **fps**: This indicates the current number of frames per second. ▸ **max**: This is the maximum number of frames per second achieved. ▸ **min**: This is the minimum number of frames per second achieved. ▸ **mspf**: This is the number of milliseconds taken to render the current frame.
gfx	This gives the information about the graphics subsystem with the following status: ▸ **PolyCount**: This is the number of polygons rendered in this frame. ▸ **DrawCalls**: This is the number of draw primitive calls in this frame. ▸ **RTChanges**: This is the number of times the render target changed in this frame.
groundCover	This gives the information about ground cover objects with the following status: ▸ **Cells**: This is the number of rendered cells in this frame. ▸ **Billboards**: This is the number of billboards rendered in this frame. ▸ **Batches**: This is the number of rendered billboard batches in this frame. ▸ **Shapes**: This is the number of rendered shapes in this frame.
imposter	This gives information about billboard imposters with the following status: ▸ **Rendered**: This is the number of rendered imposters in this frame. ▸ **Batches**: This is the number of batches of rendered imposters in this frame. ▸ **DrawCalls**: This is the number of imposter draw primitive calls in this frame. ▸ **Polys**: This is the number of imposter polygons rendered in this frame. ▸ **RtChanges**: This is the number of times the render target changed during imposter rendering in this frame.

Metric	Description
light	This gives information about advanced rendering lights with the following status:
	▸ **Active**: This indicates the number of lights used in this frame.
	▸ **Culled**: This is the number of lights in the level but not used in this frame (not currently used).
net	This gives the information about client/server networking with the following status:
	▸ **BitsSent**: While this parameter has the name bits in it, it is actually the number of bytes sent during the last packet send operation.
	▸ **BitsRcvd**: While this parameter has the name bits in it, it is actually the number of bytes received during the last packet send operation.
	▸ **GhostUpd**: This is the total number of ghosts added, removed, and/or updated on the client during the last packet process operation.
particle	This gives information about particle objects (not currently used).
reflect	This gives the information about reflections (only available in debug builds) with the following status:
	▸ **Objects**: This is the number of objects registered as reflector.
	▸ **Visible**: This is the number of visible reflector objects in this frame.
	▸ **Occluded**: This is the number of occluded reflector objects in this frame.
	▸ **Updated**: This is the number of reflections updated in this frame.
	▸ **Elapsed**: This is the number of milliseconds taken to update reflection in this frame.
	▸ **Allocated**: This is the number of allocated reflection textures allocated in this frame.
	▸ **Pooled**: This is the total number of reflection textures that are pooled.
	▸ **Name**: This is the name of the reflect render target profile, if any.
	▸ **Active**: This is the total number of reflection textures that are pooled (same as the Pooled parameter).
	▸ **Memory**: This is the amount of storage currently allocated.

Metric	Description
render	This gives information about rendered instance types (not currently used).
sfx	This gives information about sound effects with the following status:

> ▸ **Sounds**: This is the number of SFXSound object instances.
>
> ▸ **Lists**: This is the number of SFXSource object instances that are neither SFXSound nor FMOD event sources. These are also known as **controllers**.
>
> ▸ **Events**: This is the number of FMOD event sources.
>
> ▸ **Playing**: This is the number of sounds that are in a playing state
>
> ▸ **Culled**: This is the number of SFXSound instances that are in a virtualized playback mode.
>
> ▸ **Voices**: This is the number of voices that are allocated on the sounds device.
>
> ▸ **Buffers**: This is the number of buffers that are allocated on the sound device.
>
> ▸ **Memory**: This is the amount of memory used by the sound device buffers.
>
> ▸ **Time/S**: This is the number of milliseconds spent on the last SFXSource update loop.
>
> ▸ **Time/P**: This is the number of milliseconds spent on the last SFXParameter update loop.
>
> ▸ **Time/A**: This is the number of milliseconds spent on the last ambient audio update.

Metric	Description
SFXSources	This gives information about all current SFXSource instances with the following status: ▸ **ID**: This is the SimObject ID of the source. ▸ **type**: This is the type of sound source. It can be any one of the following: group, sound, list, or other. ▸ **status**: This is the source status. It can be any one of the following: playing, paused, stopped, or unknown. ▸ **blocked**: This indicates if the source is currently blocked. ▸ **volume**: This is the attenuated volume of the sound source. ▸ **priority**: This is the effective priority of the source. ▸ **virtual**: This indicates if the source is currently virtualized. ▸ **looping**: This indicates if the source is set to loop. ▸ **3d**: This indicates if this is a 3D-sound source. ▸ **group**: This is the group name of the source, if any. ▸ **playtime**: This is the elapsed play time for the sound source. ▸ **playOnce**: This indicates if the sound is set to play once and then delete itself. ▸ **streaming**: This indicates if this is a streaming sound source. ▸ **hasVoice**: This indicates if this source currently has a voice assigned. ▸ **track**: This is the source's track name, if any.
SFXState	This provides a list of all active sound effect state object names.
shadow	This gives information about shadow maps with the following status: ▸ **Active**: This is the number of active shadow maps in this frame. ▸ **Updated**: This is the number of shadow maps that were updated this frame. ▸ **PolyCount**: This is the number of triangles used for shadow map rendering in this frame. ▸ **DrawCalls**: This is the number of draw primitive calls used for shadow map rendering in this frame. ▸ **RTChanges**: This is the number of render target changes used for shadow map rendering in this frame. ▸ **PoolTexCount**: This is the number of shadow textures in the shadow texture pool. ▸ **PoolTexMB**: This is the approximate memory usage for the shadow texture pool.

Metric	Description
terrain	This gives information about the TerrainBlock objects with the following status: ▸ **Cells**: This is the number of TerrainBlock cells rendered in this frame. ▸ **Override Cells**: This is the number of TerrainBlock cells rendered during the shadow pass. ▸ **DrawCalls**: This is the number of draw primitive calls used during TerrainBlock rendering in this frame.
time	This gives information about the time of simulation with the following status: ▸ **Sim Time**: This is the current simulation time in milliseconds since the game started. ▸ **Mod**: This is the remainder of the simulation time divided by the number of milliseconds per simulation tick (32).

Creating game-specific metrics

It can be very handy to provide game-specific metrics while developing a game. For example, we could display the number of active NPCs and how many are in a particular state, or the player's current game play attributes.

To create a set of custom metrics, we need to define a metrics callback function named xxxMetricsCallback() where the xxx prefix is replaced with the name of our metrics. Using the example of NPC metrics (and assuming we had already built some NPC manager class), we could have the following function:

```
function npcMetricsCallback()
{
    return "  | NPC |" @
            "  Active: " @ NPCSimSet.getCount() @
            "  Hungry: " @ NPCManager.getHungryCount() @
            "  Sleepy: " @ NPCManager.getSleepyCount() @
            "  In Combat: " @ NPCManager.getCombatCount();
}
```

The returned text follows the standard form as used by other metric callbacks. Now we can type the following in the console to see our new metrics:

```
metrics("npc");
```

If we wanted to display our custom metrics along with the standard **FPS** and **GFX** metrics, we could type the following in the console:

```
metrics("fps gfx npc");
```

Making use of a metrics callback allows us to return any possible information that would be useful during the development of a game.

Displaying a list of all game objects

While developing a game, it would be great to have a list of all objects in the game along with their properties. The *World Editor* can be used to some extent, but it only provides access to those objects that were loaded by the level. It doesn't provide access to objects dynamically created by the game play scripts. In this recipe, we'll look into gaining access to all objects in a game, regardless of how they were generated.

Getting ready

For this recipe we will be working with the console while a game is running. Start up your own game or launch the `FPS Tutorial` game that comes with Torque 3D, and load a level to run your character through.

How to do it...

In the following steps we will discover how to view a list of all objects in the game engine:

1. Open the console using the tilde (~) key.

2. Enter the following at the bottom of the screen:

   ```
   tree();
   ```

3. The **Torque SimView** window will open, displaying a tree list of all objects on the left-hand side, and the properties of the currently selected object on the right-hand side. This window may be resized as needed.

4. Close the console using the tilde (~) key again to gain access to the **Torque SimView** window.

The next screenshot shows the **Torque SimView** window displayed over the top of the FPS Tutorial game with a Player class object selected:

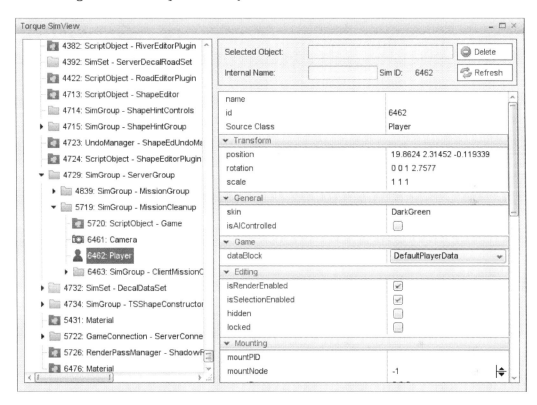

How it works...

The **Torque SimView** window starts at the RootGroup object, the grandparent of all SimObject instances. From there we have access to all SimObject instances, SimGroup instances, and SimSet instances that currently exist within the game. This allows us to look at the properties of any object, and modify them while the game is running.

Any changes we've made to an object's properties using the Torque SimView window will not be automatically saved. If we want any changes to the objects of a level to be persistent, those changes will need to be done using the *World Editor*. The **Torque SimView** window is purely for inspecting and modifying run-time values.

Displaying a level at the main menu

Torque 3D's example projects come with a static main menu that includes buttons to start playing a level or join a server. Often, a game developer will just drop in a nice picture as the backdrop of the main menu. In this recipe, we will take this customization one step further by displaying an actual game level in the background of the main menu to add a level of professionalism to the game.

Getting ready

For this recipe we will be working with a fresh copy of the `Full` template and make a number of script changes and additions. If you haven't done so already, use the Torque Project Manager (`Project Manager.exe`) to create a new project from the `Full` template. It will be found under the `My Projects` directory. Then start up your favorite script editor, such as Torsion, and let's get going!

How to do it...

In the following steps we will set up a level that will be displayed in the background of main menu of the game:

1. We'll begin by creating the level that will be displayed in the background of the main menu. Create a new directory just under the `game` directory of the project and name it `mmlevels`. We don't want to put our main menu level in the `Standard Levels` directory since it will show up as a valid level for the user to play.

2. Copy the `levels/Empty Terrain.mis` mission file into our new `mmlevels` directory. Rename this new mission file as `mmlevels/MainMenuLevel.mis`.

3. Open this mission in your text editor and modify the `LevelInfo` object to include the `gameType` property, as follows:

```
new LevelInfo(theLevelInfo) {
    nearClip = "0.1";
    visibleDistance = "2000";
    decalBias = "0.0015";
    fogColor = "1 1 0.6 1";
    fogDensity = "0.001";
    fogDensityOffset = "10";
    fogAtmosphereHeight = "100";
    canvasClearColor = "233 220 143 255";
    advancedLightmapSupport = "0";
        desc0 = "Displays in the background of the
                    main menu.";
        LevelName = "Main Menu Level";
    gameType = "MainMenuLevel";
};
```

4. Next we will create the main menu's GUI itself. This is based on the `GameTSCtrl` class, which is used to render the level. It also includes the standard **Play**, **Join**, **Options**, and **Exit** buttons. Create a new `art/gui/mainmenulevel.gui` file with the following contents:

```
%guiContent = new GameTSCtrl(MainMenuLevelGui) {
    canSaveDynamicFields = "1";
    isContainer = "1";
    Profile = "GuiContentProfile";
    HorizSizing = "right";
    VertSizing = "bottom";
    position = "0 0";
    Extent = "1024 768";
    MinExtent = "8 8";
    canSave = "1";
    Visible = "1";
    tooltipprofile = "GuiToolTipProfile";
    hovertime = "1000";
    Margin = "0 0 0 0";
    Padding = "0 0 0 0";
    AnchorTop = "1";
    AnchorBottom = "0";
    AnchorLeft = "1";
    AnchorRight = "0";
    cameraZRot = "0";
    forceFOV = "0";
        Enabled = "1";
        helpTag = "0";
        noCursor = "0";

        new GuiButtonCtrl() {
            canSaveDynamicFields = "0";
            Enabled = "1";
            isContainer = "0";
            Profile = "GuiMenuButtonProfile";
            HorizSizing = "relative";
            VertSizing = "bottom";
            Position = "9 114";
            Extent = "289 75";
            MinExtent = "8 8";
            canSave = "1";
            isDecoy = "0";
            Visible = "1";
            Command = "Canvas.pushDialog(ChooseLevelDlg);";
            tooltipprofile = "GuiToolTipProfile";
            hovertime = "1000";
            text = "Play";
```

```
            groupNum = "-1";
            buttonType = "PushButton";
            useMouseEvents = "1";
         };
         new GuiButtonCtrl() {
            canSaveDynamicFields = "0";
            Enabled = "1";
            isContainer = "0";
            Profile = "GuiMenuButtonProfile";
            HorizSizing = "relative";
            VertSizing = "bottom";
            Position = "9 190";
            Extent = "289 75";
            MinExtent = "8 8";
            canSave = "1";
            isDecoy = "0";
            Visible = "1";
            Command = "Canvas.pushDialog(JoinServerDlg);";
            tooltipprofile = "GuiToolTipProfile";
            hovertime = "1000";
            text = "Join";
            groupNum = "-1";
            buttonType = "PushButton";
            useMouseEvents = "0";
         };
         new GuiButtonCtrl() {
            canSaveDynamicFields = "0";
            Enabled = "1";
            isContainer = "0";
            Profile = "GuiMenuButtonProfile";
            HorizSizing = "relative";
            VertSizing = "bottom";
            Position = "9 267";
            Extent = "289 75";
            MinExtent = "8 8";
            canSave = "1";
            isDecoy = "0";
            Visible = "1";
            Command = "Canvas.pushDialog(optionsDlg);";
            tooltipprofile = "GuiToolTipProfile";
            hovertime = "1000";
            text = "Options";
            groupNum = "-1";
            buttonType = "PushButton";
            useMouseEvents = "0";
         };
```

```
        new GuiButtonCtrl() {
            canSaveDynamicFields = "0";
            Enabled = "1";
            internalName = "ExitButton";
            isContainer = "0";
            Profile = "GuiMenuButtonProfile";
            HorizSizing = "relative";
            VertSizing = "bottom";
            Position = "9 344";
            Extent = "289 75";
            MinExtent = "8 8";
            canSave = "1";
            isDecoy = "0";
            Visible = "1";
            Command = "quit();";
            tooltipprofile = "GuiToolTipProfile";
            hovertime = "1000";
            text = "Exit";
            groupNum = "-1";
            buttonType = "PushButton";
            useMouseEvents = "0";
        };
    };
```

5. The last GUI file we'll need is a splash screen to display while the main menu level is loading. We'll just use a white background with the Torque 3D logo. Create a new `art/gui/mainmenulevelsplash.gui` file with the following contents:

```
%guiContent = singleton GuiChunkedBitmapCtrl
(MainMenuLevelSplashGui) {
    canSaveDynamicFields = "0";
    Enabled = "1";
    isContainer = "1";
    Profile = "GuiContentProfile";
    HorizSizing = "width";
    VertSizing = "height";
    Position = "0 0";
    Extent = "800 600";
    MinExtent = "8 8";
    canSave = "1";
    Visible = "1";
    tooltipprofile = "GuiToolTipProfile";
    hovertime = "1000";
    bitmap = "art/gui/background";
    useVariable = "0";
    tile = "0";
```

```
new GuiControl() {
    canSaveDynamicFields = "0";
    Enabled = "1";
    isContainer = "1";
    Profile = "GuiDefaultProfile";
    HorizSizing = "center";
    VertSizing = "center";
    Position = "151 217";
    Extent = "497 166";
    MinExtent = "8 8";
    canSave = "1";
    Visible = "1";
    tooltipprofile = "GuiToolTipProfile";
    hovertime = "1000";

    new GuiBitmapCtrl() {
        canSaveDynamicFields = "0";
        Enabled = "1";
        isContainer = "0";
        Profile = "GuiDefaultProfile";
        HorizSizing = "center";
        VertSizing = "bottom";
        Position = "27 6";
        Extent = "443 139";
        MinExtent = "8 2";
        canSave = "1";
        Visible = "1";
        tooltipprofile = "GuiToolTipProfile";
        hovertime = "1000";
        bitmap = "art/gui/Torque-3D-logo.png";
        wrap = "0";
    };
  };
};
```

6. We will now create the first of two TorqueScript files. This one will be used from the client side to override a number of standard script functions. Create a new file named `scripts/client/mainmenulevel.cs` with the following contents:

```
// Load our special main menu GUI that will include a
// loaded level in the background.
function loadMainMenu()
{
    // We need to track when we're displaying the
    // main menu level
    $UsingMainMenuLevel = true;
```

```
      // Startup the client with the Main menu...
      Canvas.setContent( MainMenuLevelGui );

      // Load the main menu level.  We could have this be
      // chosen from a random list of levels if we wanted
      // a different one each time the user returned to
      // the main menu.
      loadLevel("mmlevels/mainmenulevel.mis");
}

// Load a single player level on the local server.  This
// function differs from the standard one by displaying
// our splash screen rather than the normal loading screen.
function loadLevel( %missionNameOrFile )
{
   // Expand the mission name... this allows you to enter
   // just the name and not the full path and extension.
   %missionFile = expandMissionFileName( %missionNameOrFile );
   if ( %missionFile $= "" )
      return false;

   // Show the splash screen screen immediately.
   Canvas.setContent("MainMenuLevelSplashGui");
   Canvas.repaint();

   // Prepare and launch the server.
   return createAndConnectToLocalServer( "SinglePlayer",
                                         %missionFile );
}

// This function is called each time the main menu
// level's progress should be updated.  We're using a
// static splash screen that doesn't require to be
// notified of the loading progress.
function loadLoadingGui(%displayText)
{
   // Do nothing as our splash screen does not
   // display progress.
}

// This function is called any time the user disconnects
// from a level, including our main menu level. The
// only difference between this function and the
// standard one is that we check if we should switch
// to the main menu GUI and level, or if we just came
// from there.
function disconnectedCleanup()
{
   // End mission, if it's running.
```

```
if( $Client::missionRunning )
   clientEndMission();

// Disable mission lighting if it's going, this is
// here in case we're disconnected while the mission
// is loading.

$lightingMission = false;
$sceneLighting::terminateLighting = true;

// Clear misc script stuff
HudMessageVector.clear();

//
LagIcon.setVisible(false);
PlayerListGui.clear();

// Clear all print messages
clientCmdclearBottomPrint();
clientCmdClearCenterPrint();

// We can now delete the client physics simulation.
physicsDestroyWorld( "client" );

if ($UsingMainMenuLevel)
{
   // We are displaying the main menu level so we
   // don't want to load it again.  The standard
   // level loading code will now start the chosen
   // level once we exit this function.
   $UsingMainMenuLevel = false;
}
else
{
   // We've just come from a standard level, so
   // load the main menu.  We need to do this
   // as a schedule() to allow the previous level
   // to completely clean itself up.
   schedule(0, 0, loadMainMenu);
}
}
```

7. Now we will create the second of our TorqueScript files. This one will be used from the server side to override a number of script functions based on the game type of the level. Create a new file named `scripts/server/gameMainMenu.cs` with the following contents:

```
// This package is activated when a MainMenuLevel
// type level is loaded.
package MainMenuLevelGame
{
    function GameConnection::initialControlSet(%this)
    {
        echo ("*** MainMenuLevelGame Initial Control Object");

        // The first control object has been set by the
        //server and we are now ready to go.

        // first check if the editor is active
        if (!isToolBuild() || !Editor::checkActiveLoadDone())
        {
            if (Canvas.getContent() != MainMenuLevelGui.getId())
            {
                // Display the main menu GUI with this level
                Canvas.setContent(MainMenuLevelGui);
            }
        }
    }
};

function MainMenuLevelGame::onMissionLoaded(%game)
{
    $Server::MissionType = "MainMenuLevel";
    parent::onMissionLoaded(%game);
}

// This method sets up whatever properties are required
// for the level.
function MainMenuLevelGame::initGameVars(%game)
{
    // What kind of "camera" is spawned is either controlled
    // directly by the SpawnSphere or it defaults back to
    //the values set here. This also controls which
    //SimGroups to attempt to select the spawn sphere's from
    //by walking down the list of SpawnGroups till it finds
    //a valid spawn object. These override the values set in
    // core/scripts/server/spawn.cs
    $Game::defaultCameraClass = "Camera";
    $Game::defaultCameraDataBlock = "Observer";
```

```
$Game::defaultCameraSpawnGroups =
    "CameraSpawnPoints PlayerSpawnPoints PlayerDropPoints";

    // Set the gameplay parameters
    %game.duration = 0;
    %game.endgameScore = 0;
    %game.endgamePause = 0;
    %game.allowCycling = false;
}


// This method is called when the client connects to
// the level.  In our case, this is the only client that
// will connect with the main menu level, and will be
// in a single player mode (also known as a local client).
function MainMenuLevelGame::onClientEnterGame(%game, %client)
{
    // Spawn a camera for the local client
    %cameraSpawnPoint =
        pickCameraSpawnPoint($Game::DefaultCameraSpawnGroups);
    %client.spawnCamera(%cameraSpawnPoint);
}


// This method is called when our local client is removed
// from the level, either because the main menu GUI is no
// longer the Canvas' content, or the program has been
//exited.
function MainMenuLevelGame::onClientLeaveGame(%game, %client)
{
    // Cleanup the camera
    if (isObject(%client.camera))
        %client.camera.delete();
}
```

8. With all of the GUI and script files built, we now need to have them execute when Torque 3D starts up. We will start with our GUI files. Open `scripts/client/init.cs` and add the following two lines to the `initClient()` function:

```
// Load up the Game GUIs
exec("art/gui/defaultGameProfiles.cs");
exec("art/gui/PlayGui.gui");
exec("art/gui/ChatHud.gui");
exec("art/gui/playerList.gui");
exec("art/gui/hudlessGui.gui");
exec("art/gui/controlsHelpDlg.gui");
exec("art/gui/mainmenulevel.gui");
exec("art/gui/mainmenulevelsplash.gui");
```

9. We also need to execute our new client script. In the same file and method as mentioned previously, add the following lines:

```
// Client scripts
exec("./client.cs");
exec("./game.cs");
exec("./missionDownload.cs");
exec("./serverConnection.cs");
exec("./mainmenulevel.cs");
```

10. Finally, we need to execute our new server script. Open `scripts/server/scriptExec.cs` and add the following line to the bottom of the file:

```
// Load our gametypes
exec("./gameCore.cs");      // This is the 'core' of the
                            // gametype functionality.
exec("./gameDM.cs");        // Overrides GameCore with
                            // DeathMatch functionality.
exec("./gameMainMenu.cs"); // Overrides GameCore with
                            // MainMenuLevel functionality
```

That takes care of all of the new stuff. Now we need to make three minor modifications to existing files to account for having a level being displayed within the main menu.

11. For the first change, open `core/art/gui/chooseLevelDlg.gui` and add the following code to the `ChooseLevelDlgBtn::onMouseUp()` method:

```
function ChooseLevelDlgGoBtn::onMouseUp( %this )
{
    // If we are displaying a mission during the main
    // menu, then disconnect.
    if (isObject(MainMenuLevelGui) &&
        Canvas.getContent() $= MainMenuLevelGui.getId())
    {
        disconnect();
    }

    // So we can't fire the button when loading is in
    //progress.
    if ( isObject( ServerGroup ) )
        return;

    // Launch the chosen level with the editor open?
    if ( ChooseLevelDlg.launchInEditor )
    {
```

```
         activatePackage( "BootEditor" );
         ChooseLevelDlg.launchInEditor = false;
         StartLevel("", "SinglePlayer");
      }
      else
      {
         StartLevel();
      }
   }
```

This addition ensures that the **GO** button of the **Choose Level** dialog correctly exits the main menu level prior to loading the level of the game.

12. For the second change, open `core/scripts/gui/chooseLevelDlg.cs` and add the highlighted code to the `getLevelInfo()` function:

```
while ( !%file.isEOF() ) {
    %line = %file.readLine();
    %line = trim( %line );

    if( %line $= "new ScriptObject(LevelInfo) {" )
        %inInfoBlock = true;
    else if( %line $= "new LevelInfo(theLevelInfo) {" )
    {
        // We need to modify the level info line to not
        // include a name as that could conflict with a
        // currently loaded level.  This does not affect
        // the operation of the level info processing as
        // it uses the object's SimObject ID.
        %line = "new LevelInfo() {";
        %inInfoBlock = true;
    }
    else if( %inInfoBlock && %line $= «};» ) {
        %inInfoBlock = false;
        %LevelInfoObject = %LevelInfoObject @ %line;
        break;
    }

    if( %inInfoBlock )
    %LevelInfoObject = %LevelInfoObject @ %line @ " ";
}
```

This code is used by the **Choose Level** dialog box to display some information about each game level. Our modification removes the name from the LevelInfo class of the inspected level to make sure it doesn't conflict with our LevelInfo object loaded by the level of the main menu.

13. For the final change, open art/gui/joinServerDlg.gui and add the following code to the JoinServerDlg::join() method:

```
function JoinServerDlg::join(%this)
{
   cancelServerQuery();
   %index = JS_serverList.getSelectedId();

   // The server info index is stored in the row along
   // with the rest of displayed info.

   // If we are displaying a mission during the main
   // menu, then disconnect.
   if (isObject(MainMenuLevelGui) &&
      Canvas.getContent() $= MainMenuLevelGui.getId())
   {
      disconnect();
   }

   if( setServerInfo( %index ) )
   {
      Canvas.setContent("LoadingGui");
      LoadingProgress.setValue(1);
      LoadingProgressTxt.setValue("WAITING FOR SERVER");
      Canvas.repaint();

      %conn = new GameConnection(ServerConnection);
      %conn.setConnectArgs($pref::Player::Name);
      %conn.setJoinPassword($Client::Password);
      %conn.connect($ServerInfo::Address);
   }
}
```

This addition ensures that the **Join Server!** button of the **Join Server** dialog box correctly exits the main menu level prior to connecting to the remote server.

With all of our changes complete, we can now launch our game and see the new main menu in action rendering our 3D level in the background.

How it works...

The GameTSCtrl class used for the background of a new main menu does all the work of rendering a loaded level. This is the same class that is used by the PlayGui control during a normal game play. The only difference in how we use the GameTSCtrl class for our MainMenuLevelGui control is with setting its noCursor property to 0. This shows the mouse pointer and allows the mouse to click on other GUI controls. If the noCursor property was set to 1, as it is with the PlayGui control, the mouse pointer would be hidden and locked to the control.

Another key element to having a level displayed with the main menu is setting the gameType property of the LevelInfo object of the level. By setting the value of this property to MainMenuLevel, it allows us to override the standard game play code that is executed while a level is being played.

The game type is used as a TorqueScript namespace and allows us to write methods against it. When used in this way, the `Game` word is appended to the game type when referencing this new namespace. In our case, we've defined the `MainMenuLevelGame::onClientEnterGame()` method to only create a camera object, and not a player object as a normal game level would.

There's more...

There is a lot more that could be done with the main menu level to make it more dynamic. Let's take a look at some examples.

Making the main menu level more interesting

Our main menu level example is quite plain and doesn't provide much more beyond a simple background image. Here are some ideas on how to improve on it to take advantage of it being a live game level:

- Add some `GroundCover` instances to the level with the wind feature turned on. This provides some quick motion elements to the level.

- Add a `CloudLayer` instance to the level that includes a wind speed.

- Add a `TimeOfDay` class to the level. This provides some variation in the level's lighting while the main menu is up. You may want to adjust the `ScatterSky` instance for night time colors so that they are not too dark.

- Add a path to the level and have the camera move along it.

- Add some nice sound effects to the level. Perhaps a gentle wind blowing, or some ambient music.

Of course, you're free to design your own level from scratch and include the full range of objects that Torque 3D provides.

Performance considerations

While it is possible to use any Torque 3D level for the main menu, we need to keep in mind how long it takes to load in all of the objects and materials. The more items that need to be loaded, the longer it takes before the user can interact with the main menu.

Dragging and dropping between two windows

All modern graphical user interfaces include being able to drag-and-drop objects from one location to another. Torque 3D's GUI also supports drag-and-drop operations with a little bit of setup. In this recipe, we will create two windows that demonstrate how to drag-and-drop items between them. The first window will stand for an RPG inventory, while the second window will represent an RPG paper doll display.

Getting ready

For this recipe, we will be working with the *GUI Editor*, a text editor such as Torsion, and the console. We begin by starting up our game (such as the one built using the `Full` template) with the main menu currently displayed.

How to do it...

In the following steps, we will be creating two windows to perform a drag-and-drop operation between. We will then test out our work.

1. On the main menu screen, open the *GUI Editor* by pressing *F10*.
2. We will now build the inventory window. From the **File** menu select **New Gui**. The **Create new GUI** dialog box will open. Fill in the **GUI Name** field of `InventoryGUI` and keep the **GUI Class** field set to `GuiControl`. Finally, click on the **Create** button of the dialog box.
3. Select the **Library** tab in the upper-right corner of the *GUI Editor* and open the **Containers** rollout. Drag out a new `GuiWindowCtrl` instance and place it near the left-hand side of the screen. Use sizing handles of the new window control to make it a square. This will be our inventory window.
4. Select the **GUI** tab in the upper-right corner of the *GUI Editor* and make sure the window control is selected in the **Tree View** panel. Give the `name` property of the window a value of `InventoryGuiWindow`, and make sure the `edgeSnap` property of the window is unchecked (which ensures that the window doesn't try to fill the whole screen when it is added to the Canvas). Give the window a title by setting its `text` property to `Inventory`.
5. In order that the user may close the **Inventory** window, enter the following for the `closeCommand` property of the window:

    ```
    Canvas.getContent().remove(InventoryGuiWindow);
    ```

6. We will now create four buttons that will hold our inventory items by creating one button and copying it three times. Select the **Library** tab and open the **Buttons** rollout. Drag out a `GuiBitmapButtonCtrl` control and place it at the top-left corner of the content area of the **Inventory** window.

7. Select the **GUI** tab and choose the newly added bitmap button control from the tree list. Modify the properties of the button, as follows:

   ❑ Set the `profile` property to `GuiButtonProfile`

   ❑ Set the `extent` property to `64 64`

   ❑ Make sure the `useMouseEvents` property is selected

   ❑ Set the `class` property to `DragControl`

8. Click on the **File Select** button to the right-hand side of the `bitmap` property of the button control. Select some fitting bitmap, such as `art/gui/weaponHud/ryder.png`.

9. Copy this `GuiBitmapButtonCtrl` control thrice and arrange the buttons in a 2 x 2 grid. Select a different bitmap for each button. We now have something similar to the following:

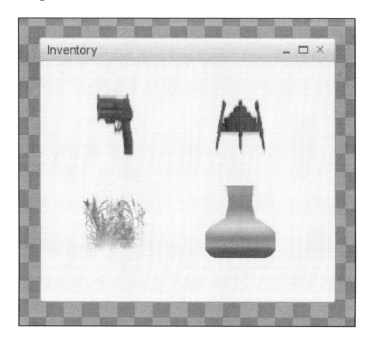

10. From the **File** menu choose **Save As**. Save this GUI as `art/gui/InventoryGUI.gui`.

11. We will now build the paper doll window. From the **File** menu select **New Gui**. The **Create new GUI** dialog box will open. Fill in the **GUI Name field** with `PaperDollGUI` and keep the **GUI Class** field set to `GuiControl`. Finally, click on the **Create** button of the dialog box.

12. Select the **Library** tab in the upper-right corner of the *GUI Editor* and open the **Containers** rollout. Drag out a new `GuiWindowCtrl` control and place it near the right-hand side of the screen. Use sizing handles of the new window control to make it a tall rectangle. This will be our paper doll window.

13. Select the **GUI** tab in the upper-right corner of the *GUI Editor* and make sure the window control is selected in the **Tree View** panel. Give a value of `PaperDollGuiWindow` to the `name` property of the window, and make sure the `edgeSnap` property of the window is unchecked (which ensures that the window doesn't try to fill the whole screen when it is added to the `Canvas`). Give the window a title by setting its `text` property to `Paper Doll`.

14. In order that the user may close the paper doll window, enter the following for the `closeCommand` property of the window:

```
Canvas.getContent().remove(PaperDollGuiWindow);
```

15. We will now create four buttons that will hold our items by creating one button and copying it three times. Select the **Library** tab and open the **Buttons** rollout. Drag out a `GuiBitmapButtonCtrl` control and place it within the content area of the `Paper Doll` window.

16. Select the **GUI** tab and choose the newly added bitmap button control from the **Tree View** panel. Modify the properties of the button, as follows:

    ❑ Set the `profile` property to `GuiButtonProfile`

    ❑ Set the `extent` property to `64 64`

    ❑ Make sure the `useMouseEvents` property is checked

    ❑ Set the `class` property to `DragControl`

17. Copy this `GuiBitmapButtonCtrl` control three times and arrange these blank buttons as two hands and two feet. Leave some space at the top for a head.

18. We will now create the head image control. Select the **Library** tab and open the **Images** rollout. Drag out a `GuiBitmapCtrl` control and place it at the top center of the content area of the `Paper Doll` window.

19. Select the **GUI** tab and choose the newly added image control from the **Tree View** panel. Modify the properties of the image control as follows:

    ❑ Set the `extent` property to be `64 64`

    ❑ Set the `bitmap` property to be `art/shapes/actors/Gideon/head_d.png`

We now have something similar to this:

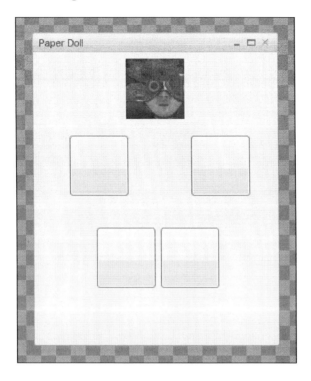

20. From the **File** menu choose **Save As**. Save this GUI as `art/gui/PaperDollGui.gui`.

21. We are now done with the *GUI Editor* and can return to the game as we'll need to enter some text into the console later on. From the drop-down menu at the top-left corner of the *GUI Editor* (it should contain the name of our control, `PaperDollGUI`), choose `MainMenuGui`. Doing this takes us back to the main menu GUI.

22. Press *F10* to exit the GUI Editor and return to the main menu screen.

23. With the two windows now built we need to make sure their files are executed by the game. Open `scripts/client/init.cs` in a text editor and add the highlighted lines to the `initClient()` function:

```
// Load up the shell GUIs
if($platform !$= "xenon")
// Use the unified shell instead
    exec("art/gui/mainMenuGui.gui");
exec("art/gui/joinServerDlg.gui");
exec("art/gui/endGameGui.gui");
exec("art/gui/StartupGui.gui");
```

```
// Load up drag and drop GUIs
exec("art/gui/InventoryGui.gui");
exec("art/gui/PaperDollGui.gui");
```

24. The next step is to write the supporting TorqueScript for the drag-and-drop operations. Create a new `scripts/client/dragAndDrop.cs` file and open it in a text editor. The first method that we'll add to this file handles the user starting to drag an inventory item, as follows:

```
// This method will start the drag and drop operation
function DragControl::onMouseDragged( %this )
{
    // Only perform a drag and drop operation if the
    // button has a bitmap defined.
    if (%this.bitmap $= "")
        return;

    // Create the temporary control that forms the payload
    // for the drag operation.
    %payload = new GuiBitmapButtonCtrl();

    // Copy the fields from this control into the payload
    %payload.assignFieldsFrom( %this );

    // Reset the payload's position
    %payload.position = "0 0";

    // Store where this payload cam from.
    %payload.dragSourceControl = %this;

    // Calculate the local center of the payload.  We use
    // this to center the control on the cursor.
    %xOffset = getWord( %payload.extent, 0 ) / 2;
    %yOffset = getWord( %payload.extent, 1 ) / 2;

    // Calculate the initial position of the
    // GuiDragAndDropControl we are about to create.
    %cursorpos = Canvas.getCursorPos();
    %xPos = getWord( %cursorpos, 0 ) - %xOffset;
    %yPos = getWord( %cursorpos, 1 ) - %yOffset;

    // Create the drag control
    %ctrl = new GuiDragAndDropControl()
    {
```

```
            profile         = "GuiSolidDefaultProfile";
            position        = %xPos SPC %yPos;
            extent          = %payload.extent;
            // Allow this control to automatically delete
            // itself on mouse up. When the drag is aborted
            // this will also delete the payload.
            deleteOnMouseUp = true;

            // Use the class field to differentiate between
            // types of drags.
            class           =
                    "GuiDragAndDropControlType_Inventory";

            // Indicate that the payload has not yet been
            // delivered.  This is used to return the payload
            // back to the original owner if it was dropped
            // on an invalid location.
            payloadDelivered = false;
        };

        // Add the payload
        %ctrl.add( %payload );

        // Remove the bitmap from this control as it is now
        // within the payload.
        %this.bitmap = "";

        // Start the drag by adding the control to the Canvas
        Canvas.getContent().add( %ctrl );
        %ctrl.startDragging( %xOffset, %yOffset);
    }
```

25. The second method we'll add handles the user dropping an inventory item onto a control, as follows:

```
// This method is triggered when the mouse is released
// over the control while in the middle of a drag and
// drop operation.
function DragControl::onControlDropped( %this, %payload,
                                        %position )
{
    // Make sure this is an inventory type drop
    if (!%payload.parentGroup.isInNamespaceHierarchy(
        "GuiDragAndDropControlType_Inventory" ))
    {
```

```
         return;
      }

      // Check if this control already has a bitmap
      // assigned.  If so then we'll abort the operation.
      if (%this.bitmap !$= "")
      {
         // Send the bitmap back home
         %payload.dragSourceControl.bitmap = %payload.bitmap;
         return;
      }

      // Copy the bitmap to us from the payload
      %this.bitmap = %payload.bitmap;

      // Indicate that the payload has been delivered
      %payload.parentGroup.payloadDelivered = true;
   }
```

26. The final method we'll add handles the user dropping an inventory item over an invalid target, as follows:

```
// This method is called when our drag and drop object
// is deleted.
function GuiDragAndDropControlType_Inventory::onRemove(%this)
{
   // Has the payload been delivered?  If not, send it back
   // to the owner.
   if (!%this.payloadDelivered)
   {
      %payload = %this.getObject(0);
      %owner = %payload.dragSourceControl;

      // Give the bitmap back to the original owner
      %owner.bitmap = %payload.bitmap;
   }
}
```

27. We now need to make sure our new script file is executed. Open `scripts/client/init.cs` in a text editor and add the following to the `initClient()` method:

```
// Gui scripts
exec("./playerList.cs");
exec("./chatHud.cs");
exec("./messageHud.cs");
exec("scripts/gui/playGui.cs");
exec("scripts/gui/startupGui.cs");

// Load the drag and drop scripts
exec("./dragAndDrop.cs");
```

28. All of the setup is now complete, so it is time to try everything out. Start up the game and at the main menu open the console using the tilde (~) key. Type the following lines into the bottom of the console:

```
Canvas.getContent().add("InventoryGuiWindow");

Canvas.getContent().add("PaperDollGuiWindow");
```

29. The inventory window will now be on the left-hand side and the `Paper Doll` window will now be on the right-hand side, as shown in the next screenshot:

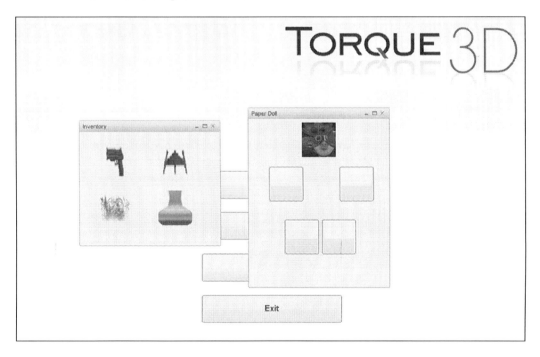

30. We can now drag items from the inventory to the empty `Paper Doll` locations. We can also drag items back into the inventory. If we ever drop an item in an invalid location, it will pop back to its starting location. Here is what the **Inventory** and **Paper Doll** windows look like after dragging a couple of items across:

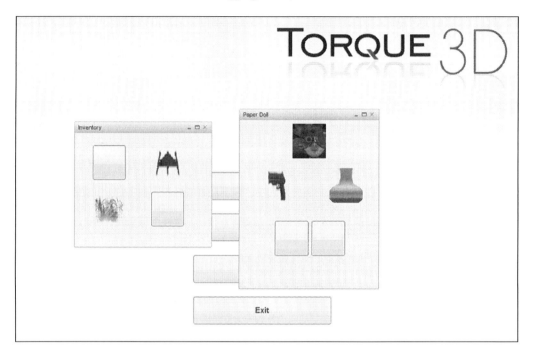

How it works...

The key to having drag-and-drop work is the `GuiDragAndDropControl` class and its defined payload. Its payload may consist of a single `GuiControl` object, although the payload object itself may have any number of children as required. When the user starts the drag operation, we create a new `GuiDragAndDropControl` object and assign its payload. We then add this object to the Canvas and start the dragging of the object. All of this is done in our `DragControl::onMouseDragged()` method.

When the dragged object is dropped, the `GuiControl` class, immediately underneath the dropped object, has its `onControlDropped()` method called. It is up to the `GuiControl` class to decide what to do with the given payload. We take care of this logic in the `DragControl::onControlDropped()` method.

Any of the available button GUI controls make excellent drag sources so long as their `useMouseEvents` property is set to `true`. We will then receive the `onMouseDragged()` callbacks whenever the user holds the mouse down on the button control and starts to move it. In our example we're using the `GuiBitmapButtonCtrl` class to display a bitmap that represents our inventory item. We've also set the `class` property of each of the button to `DragControl` so they'll automatically make use of our two methods.

If the user drops an inventory item onto an invalid drop target, we want the item to return to the `GuiBitmapButtonCtrl` it came from. We've set the `deleteOnMouseUp` property of the `GuiDragAndDropControl` object to `true` so that it is automatically deleted whenever it has been dropped. We take advantage of this automatic deletion by performing a check within the `onRemove()` method of the dragged object.

When an inventory item has been dropped on a valid target, we set a flag on the `GuiDragAndDropControl` object to indicate success (`%payload.parentGroup. payloadDelivered = true;`). If this flag has not been set by the time we get to the drag object's `onRemove()` method, we know that the drop was on an invalid `GuiControl`. We then return the bitmap back to its original owner to indicate that the inventory item has not been successfully moved.

There's more...

Let's explore the drag-and-drop operation a little further.

Dialog boxes and the drag-and-drop operation

In our previous example, you'll notice that we didn't use the typical `Canvas` methods `pushDialog()` and `popDialog()` when displaying our `Inventory` and `Paper Doll` windows. Instead, we used `Canvas.getContent().add()` and put the window control itself onto the Canvas. The reason we need to do this comes down to the `Canvas` layers.

The `Canvas` content (such as the main menu) resides at the bottom with any pushed dialog boxes residing on a layer just above it (layer 0 by default). When we add the `GuiDragAndDropControl` object to the Canvas for dragging, it gets placed onto the content layer. As the user drags this object around, it will therefore be rendered behind any dialog windows. This makes it very hard to drop an item onto one of these windows. By placing our inventory and paper doll windows onto the content layer itself, the `GuiDragAndDropControl` object will now render over the top of all other content of the `GuiControl` objects, and we can easily drop it on the appropriate spot.

How to use the inventory and paper doll windows in a game

In order to use our `Inventory` and `Paper Doll` windows within the `Full` template FPS game, we'll need to assign some key bindings. Open `scripts/client/default.bind.cs` in a text editor and add the following to the bottom:

```
function toggleInventoryWindow()
{
   if (Canvas.getContent().isMember(InventoryGuiWindow))
   {
      // The Inventory window is already open
      Canvas.getContent().remove(InventoryGuiWindow);
   }
   else
   {
      // The Inventory window is not yet open
      Canvas.getContent().add(InventoryGuiWindow);
   }
}


function togglePaperDollWindow()
{
   if (Canvas.getContent().isMember(PaperDollGuiWindow))
   {
      // The Paper Doll window is already open
      Canvas.getContent().remove(PaperDollGuiWindow);
   }
   else
   {
      // The Paper Doll window is not yet open
      Canvas.getContent().add(PaperDollGuiWindow);
   }
}


function toggleMouseLock()
{
   Canvas.getContent().noCursor =
         !Canvas.getContent().noCursor;
   Canvas.checkCursor();
}

moveMap.bindCmd(keyboard, i, "toggleInventoryWindow();", "");
moveMap.bindCmd(keyboard, p, "togglePaperDollWindow();", "");
moveMap.bindCmd(keyboard, m, "toggleMouseLock();", "");
```

These functions place the `Inventory` window on the *i* key and the `Paper Doll` window on the *p* key. Now after we launch the game and start a level, we can press those keys to toggle our windows. Look at the following screenshot showing the result:

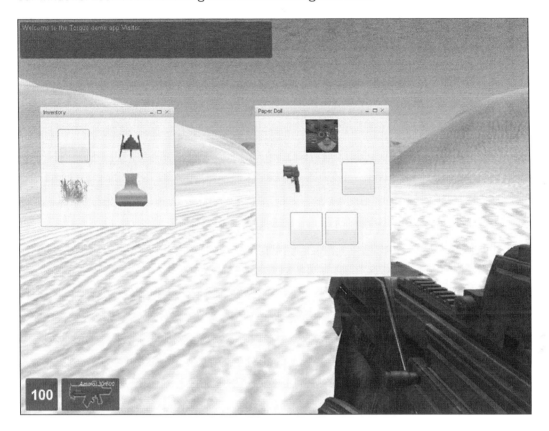

The only problem is that we need access to the mouse pointer within the FPS game (which normally has the mouse locked and hidden). In the previous code, we've placed a mouse toggle on the *m* key. Now we can use the *m* key to show the mouse and drag some inventory items, and then press the *m* key again to go back to the normal FPS operations.

How to pass along game play information with the dragged controls

In our previous example, we are only passing around a bitmap file path between controls when dragging and dropping. In a real game, we would likely need to pass along a lot more information.

Fortunately, TorqueScript allows us to define any dynamic variables we want on the drag-and-drop payload object. This payload information could include some item identifier that is used to verify that the drop is valid within the `onControlDropped()` method. We could also include a quantity value for when we are dragging multiple items in the same stack at once; for example look at the following code:

```
%payload.itemId = %itemId;
%payload.quantity = 1;
```

4
Camera and Mouse Controls

In this chapter we will cover:

- ▶ Locking and hiding the mouse while the right mouse button is down
- ▶ Clicking on an object in the scene (client-side)
- ▶ Clicking on an object in the scene (server-side)
- ▶ Picking up an item in the scene while the mouse is locked and hidden
- ▶ Changing the camera's view and control mode
- ▶ Giving the camera a smooth movement
- ▶ Having the camera follow a path

Introduction

Torque 3D provides complete access to how the mouse functions—from the standard input that any application provides, to tracking relative movements while the mouse pointer is hidden. This allows for its use in a variety of games, from a first-person shooter to a role-playing game. In this chapter, we discuss setting up the mouse beyond the default first-person shooter control scheme that Torque 3D ships with, as well as how to use the mouse to interact with the 3D environment.

Torque 3D also provides a variety of options when it comes to manipulating the virtual camera used to render its 3D environment. In this chapter, we will discuss the various camera types and their control by both the user, and automatically by the game.

Locking and hiding the mouse while the right mouse button is down

Using the left mouse button to select and the right mouse button to activate camera rotation is a common control scheme found in many games that allow for free looking, such as role-playing games. In this recipe, we will modify the default FPS (First Person Shooter) camera control behavior of Torque 3D and allow holding down the right mouse button to control the rotation of the camera to freely look around.

Getting ready

We will be making TorqueScript changes in a project based on the Torque 3D `Full` template, and will try them out using the `Empty Terrain` level. If you haven't already, use the Torque Toolbox Project Manager (`Project Manager.exe`) to create a new project from the `Full` template. This template can be found under the `My Projects` folder. Next, start up your favorite script editor, such as Torsion, and let's get going!

How to do it...

In the following steps we will alter Torque 3D's default mouse behavior to freely look around while holding the right mouse button:

1. Open `art/gui/playGui.gui` in a text editor, such as Torsion.
2. Find the `PlayGui GameTSCtrl` class reference at the top.
3. Change its `noCursor` property from a value of `1` to a value of `0`.
4. Save the changes.
5. Open `scripts/gui/playGui.cs` in a text editor.
6. Add the following two functions to the end of the file and save it:

```
function PlayGui::onRightMouseDown(%this, %screenPos,
                                   %cameraPos, %worldDir)
{
   Canvas.alwaysHandleMouseButtons = true;
   hideCursor();
}

function PlayGui::onRightMouseUp(%this, %screenPos,
                                 %cameraPos, %worldDir)
{
   showCursor();
   Canvas.alwaysHandleMouseButtons = false;
}
```

7. Start up the game and load the `Empty Terrain` level. The mouse cursor should be visible.

8. Hold down the right mouse button somewhere on the screen and drag the mouse. The camera will rotate with the mouse.

9. Let go of the right mouse button and the mouse cursor will return.

How it works...

There are a couple of things at work here. The first has to do with the `noCursor` property of the `PlayGui` control. When the `Canvas.setContent()`, `Canvas.pushDialog()`, or `Canvas.popDialog()` methods are called, each root control is checked for the `noCursor` property. If any of the root controls have this property not defined or set to `false` (or `0`), the mouse cursor will be shown. However, if all of the root controls on the canvas have the `noCursor` property set to `true` (or `1`), the mouse cursor will be automatically hidden and locked to the window.

In the case of the `Full` template's game, the `PlayGui` control is normally the only root control on the canvas, and its `noCursor` property is set to `1`. By default, the mouse cursor is hidden. By setting this property to `0`, as we did in the previous example, the mouse cursor will now always be shown.

When the mouse cursor is shown, the GUI controls have a chance of handling mouse events. With the `PlayGui::onRightMouseDown()` method we added previously, we hide the mouse cursor. With the cursor hidden, all mouse events now go to the `ActionMap` system. This is what allows the mouse to rotate the camera (as already defined by the `moveMap` instance in another client-side script file, such as `default.bind.cs`).

With the `PlayGui::onRightMouseUp()` method we once again show the mouse cursor when the right mouse button is released. However, if hiding and showing the mouse cursor was all we did within these new methods, we would hit a problem. When the mouse cursor is hidden in `PlayGui::onRightMouseDown()`, the `PlayGui` control will never see the right mouse up message and it will be consumed by the current `ActionMap` class.

To overcome this issue, we use the `alwaysHandleMouseButtons` property of the `Canvas` class. When this property is set to `true`, then `Canvas` will first check if there is a defined method to handle the given mouse button event. If there is, the mouse event will be passed to that method. If there is no method defined, then the mouse event will be passed on to the current `ActionMap` class as usual.

In our previous code, we set the `alwaysHandleMouseButtons` property to `true` when the right mouse button is held down. This allows the `PlayGui` control to receive the right mouse button being released rather than it going straight to an `ActionMap` class. And when we receive the right mouse button up event, we set the `Canvas` class' `alwaysHandleMouseButtons` property to `false` to return it to its default value to clean up after ourselves.

There's more...

For these TorqueScript additions to work, we need to make sure that the right mouse button events make their way to the `PlayGui` control. If any child control is set to consume button events, they will receive the events instead of the `PlayGui` control.

In the case of the `Full` template, the `PlayGui` root has the `DamageHUD` control as a child. This GUI control is found at the center of the screen, extending outwards past the cross hairs. If we right-click on this region, we'll find that the mouse cursor will not be hidden. This is because `DamageHUD` uses the `GuiDefaultProfile` profile. The `GuiDefaultProfile` profile has its `modal` property set to `true`, which means it accepts mouse events.

To stop `DamageHUD` from consuming the mouse events (it doesn't make use of them), we need to choose a profile that has its `modal` property set to `false`. A good profile to use is the `GuiModelessDialogProfile` (you'll find other `PlayGui` children also make use of this profile). If we modify the `art/gui/playGui.gui` script file so that the `DamageHUD` display's `profile` property is set to `GuiModelessDialogProfile` (or use the GUI editor to change its `profile` property) we will find that a right mouse click now correctly passes on to the `PlayGui` root control.

Clicking on an object in the scene (client-side)

Clicking on an object within the 3D world with the mouse is a common action in many games. Torque 3D allows for the processing of this action to occur on either the client or server side, depending on what is appropriate. Handling this on the client side is useful when the act of clicking on an object doesn't need to be authorized by the server, or we don't need all of the server-side gameplay information on an object in order to work with it. In this recipe, we will look into clicking on an object from the client and processing it on the client side.

Getting ready

We will be making TorqueScript changes in a project based on the Torque 3D `Full` template, and try them out using the `Empty Terrain` level. If you haven't already, use the Torque Project Manager (`Project Manager.exe`) to create a new project from the `Full` template. It will be found under the `My Projects` folder.

How to do it...

In the following steps we will add an object to the scene and play a sound when the user clicks on it:

1. We will begin by adding an object to the level that we can click on. Start up the `Full` template-based game with the `Empty Terrain` level.
2. Press *F11* to open the *World Editor*.
3. Make sure the *Object Editor* is active by pressing *F1* or by choosing it from the **Editors** menu.
4. Select the **Library** tab of the **Scene Tree** window.
5. Click on the **Meshes** tab and double-click on **art/shapes/trees/defaulttree/ defaulttree** to place a tree into the scene.
6. Click on the new tree if it is not already selected and use the axis gizmo to place it appropriately within the level.
7. Using the **Inspector** pane on the right-hand side, change the new tree's **name** property to **ThunderTree**.
8. Also with the **Inspector** pane, make sure that the tree's **collisionType** property is set to **Collision Mesh**.

9. Save the level and quit the game.

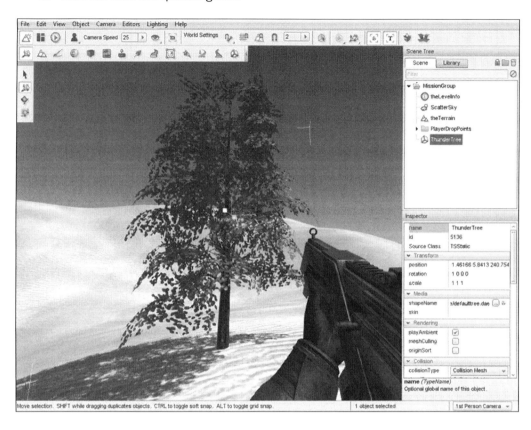

10. Next, we will make the necessary script changes to allow for clicking on our tree. Open `scripts/gui/playGui.cs` in a text editor and add the following function to the end of the file:

```
// Called when left mouse button is clicked.
// %screenPos - The 2D screen position of the mouse click
// %cameraPos - The 3D position of the camera in the world
// %worldDir  - The normalized ray that goes from the camera
//              to the mouse click
function PlayGui::onMouseDown(%this, %screenPos, %cameraPos,
                             %worldDir)
{
   // The farthest distance we want to search in the scene
   %range = 500;

   // Scale the direction ray to the range distance.
   %dirScaled = VectorScale(%worldDir, %range);
```

```
// Calculate the ray cast end point.  The start will be
// the camera position.
%endPoint = VectorAdd(%cameraPos, %dirScaled);

// Perform the ray cast.  This function takes the
// following parameters:
// 1. The ray's start position in the world
// 2. The ray's end position in the world
// 3. A bit mask of the types of objects to search for
// 4. An object to exempt from the ray cast, such as
//    the player
// 5. Whether to use the client scene graph (when true)
//    or the server one
%result = containerRayCast(%cameraPos, %endPoint,
            $TypeMasks::StaticShapeObjectType,
            ServerConnection.getControlObject(), true);

echo("@@@ Ray cast result: " @ %result);

// Check if an object has been hit by our ray
if (getWordCount(%result) > 0 &&
    getWord(%result, 0) !$= "0")
{
    // We have hit an object.  If it is a TSStatic then
    // it is our tree (the only TSStatic in the scene).
    %obj = getWord(%result, 0);
    if (%obj.getClassName() $= "TSStatic")
    {
        // Play a thunder sound on the client
        sfxPlayOnce(ThunderCrash1Sound);
    }
}
}
```

11. Follow the steps in the *Locking and hiding the mouse while the right mouse button is down* recipe to allow the mouse cursor to be shown while the game is running. Also make note of how that recipe deals with GUI objects that may block our mouse clicks.

12. Start up the game again with the `Empty Terrain` level. Walk around and find the tree that we placed in the level and click on it. A thunder-crash sound will play.

How it works...

The key to finding the object that the user has clicked on is the 3D ray, or line, which we pass through the scene and determine the first object that the ray intersects with. To build this ray, we use the parameters provided by the `PlayGui::onMouseDown()` method. The provided camera world position forms the starting point of the ray. We then calculate the ray's end point using the provided directional vector that is generated by the engine based on where the user clicked, and multiply this vector by a chosen range. This range is the maximum distance from the camera that we wish to check.

With the ray's two points in space known, we now use the `containerRayCast()` function to determine the first object that intersects with our ray. This function also takes a bit mask that allows us to limit the objects that should be checked for, as well as an object that we want to ignore (often this is the player object). The final parameter to this function is if we should search the client scene graph or the server scene graph. For this recipe we've chosen to use the client scene graph.

If an object is found to intersect the given ray, the returned results are a space-delimited string with the following seven components:

- The `SimObject` ID of the found object
- The x, y, and z world position of the point the ray has struck
- The x, y, and z vector of the normal of the face the ray has struck

We can now work with the returned object, if any. In the previous example we play a thunder sound when any `TSStatic` object is clicked on.

There's more...

Let's continue with the discussion of working with the `containerRayCast()` function.

Collision mesh required

The `containerRayCast()` function will only find those objects that have a collision mesh. For a `TSStatic` object-based object we just need to make sure its `collisionType` property is set to something other than `None`. For `ShapeBase` derived objects, the collision mesh must be found within the shape file itself, as defined by the artist (or with the *Shape Editor* window).

Client-side-only limitations

When using `containerRayCast()` with the client scene graph, it will return a client `SimObject` object. Client objects do not possess all of the information that server objects do, such as the object's `name` property. If we were to call the `getName()` method on the returned tree object in our previous example, we would get an empty string rather than the **ThunderTree** name as entered in the *Object Editor*.

Please see the *Clicking on an object in the scene (server-side)* recipe for how to work with the server-side object instead.

Single-player games

In Torque 3D, a single-player game still makes use of a server and client split when it comes to objects and scene graphs. However, these two halves exist in the same executable and it is easy to switch between them. We can use this to avoid any client-side limitations when it comes to object properties.

When it comes to clicking on an object in the scene, we could simply use the server scene graph instead of the client one. To do so, we change the last parameter of `containerRayCast()` from `true` to `false`. We also need to make sure we exclude the server instance of the player object rather than the client instance. To make this change we use the special `LocalClientConnection` object that is only available when both the client and server code is running within the same executable, such as a single-player game. This makes our previous example look like this:

```
%result = containerRayCast(%cameraPos, %endPoint,
          $TypeMasks::StaticShapeObjectType,
          LocalClientConnection.getControlObject(),
          false);
```

Now the returned object will be from the server side. If we were to call the `getName()` method on the returned tree object in our previous example, we would get the **ThunderTree** name.

If we want to convert from this server object into the client object for some reason (perhaps to toggle a special rendering feature without having to go through the overhead of the networking system that still exists in a single-player game), we can make use of the `serverToClientObject()` function. We pass in the server object ID and get the client-side `SimObject` ID in return. This shortcut, of course, only works when the server and client are running in the same process, such as with a single-player game.

Type masks

Type masks are used to limit the `containerRayCast()` function to only search for objects of a specific type. If we want to search for objects with more than one type mask, we just use the logical OR operator to join them together. For example, to search for both static shapes and `Item` class objects we would use:

```
%typemask = $TypeMasks::StaticShapeObjectType |
            $TypeMasks::ItemObjectType;
```

Here is a list of all the available type masks:

Type mask (add the $TypeMasks:: prefix to use)	Object classes the mask is used by
CameraObjectType	Camera and PathCamera
CorpseObjectType	Disabled/dead Player and AIPlayer
DebrisObjectType	Debris and PhysicsDebris
DynamicShapeObjectType	Debris, PhysicsDebris, PhysicsShape, all Vehicle classes, Item, Player, Projectile, RigidShape, and all TurretShape and AITurretShape objects that are not at rest (not static)
EnvironmentObjectType	BasicClouds, CloudLayer, ScatterSky, SkyBox, Sun, TimeOfDay, Forest, ForestWindEmitter, DecalManager, Lighting, LightBase and its derivatives, and ParticleEmitterNode
ExplosionObjectType	Explosion
GameBaseObjectType	GameBase and its derivatives (all classes that use datablocks)
InteriorObjectType	InteriorInstance
ItemObjectType	Item, TurretShape, AITurretShape, ProximityMine
LightObjectType	ScatterSky, Sun, Explosion, LightBase and its derivatives, Projectile, and ShapeBase and its derivatives
MarkerObjectType	Marker, SFXEmitter
PhysicalZoneObjectType	PhysicalZone
PlayerObjectType	Enabled/alive Player and AIPlayer
ProjectileObjectType	Precipitation, Projectile
ShapeBaseObjectType	ShapeBase and its derivatives
StaticObjectType	BasicClouds, CloudLayer, DecalRoad, MeshRoad, ScatterSky, SkyBox, Sun, River, WaterBlock, WaterPlane, Forest, ForestWindEmitter, InteriorInstance, fxFoliageReplicator, fxShapeReplicator, GroundCover, Lightning, TurretShape and AITurretShape at rest, ConvexShape, GroundPlane, MissionMarker, WayPoint, SpawnSphere, CameraBookmark, Portal, Prefab, StaticShape, TSStatic, and TerrainBlock

Type mask (add the $TypeMasks:: prefix to use)	Object classes the mask is used by
StaticShapeObjectType	DecalRoad, MeshRoad, Forest, InteriorInstance, GroundCover, TurretShape and AITurretShape at rest, GroundPlane, ProximityMine, ScopeAlwaysShape, StaticShape, TSStatic, and TerrainBlock
TerrainObjectType	TerrainBlock
TriggerObjectType	Trigger
VehicleBlockerObjectType	VehicleBlocker
VehicleObjectType	TurretShape, AITurretShape, Vehicle and its derivatives, and RigidShape
WaterObjectType	River, WaterBlock, WaterPlane

See also

▸ *Locking and hiding the mouse while the right mouse button is down*

▸ *Clicking on an object in the scene (server-side)*

Clicking on an object in the scene (server-side)

Clicking on an object within the 3D world with the mouse is a common action in many games. Torque 3D allows for the processing of this action to occur on either the client or server side depending on what is appropriate. Handling this action on the server is useful when the act of clicking needs to be authorized by the server (such as making sure an object is in the player's line of sight and they are not cheating), or we need to make use of the gameplay information on an object in order to work with it. In this recipe, we will look into clicking on an object from the client and processing it on the server side.

Getting ready

We will be making TorqueScript changes in a project based on the Torque 3D Full template, and try them out using the Empty Terrain level. If you haven't already, use the Torque Project Manager (Project Manager.exe) to create a new project from the Full template. It will be found under the My Projects directory. Then start up your favorite script editor, such as Torsion, and let's get going!

How to do it...

In the following steps, we will add an object to the scene and have the server tell the client to play a sound when the user clicks on the object.

1. Perform steps 1-9 from the *Clicking on an object in the scene (client-side)* recipe.

2. Next, we will make the necessary script changes. Open `scripts/gui/playGui.cs` in a text editor and add the following function to the end of the file:

```
// Called when left mouse button is clicked.
// %screenPos - The 2D screen position of the mouse click
// %cameraPos - The 3D position of the camera in the world
// %worldDir  - The normalized ray that goes from the camera
//              to the mouse click
function PlayGui::onMouseDown(%this, %screenPos, %cameraPos,
                             %worldDir)
{
    // Send a command to the server with the ray generated
    // by the mouse click.  This will be used on the server
    // to determine which object has been clicked on.
    commandToServer('ClickOnObject', %worldDir);
}
```

3. Open `scripts/server/commands.cs` in a text editor and add the following function to the end of the file:

```
// Called by the client when the user has clicked on
// an object.
// %client   - The client that made the call
// %worldDir - The ray produced by the user clicking the mouse
function serverCmdClickOnObject(%client, %worldDir)
{
    // The farthest distance we want to search in the scene
    %range = 500;

    // The position of the camera for the client
    %camera = %client.getCameraObject();
    %cameraPos = %camera.getPosition();

    // Scale the direction ray to the range distance.
    %dirScaled = VectorScale(%worldDir, %range);

    // Calculate the ray cast end point.  The start will be
    // the camera position.
    %endPoint = VectorAdd(%cameraPos, %dirScaled);
```

```
// Perform the ray cast.  This function takes the following
// parameters:
// 1. The ray's start position in the world
// 2. The ray's end position in the world
// 3. A bit mask of the types of objects to search for
// 4. An object to exempt from the ray cast, such as the
//    player
// 5. Whether to use the client scene graph (when true)
//    or the server one
%result = containerRayCast(%cameraPos, %endPoint,
            $TypeMasks::StaticShapeObjectType,
            %client.getControlObject(), false);

echo("@@@ Ray cast result: " @ %result);

// Check if an object has been hit by our ray
if (getWordCount(%result) > 0 &&
    getWord(%result, 0) !$= "0")
{
    // We have hit an object.  Check if it is our
    // ThunderTree
    %obj = getWord(%result, 0);
    if (%obj.getName() $= "ThunderTree")
    {
        // Play a thunder sound on the client
        %client.play2D(ThunderCrash1Sound);
    }
}
}
```

4. Follow the steps in the *Locking and hiding the mouse while the right mouse button is down* recipe to allow for the mouse cursor to be shown while the game is running. Also make a note of how that recipe deals with GUI objects that may block our mouse clicks.

5. Start up the game again with the `Empty Terrain` level. Walk around and find the tree we placed in the level and click on it. A thunder-crash sound will play.

How it works...

This recipe requires cooperation between the client and server for it to work. On the client side, the user clicks the left mouse button somewhere on the scene. For example, he or she clicks on our tree. This action calls our new `PlayGui::onMouseDown()` method with a number of parameters describing where the mouse was clicked.

The only parameter of the `onMouseDown()` method we're interested in is `%worldDir`, which is the 3D-normalized vector that points to where the mouse was clicked from the camera's point of view. We will pass this vector on to the server to perform the calculations to determine what has been clicked on. We don't pass along the client's camera position as the server will already have that information. This also prevents cheating by hacking this position before passing it to the server (which could allow the user to click on objects that are not in view).

To send the mouse-click vector to the server, we use the `commandToServer()` function, which has a form of:

```
commandToServer( functionName, [params] );
```

In the previous code snippet, the `functionName` parameter is the name of the function to call on the server, and the `params` parameter is actually an optional set of zero or more parameters to pass to the server's function. This is a generic function that allows us to send data from the client to the server. In our case, the TorqueScript function we want to call on the server is `ClickOnObject`, and the single parameter we will send is the mouse-click vector. We are now done with the client side.

On the server we define the `ClickOnObject` TorqueScript function the client wishes to call. Any function that the client may call is prefixed with `serverCmd`, which makes sure the client may only call those functions we've specifically defined. By combining this prefix with the name of our function, we end up with the following function definition on the server:

```
function serverCmdClickOnObject(%client, %worldDir)
{
   ...
}
```

In the previous code, the `%client` parameter is the `NetConnection` client object that made the call to the server, and the `%worldDir` parameter is the only parameter passed by the client.

This TorqueScript server function is the meat of this recipe. This is where we calculate the starting and ending point of a ray that will be used to collide with the objects in the scene. The starting point of our ray is the client's current camera position. To calculate the ending point of the ray, we multiply the given mouse-click vector from the client by a chosen range. This determines how far into the scene we wish the mouse click to reach. Adding this scaled vector to the camera position gives us the ray's end point.

The function we use to test if our ray collides with any objects in the scene is `containerRayCast()`. This function has a form of:

```
%result = containerRayCast(rayStart, rayEnd, bitmask, exclude,
                           useClientScene);
```

In the previous code, the `rayStart` parameter is the starting point of the ray, the `rayEnd` parameter is the ending point of the ray, the `bitmask` parameter is used to restrict the types of objects to test against, the `exclude` parameter is an object to exclude from the ray test (often this is the player object), and the `useClientScene` parameter is set to `true` if the client scene graph should be used, or `false` if the server scene graph is to be used.

In our example, we have the `bitmask` parameter set up to only test against static shape type objects. There are a number of different type masks that may be used and combined together, depending on what we want to cast the ray against. Please see the *Clicking on an object in the scene (client-side)* recipe for a complete list of all the available type masks.

Our example also excludes the client's current control object. Usually this is the player object, but if the player is currently mounted in a vehicle, this will exclude the vehicle itself. By excluding the player from the ray cast, we don't need to worry about accidentally selecting it with our mouse click. When it comes to the `Player` class, this ray cast exclusion also excludes any items mounted on the player, such as weapons and torches, among other items.

With all of its parameters set up, `containerRayCast()` returns the result of the ray cast. If an object is found to intersect the given ray, the returned results are a space-delimited string with the following seven components:

- The `SimObject` object ID of the found object
- The x, y, and z world position of the point the ray has struck
- The x, y, and z vector of the normal of the face the ray has struck

In our example, we retrieve the name of the returned `SimObject`. If it matches the name of the tree we added to the scene (**ThunderTree**), we tell the client to play a thunder sound.

There's more...

Let's continue the discussion of working with the `containerRayCast()` function.

Collision mesh required

The `containerRayCast()` function will only find those objects that have a collision mesh. For a `TSStatic` object-based object, we just need to make sure its `collisionType` property is set to something other than `None`. For `ShapeBase` derived objects, the collision mesh must be found within the shape file itself as defined by the artist (or with the *Shape Editor*).

See also

- *Locking and hiding the mouse while the right mouse button is down*
- *Clicking on an object in the scene (client-side)*

Picking up an item in the scene while the mouse is locked and hidden

While the mouse is locked and hidden, such as during a typical first-person shooter game where the mouse position is locked as the targeting reticle, there are times when the player needs to interact with the environment in a means other than colliding with it. For example, we may want to pick up a cache of ammo we are looking at, or activate a switch. In this recipe, we will pick up an object on the ground based on where the player is looking.

Getting ready

We will be making TorqueScript changes in a project based on the Torque 3D `Full` template, and try them out using the `Empty Terrain` level. If you haven't already, use the Torque Project Manager (`Project Manager.exe`) to create a new project from the `Full` template. It will be found under the `My Projects` directory.

How to do it...

In the following steps we will add some objects to the scene and allow the user to pick them up by pressing a key while looking at an object:

1. We will begin by adding three objects to the level that we can interact with. Start up the `Full` template-based game with the `Empty Terrain` level.

2. Press *F11* to open the *World Editor*.

3. Make sure the *Object Editor* is active by pressing *F1* or by choosing it from the **Editors** menu.

4. Select the **Library** tab of the **Scene Tree** window.

5. Click on the **Meshes** tab and double-click on **art/shapes/items/kit/healthkit** to place a backpack into the scene.

6. Click on the new backpack if it is not already selected and use the axis gizmo to place it somewhere on the terrain.

7. Using the **Inspector** pane on the right, change the backpack's *class* property to `SoldierPack`.

8. With the axis gizmo set to move mode, hold down the *Shift* key and drag the backpack to make a copy. Place this copy somewhere on the terrain. Do this again to make a total of three backpacks in the scene.

9. Save the level and quit the game.

10. Next, we will make the necessary script changes that will enable us to interact with this object using the mouse and keyboard. Open `scripts/client/default.bind.cs` in a text editor and add the following code to the end of the file:

```
moveMap.bindCmd(keyboard, g,
                "commandToServer(\'pickupObject\');", "");
```

11. Open `scripts/server/commands.cs` in a text editor and add the following function to the end of the file:

```
function serverCmdPickupObject(%client)
{
    // The farthest distance we want to search in the scene
    %range = 5;

    // Get the control object for the client
    %control = %client.getControlObject();

    // Use the ShapeBase::getLookAtPoint() method to perform
    // the ray cast.  This uses the object's eye point and
    // vector to determine the ray's origin and direction.
```

```
// This method takes two parameters:
// 1. The range to cast the ray out to (ray length)
// 2. A bitmask of the object types to search for
%result = %control.getLookAtPoint(%range,
                    $TypeMasks::StaticShapeObjectType);

echo("@@@ Ray cast result: " @ %result);

// Check if an object has been hit by our ray
if (getWordCount(%result) > 0 &&
    getWord(%result, 0) !$= "0")
{
    // We have hit an object.  Check if it is a
    // backpack object
    %obj = getWord(%result, 0);
    if (%obj.getClassNamespace() $= "SoldierPack")
    {
        // Play a pickup sound at the position of the
        // backpack that all clients within range will hear
        ServerPlay3D(AmmoPickupSound, %obj.getTransform());

        // Remove the object from the scene and increment
        // the soldier pack count on the player
        %obj.delete();
        %control.soldierPackInventory += 1;
    }
}
```

12. Start up the game again with the `Empty Terrain` level. Walk around and find the three backpacks on the ground. Point the crosshairs at the first pack and press the *g* key. The pack will disappear and a sound will play.

How it works...

This recipe requires cooperation between the client and server for it to work. On the client side, we've bound the *g* key to call the `commandToServer()` function, which has a form of:

```
commandToServer( functionName, params );
```

In the previous code, the `functionName` parameter is the name of the function to call on the server, and the `params` parameter is actually an optional set of zero or more parameters to pass to the server's function. In our case, the TorqueScript function we want to call on the server is `PickupObject` without any parameters. We are now done with the client side.

On the server we define the `PickupObject` TorqueScript function the client wishes to call. Any function that the client may call is prefixed with `serverCmd`, which makes sure the client may only call those functions we've specifically defined. By combining this prefix with the name of our function, we end up with the following function definition on the server:

```
function serverCmdPickupObject(%client)
{
...
}
```

In the previous code, the `%client` parameter is the `NetConnection` client object that made the call to the server. The client doesn't send along any additional parameters in our example, so we are done with the function definition.

This TorqueScript server function is the meat of this recipe. This is where we cast a ray within the scene and determine if it hits any of the objects we are interested in. We start by obtaining the object that is controlled by the given client. In our example, this is a `Player` class object. We then take advantage of a `ShapeBase` method (from which the `Player` class is derived from) that will cast a ray based on where the object is looking:

```
%result = %control.getLookAtPoint( range, bitmask );
```

In the previous code, the `range` parameter is the length of the ray that will be cast from the player's eye node, and the `bitmask` parameter is used to restrict the types of objects to test against. Please see the *Clicking on an object in the scene (client-side)* recipe for a list of available type masks and how to use them.

If an object of the request type is found to intersect the internally generated ray, the returned results are a space-delimited string with the following five components:

- The `SimObject` ID of the found object
- The x, y, and z world position of the point the ray has struck
- The `SimObject` ID of the material that has been struck (this is optional and not always present in the results)

We can now work with the returned object, if any. In the previous example, if the returned object has a class namespace of `SoldierPack`, then we play a 3D sound that all the nearby clients will hear, delete the object from the scene (making it disappear), and increment a dynamic variable on the `Player` object that keeps track of the number of backpacks picked up.

There's more...

Unfortunately, the ray casting that is done by `ShapeBase::getLookAtPoint()` does not automatically exclude the object that the ray originates from, such as the `Player` object. This means that if we use a type mask that would include the ray casting object, it may be possible that the object itself will be returned in the results. The easiest way around this is to not include the `$TypeMasks::PlayerObjectType` type mask in the method call (assuming the client-controlled object is a `Player` class instance).

If we need more control over the ray being cast and need to explicitly exclude the originating object, we can fall back to the more general `containerRayCast()` function as detailed in the *Clicking on an object in the scene (server-side)* recipe. In order to use this function we will need to obtain the player's eye position and direction vector (the equivalent to the camera position and world direction used in the other recipe):

```
...
// Get the control object for the client
%control = %client.getControlObject();

// Get the eye position for the control object (player).
// This will be used as the camera position for the ray cast.
%eyePos = %control.getEyePoint();

// Get the eye vector for the control object.  This will be
// used to calculate the end point of the ray, and is the
// equivalent to the %worldDir used in other recipes.
%eyeVec = %control.getEyeVector();
...
```

We now have enough information to proceed with using the `containerRayCast()` function.

See also

 ▶ *Clicking on an object in the scene (client-side)*
 ▶ *Clicking on an object in the scene (server-side)*

Changing the camera's view and control mode

Torque 3D offers a number of different camera modes that affect what the camera sees and how the user interacts with it. In this recipe, we will modify the standard camera's behavior and go through the available modes.

Getting ready

We will be making TorqueScript changes in a project based on the Torque 3D `Full` template, and try them out using the `Empty Terrain` level. If you haven't already, use the Torque Project Manager (`Project Manager.exe`) to create a new project from the `Full` template. It will be found under the `My Projects` directory. Then start up your favorite script editor, such as Torsion, and let's get going!

How to do it...

In the following steps we will modify the third-person camera's behavior to allow only for rotation:

1. Open `scripts/server/gameCore.cs` in a text editor, such as Torsion.

2. Add the following lines to `GameCore::onClientEnterGame()`:

   ```
   function GameCore::onClientEnterGame(%game, %client)
   {
   ...
      // Find a spawn point for the camera
      // This function currently relies on some helper functions
      // defined in core/scripts/server/spawn.cs. For custom
      // spawn behaviors one can either override the properties
      // on the SpawnSphere's or directly override the
      // functions themselves.
      %cameraSpawnPoint =
         pickCameraSpawnPoint($Game::DefaultCameraSpawnGroups);
      // Spawn a camera for this client using the
      // found %spawnPoint
      %client.spawnCamera(%cameraSpawnPoint);

      // Change the camera's mode to only allow rotation and
      // no movement
      %client.camera.controlMode = "FreeRotate";

      // Setup game parameters, the onConnect method currently
      // starts everyone with a 0 score.
      %client.score = 0;
      %client.kills = 0;
      %client.deaths = 0;
   ...
   }
   ```

3. Start up the game and load the `Empty Terrain` level.

4. Press *Alt + C* to switch to the third-person camera. We can now rotate the camera but cannot move it around with the WASD keys (unlike the default Torque 3D camera).

How it works...

The `Camera` class supports a set of basic and advanced modes. All of the basic modes may be set by modifying a camera's `controlMode` property as seen in our preceding example. The basic modes and their functions are as follows:

The `controlMode` property	**Description**
`Stationary`	Camera cannot be moved or rotated by the user
`FreeRotate`	Camera may only be rotated by the user
`Fly`	Camera may be moved and rotated by the user
`Overhead`	Camera may be rotated by the user but only moves along the world's x and y planes

The advanced modes require additional information and therefore must be set using a specific method:

Advanced mode method	**Description**
`setOrbitObject()`	This sets the camera to orbit around a given object. The user controls the rotation around the object (can be turned off), but cannot move the camera.
`setOrbitPoint()`	This method sets the camera to orbit around a given world point. The user controls the rotation about the point (can be turned off), but cannot move the camera.
`setTrackObject()`	This method sets the camera to always face the given object. The user may not rotate or move the camera.

Please see the `Camera` class reference in `Torque 3D - Script Manual.chm` found in the Torque 3D documentation for a complete list of each advanced method's parameters.

See also

▸   *Giving the camera smooth movement*

Giving the camera smooth movement

Torque 3D's standard camera motion causes the camera to start and stop instantaneously, which is a common behavior found in many games. However, there are times when the camera should accelerate and decelerate into its motion. One example of this is when recording a fly-through for a game's video to keep all movement appear smooth. In this recipe, we will set up the camera to smoothly go from standing still to full speed, and back to being stationary.

Getting ready

We will be making TorqueScript changes in a project based on the Torque 3D `Full` template, and try them out using the `Empty Terrain` level. If you haven't already, use the Torque Project Manager (`Project Manager.exe`) to create a new project from the `Full` template. It will be found under the `My Projects` directory. Then start up your favorite script editor, such as Torsion, and let's get going!

How to do it...

In the following steps, we will modify how the camera moves in response to the user's input:

1. Open `scripts/server/gameCore.cs` in a text editor, such as Torsion.

2. Add the following lines to `GameCore::onClientEnterGame()`:

```
function GameCore::onClientEnterGame(%game, %client)
{
...
   // Find a spawn point for the camera
   // This function currently relies on some helper functions
   // defined in core/scripts/server/spawn.cs. For custom
   // spawn behaviors one can either override the properties
   // on the SpawnSphere's or directly override the
   // functions themselves.
   %cameraSpawnPoint =
      pickCameraSpawnPoint($Game::DefaultCameraSpawnGroups);
   // Spawn a camera for this client using the
   // found %spawnPoint
   %client.spawnCamera(%cameraSpawnPoint);

   // Change the camera's mode to allow full movement and
   // rotation.  Also enable smooth movement, known as
   // Newton Mode.
```

```
%client.camera.controlMode = "Fly";
%client.camera.newtonMode = true;

// Setup game parameters, the onConnect method currently
// starts everyone with a 0 score.
%client.score = 0;
%client.kills = 0;
%client.deaths = 0;
...
}
```

3. Start up the game and load the `Empty Terrain` level.

4. Press *Alt + C* to switch to the third-person camera. As expected, we can freely move and rotate the camera. However, all movement now has smooth acceleration and deceleration.

How it works...

When a `Camera` object has its `newtonMode` property set to `true`, it uses Newton's 2nd Law of Motion (force = mass x acceleration) to move the camera in the scene. This provides acceleration up to maximum speed when a move has been requested, and deceleration down to a stop when the move has been stopped.

While the Newton mode is active, the `Camera` object provides a number of properties to fine-tune the camera's motion. The first of these is the `force` property. This determines how much force is applied to move the camera. The greater the force, the faster the camera will accelerate up to top speed. The second property is `drag`, which determines how quickly the camera slows down when all movement input has stopped. The greater the drag, the faster the camera will decelerate to a stop.

The third `Camera` property used by the Newton mode is `mass`. A camera's mass affects its acceleration, but doesn't take part in the deceleration calculations. Often, we will just tweak a camera's `force` and `drag` properties until the motion is just right and leave its `mass` alone.

There's more...

Let's continue our discussion of the `Camera` object's smooth motion.

Camera speed boost and brakes using triggers

A `Camera` object listens to input triggers `0` and `1` (`$mvTriggerCount0` and `$mvTriggerCount1` on the client) and modifies its Newton mode motion based on these inputs. When trigger `0` is active, the camera is given a speed boost according to its `speedMultiplier` property. This speed boost takes the form of the camera's `force` property being multiplied by its `speedMultiplier` property.

When trigger 1 is active, it is as if the camera has air brakes applied. This extra slowdown takes the form of the camera's `drag` property multiplied by its `brakeMultiplier` property. This is useful when we want the camera to slow down quicker than its usually-gentle deceleration.

Smooth camera rotation

In addition to smooth movement, Torque 3D's `Camera` object also supports smooth rotation, which is called **Newton Rotation**. This ease-in and ease-out rotation may be set independent of a camera's smooth movement so we may have one or the other, or both set at the same time. To activate smooth rotation for a `Camera` object we set its `newtonRotation` property to `true`.

While the Newton Rotation is active, the `Camera` object provides a number of properties to fine-tune the camera's rotation. The first of these is the `angularForce` property. This determines how much force is applied to rotate the camera. The greater the force, the faster the camera will accelerate up to its top rotation speed. The second property is `angularDrag`, which determines how quickly the camera slows down when all rotation input has stopped. The greater the angular drag, the faster the camera will decelerate to a stop.

The third `Camera` property used by Newton Rotation is `mass`. A camera's mass affects its rotational acceleration but doesn't take part in the rotational deceleration calculations. Often we will just tweak a camera's `angularForce` and `angularDrag` properties until the rotation is just right and leave its `mass` property alone.

Having the camera follow a path

While Torque 3D has the camera under user control most of the time, there are times when we want the camera to follow a defined path through the scene. This can be useful during an in-game cinematic, or as part of a shooter-on-rails game. In this recipe, we will set up a path using the *World Editor* and have the camera follow it.

Getting ready

We will be making TorqueScript changes in a project based on the Torque 3D `Full` template, and try them out using the `Empty Terrain` level. If you haven't already, use the Torque Project Manager (`Project Manager.exe`) to create a new project from the `Full` template. It will be found under the `My Projects` directory.

How to do it...

In the following steps we will add a path to a level and have the camera follow it:

1. We will begin by adding an object to the level that we can click on. Start up the `Full` template-based game with the `Empty Terrain` level.

2. Press *F11* to open the *World Editor*.

3. Make sure the *Object Editor* is active by pressing *F1* or choosing it from the **Editors** menu.

4. Press *Alt + C* to go into the **Standard Camera** mode. Fly to an open area of the terrain.

5. Select the **Library** tab of the **Scene Tree** window.

6. Click on the **Level** tab and double-click on the **Path** item (this is shown in the previous screenshot). This will place a new **Path** object in the **Scene Tree** window, but it does not have a position within the 3D world (you cannot click on it in the scene).

7. Select the **Scene** tab of the **Scene Tree** window.

8. Select the new **Path** object in the **Scene Tree** window. Give it a name of `CameraPath1`.

9. Uncheck the **CameraPath1** object's **isLooping** property as we want the camera's motion to have a start and an end.

10. Right-click on the **CameraPath1** object and choose **Add New Objects Here** from the context menu. All new objects will now be placed as a child of this **Path** object.

11. Go back to the **Library** tab of the **Scene Tree** window and make sure the **Level** tab is still the current one.

12. Double-click on the **Path Node** item. This will place a new **PathNode** object in the scene and will represent the first node in **CameraPath1**. Using the axis gizmo, drag this **PathNode** to an appropriate place.

13. Double-click again on the **Path Node** item to add another **PathNode** object to the scene as the second **CameraPath1** child. Place this node somewhere else wherever appropriate.

14. Create a third **PathNode** object in the scene and drag it somewhere else. The **Scene** tab is shown in the following screenshot:

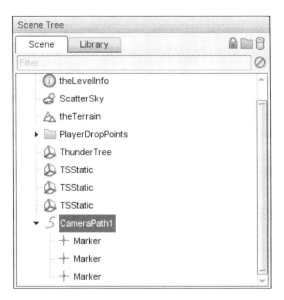

15. Go back to the **Scene** tab of the **Scene Tree** window and make sure the **CameraPath1** object is selected. You will see a bunch of green triangles forming an arc from the first path node to the last path node. This is the path that the camera is about to follow.

16. Save the level and quit the game.

17. Now we will make the necessary script changes. Open `core/art/datablocks/camera.cs` in a text editor and add the following code to the end of the file:

```
datablock PathCameraData(PathCameraDatablock)
{
};
```

18. Open `scripts/client/default.bind.cs` in a text editor and add the following code to the end of the file:

```
moveMap.bindCmd(keyboard, p,
                "commandToServer(\'togglePathCamera\');", "");
```

19. Open `scripts/server/commands.cs` in a text editor and add the following function to the end of the file:

```
function serverCmdTogglePathCamera(%client)
{
    if (!isObject(%client.pathCamera))
    {
        // Create a new path camera for this client
        %client.pathCamera = spawnObject(PathCamera,
                                         PathCameraDatablock);

        // Ensure that the camera is cleaned up when
        // the mission ends
        MissionCleanup.add(%client.pathCamera);

        // Keep the camera in scope for the client
        %client.pathCamera.scopeToClient(%client);
    }

    %camera = %client.pathCamera;

    %control = %client.getControlObject();
    if (%control != %camera)
    {
        // Store the current control object
        %client.prevControl = %control;

        // Reset the path camera's current node list.  This
        // will add a single node to the camera with the
        // camera's current transform.  For our
        // work here we will remove this default node further
        // along.
```

```
%camera.reset();

// Store the path
%camera.path = CameraPath1;

// Copy the path in to the path camera
%count = %camera.path.getCount();
for (%i=0; %i<%count; %i++)
{
    %node = %camera.path.getObject(%i);

    // Add the node to the path camera.  The 1.0 is
    // the speed of the camera as it travels to this
    // node, which we're setting to 1.0 m/s.
    %camera.pushBack(%node.getTransform(), 1.0,
                     %node.type, %node.smoothingType);
}

// Remove the front most node that was added by the
// reset() method.  This is not part of the
// CameraPath1 defined nodes.
%camera.popFront();

// Set the path camera to start at the beginning of
// the path
%camera.setPosition(0);

// Make the path camera the client's control object
%client.setControlObject(%camera);
}
else
{
    // Switch back to the regular control object
    %client.setControlObject(%client.prevControl);
}
}
```

20. Start up the game again with the Empty Terrain level. Press the *p* key and the view will change to that of the PathCamera object moving along the defined path. Press the *p* key again to go back to the player view.

How it works...

Making the camera follow a path requires that we make use of the `PathCamera` class. Rather than having a user's input move and rotate the camera, the `PathCamera` class relies on a set of nodes (or knots) that define how the camera will move over time. These path nodes could either be dynamically generated in TorqueScript, or they may come from a `Path` object defined in the scene. In our example, we're making use of a defined `Path` object.

With a `Path` object and its nodes built, we move on to building the `PathCamera` object. We begin by defining a `Datablock` definition for the camera (Torque 3D does not have one we can use by default). All `ShapeBase` objects require a `Datablock` definition and this includes the `PathCamera` class. We're not making much use of the camera's `Datablock` definition in this recipe, so an empty definition will suffice.

For our example we want the user to be able to control when to switch between the player's view and the `PathCamera` view. To do this we bind a server command, `TogglePathCamera`, to the *p* key. That is the extent of the client-side changes.

On the server, we define the `TogglePathCamera` function the client wishes to call. Any function that the client may call is prefixed with `serverCmd`, which makes sure the client may only call those functions we've specifically defined. By combining these two parts we end up with the following function definition on the server:

```
Function serverCmdTogglePathCamera(%client)
{
...
}
```

In the previous code, the `%client` parameter is `theNetConnection` client object that made the call to the server. No additional parameters are passed along by the client in our example.

It is within this TorqueScript function that all of the action takes place. The first thing we do is ensure that `PathCamera` is available for the client to use. If not, then we use the standard `spawnObject()` function that is handy for creating new `ShapeBase` objects. This function takes a class and a `Datablock` definition as its parameters and returns a new `ShapeBase` type object. We then make sure that the object will be properly cleaned up if the mission ends, and also make sure the `PathCamera` object will be sent to the client regardless of any other scene scoping (such as distance from the client's control object).

With the `PathCamera` object ready, we then copy each of the `Path` object's nodes into the camera. Instead of copying an existing path into the camera, we could have dynamically generated nodes based on some algorithm. It's also possible for us to add nodes to the `PathCamera` object while it is travelling through its internal node list. The `PathCamera` object will only stop moving when it runs out of nodes to move to (or the user explicitly tells the camera to stop, by using the `setState()` or `setTarget()` methods).

The final step in all this is to make the `PathCamera` object the control object for the client. A client's control object defines where the scene is rendered from, and is the first destination for all user input. In the case of the `PathCamera` object, all user input is ignored; although its `Datablock` definition can receive `onTrigger()` callbacks just like any other `ShapeBase` object.

There's more...

Let's continue the discussion about the `PathCamera` class.

Maximum size of node list

The `PathCamera` class supports a maximum of 128 internally defined nodes at once. If a 129th node is added to the internal list with the `pushBack()` method, the first node is removed from the list.

This can be useful if a camera's path is continuously being generated as the game plays. We don't need to worry about overflowing memory with path nodes and may add them as necessary, as long as we don't get more than 128 nodes ahead of the camera.

Manually stopping and changing direction

If left on its own, a `PathCamera` will move until it reaches the last defined path node and comes to a stop. It is also possible to have the camera stop at a particular node, or even in-between two nodes by using the `setTarget()` method.

This method's only parameter is the node index to stop at (or a fractional node index to stop somewhere between nodes). If the given node index is between the camera's current position and the start of the path, the camera will move backwards along the path. Once the camera reaches the given node, it will come to a stop.

It is also possible to make a `PathCamera` object jump to a node on the path by using the `setPosition()` method. This method's single parameter is also a node index or a fractional node index. After the `PathCamera` object has jumped to the given position, it will continue to move in the direction in which it was moving before the `setPosition()` call.

Finally, it is possible to force the camera to stop moving (and start up again) using the `setState()` method. This method takes a single string parameter of `stop`, `forward`, or `backward`, with the effect on the camera being what you would expect.

Node callback

As a `PathCamera` object reaches each path node, the `onNode()` callback is called. This callback is made on the `PathCamera` object itself, which requires that the camera have a globally unique name, has its class property defined to a TorqueScript namespace, or has the callback defined on the `PathCamera` class itself (which means it applies to all `PathCamera` objects that don't make use of the first two options).

In Torque 3D, it is a common pattern that the `ShapeBase` derived objects have all of their callbacks made on their `Datablock` definition. This allows for an object's behavior to change according to the assigned `Datablock` definition. Unfortunately, the `PathCamera` object does not follow this pattern; but it is possible to write some TorqueScript to mold it to this pattern. Add the following code to the end of `scripts/server/game.cs`:

```
function PathCamera::onNode(%this, %nodeIndex)
{
    // Forward this callback on to the camera's datablock
    %this.getDatablock().onNode(%this, %nodeIndex);
}
```

Now all the `PathCamera` objects will automatically call the `Datablock` objects' `onNode()` method. We can extend our recipe's example by adding the following code to the end of `core/art/datablocks/camera.cs`:

```
function PathCameraDatablock::onNode(%this, %camera,
                                        %nodeIndex)
{
    echo("@@@ PathCameraDatablock::onNode(): " @ %camera
        SPC %nodeIndex);
}
```

With this code, every time a `PathCamera` object using this `Datablock` definition reaches a path node, it writes some information to the console. If we want a different behavior, we could create a new `Datablock` definition and build a new `onNode()` method.

5
Your Graphics Evolved

In this chapter we will cover the following topics:

- ▶ Using the built-in video recording
- ▶ Changing the material of a `ShapeBase` object using script
- ▶ Building a custom material
- ▶ Building a custom material using advanced lighting
- ▶ Building a postFX

Introduction

Torque 3D's graphics pipeline is one of the most advanced in the industry for PC and console games. Its quality and flexibility puts it in the same category as any other high-end game engine currently available on the market, and is really only limited by the art assets you have available and how you make use of them. In this chapter, we will discuss some of the more advanced aspects of Torque 3D's graphics pipeline and how to make use of them in your own games.

Using the built-in video recording

There will come a time when we want to record a game session out to a video file. There are a number of third-party tools that can do this, and some of them support a number of different file formats. Torque 3D also supports direct recording of its display to a Theora format video file which is a cross-platform, open format. In this recipe we will start and stop video recording using a key press from within Torque 3D.

Getting ready

We will be making TorqueScript changes in a project based on the Torque 3D `Full` template, and try them out using the `Empty Terrain` level. If you haven't already, use the Torque Project Manager (`Project Manager.exe`) to create a new project from the `Full` template. It will be found under the `My Projects` directory. Then start up your favorite script editor, such as Torsion, and let's get going!

How to do it...

In the following steps we will add a key combination to start and stop video recording:

1. Open `scripts/client/default.bind.cs` in a text editor, such as Torsion.

2. Add the following to the end of the file and save it:

```
$RecordingMovie = false;

function toggleMovieRecording(%val)
{
   if (!%val)
      return;

   // Path to save our movies to.  Make sure this
   // directory exists before using this function.
   %moviePath = "movies/";

   // The number of frames per second to record at
   %movieFPS = 30;

   // The type of movie encoding.  Valid values are
   // "THEORA" and "PNG"
   %movieEncodingType = "THEORA";

   if (!$RecordingMovie)
   {
      // Find the next available file name in the
      // 'movies' directory
      %suffix = 1;
      %file = findFirstFile(%moviePath @ "movie*.*", false);
      while(%file !$= "")
      {

         // Get the number at the end of the file name
         %num = getTrailingNumber(fileBase(%file));

         // If it is greater than or equal to the current
```

```
        // suffix then make our suffix one more.
        if(%num >= %suffix)
            %suffix = %num + 1;

        // Move on to the next file
        %file = findNextFile(%moviePath @ "movie*.*");
    }

    // Using printf-style formatting, pad the suffix
    // with zeros as required to make a four digit
    // number.
    %suffix = strformat("%04d", %suffix);

    // We now have our file name to record with.
    // Note: The Theora video encoder will add
    // the .ogv extension to this file name.
    %filePath = %moviePath @ "movie" @ %suffix;

    // Start the movie recording
    echo("Recording movie to: " @ %filePath);
    recordMovie(%filePath, %movieFPS, %movieEncodingType);

    // Store our recording state
    $RecordingMovie = true;
    }
    else
    {
        // Stop the current recording
        echo("Stopped movie recording");
        stopMovie();

        // Store our recording state
        $RecordingMovie = false;
    }
}

// Use the global action map so this key binding works at
// any time and not just while in a game.
GlobalActionMap.bind(keyboard, "alt m", toggleMovieRecording);
```

3. In the same directory as the game's executable, add a `movies` directory.

4. Start the game and load the `Empty Terrain` level. Press *Alt + M* to start recording a movie. Walk around the level and fire the gun. Press *Alt + M* again to stop the recording.

How it works...

The recording of a movie within Torque 3D is quite straightforward. We call the `recordMovie()` function to start the recording, and the `stopMovie()` function to stop the recording.

```
recordMovie(%moviePath, %recordFramesPerSecond, %encoding);
stopMovie();
```

The majority of the recipe's code is in determining the movie path to which to save. Prior to recording the movie we scan through all of the files within the `movies` directory. For each file we read its trailing number (for example, `0005` for the file `movie0005.ogv`) and determine the largest value. For the new movie file we add one to this number to come up with the next sequential file. We can use this same technique any time we wish to save a file without over writing an existing file.

Something else to make note of is that we bind our movie recording key using the `GlobalActionMap` class. By using the `GlobalActionMap` class rather than the usual `MoveMap` class, we make movie recording available right from the beginning without a need to start a level first.

There's more...

While recording a movie from Torque 3D is straightforward, there are a couple of things of which to be aware.

Playing back Theora videos on Windows

The Theora OGV file format is not one that is known by the Windows Media Player by default. In order to watch a recorded Torque 3D video, you will need to download and install a DirectShow filter. The website `http://www.theora.org/faq` has all the information you will need to install the appropriate files under the **Using Theora** section.

Record to individual PNG frames

In addition to recording to a Theora OGV file, Torque 3D supports recording to individual PNG files with one PNG file per frame. These frames could later be loaded into a video editing program and made into a movie, without audio of course. To start recording a movie as individual frames, we pass PNG as the encoding format to the `recordMovie()` function. When recording to PNG files, the file path we pass in to `recordMovie()` is actually a directory path into which the individually numbered PNG files will be saved. For example:

```
recordMovie("movies/movie0001", 30, "PNG");
```

Will write the numbered PNG frames to the `movies/movie0001/` directory.

Changing the material of a ShapeBase object using script

While a game is running we may want to modify the materials used by an object based on some event. For example, in a base-capture game we want the base's flag to show the current team's colors. This process of changing an object's materials is called changing an object's skin in Torque 3D. In this recipe we will modify an object's materials at any time using TorqueScript.

Getting ready

Modifying an object's materials while a game is running is very similar to skinning using the *World Editor*. In preparation for this recipe, please see the *How to skin an object in the World Editor* recipe in *Chapter 2, Working with Your Editors*, and set up all of the materials and the object to be skinned as described there.

How to do it...

Use the `ShapeBase setSkinName()` method to change an object's materials. To modify an object from using `base_` materials to `team1_` materials, make the following method call (with the object referenced using the `%myObject` variable):

```
%myObject.setSkinName("team1");
```

How it works...

When a `ShapeBase` derived object's `setSkinName()` method is called, any of the object's referenced `Material` objects whose `mapTo` property has a prefix of `base_` will automatically be remapped to make use of the new `Material` objects. Any of the object's referenced `Material` objects that do not start with `base_` will not be touched.

There's more...

All of the rules that apply to changing an object's materials using the *World Editor* also apply when using `setSkinName()`. This includes modifying materials that do not start with `base_`, and changing multiple materials at once. Please see the *How to skin an object in the World Editor* recipe in *Chapter 2, Working with Your Editors*, for more information.

In addition to the rules when modifying an object's `skin` property in the *World Editor*, there are some additional rules of which to be aware when skinning an object during gameplay.

The setSkinName() method needs to be called on the server

The `setSkinName()` method must be called on the server-side `ShapeBase` derived object for it to work. Calling this method on the client side does nothing. This ensures that all connected clients will see the material changes.

Multiplayer considerations

The `setSkinName()` method only stores the last set of skin changes that were made, and it is this last set of changes that are sent when the object is ghosted to a client (for example, when a client first connects or the skinned object comes into scope). This means that if only a few of an object's materials are modified by one `setSkinName()` call, and then another set of materials is modified with a second `setSkinName()` call, only this second set of material changes will be transmitted when the object comes into scope for a client. This can lead to some clients not seeing the proper set of materials for an object.

To work around this issue, we need to make sure we always combine all the materials that may change into a single `setSkinName()` call, even if they are not specifically changing at this time. For example, we may want to start off our player with a chain-armor material and a particular face material based on the player's inventory:

```
%player.setSkinName("base=chain;face=face2");
```

Later on while the game is still running, the player acquires some plate armor and wears it while still maintaining the same face material. The correct `setSkinName()` call to use is:

```
%player.setSkinName("base=plate;face=face2");
```

By including all of the changed materials in every `setSkinName()` method call we ensure that all clients will always see the correct view, no matter when the object is in scope and ghosted for them.

Player class considerations

When using the `setSkinName()` method on a `Player` class object, both the first-and third-person `Player` class shapes will be skinned appropriately. By setting up our first-and third-player shape's `Material` objects correctly (such as both sets of `Material` object's `mapTo` properties starting with `base_` or sharing some other common root), we ensure that both the shapes are always in sync.

See also

> ▶ *How to skin an object in the World Editor* in *Chapter 2, Working with Your Editors*.

Building a custom material

Torque 3D's material system allows us to build nearly any type of rendered surface for our 3D objects. The appropriate shaders are automatically generated by Torque 3D based on the `Material` class properties we set. However, there are times when we need to do something special for our game that the standard material system cannot handle. In those circumstances, the `CustomMaterial` class allows us to use custom shaders with our objects. While a discussion on writing HLSL code to produce shaders is beyond the scope of this book, this recipe demonstrates how to hook up custom vertex and pixel shaders into Torque 3D's rendering pipeline.

Getting ready

We will be making TorqueScript changes in a project based on the Torque 3D `Full` template, and try them out using the `Empty Terrain` level. If you haven't already, use the Torque Project Manager (`Project Manager.exe`) to create a new project from the `Full` template. It will be found under the `My Projects` directory. Then start up your favorite script editor, such as Torsion, and let's get going!

How to do it...

In the following steps, we will be replacing the soldier's standard material with a custom material that blends the sky cube map on to polygons that are angled away from the camera:

1. Create a `new shaders/common/packt` directory.
2. Place the following vertex shader code into a new `soldierCustomV.hlsl` file in the new `packt` directory:

```
#include "shaders/common/hlslStructs.h"

// Matrix to convert into view space
uniform float4x4  modelview;

// Matrix to go from object to cube map space
uniform float3x3  cubeTrans;

// Eye position relative to the cube map
uniform float3    cubeEyePos;

// Eye position relative to the object
uniform float3    eyePos;

// The vertex shader uses one of the input structures
// as defined in hlslStructs.h.  In this particular
```

```
   // case it is the VertexIn_PNT struct.

   // Output to the pixel shader
   struct VS_OUTPUT
   {
      // Standard position not passed to the pixel shader
      float4 pos         : POSITION;
      // Texture coordinates
      float2 uv0         : TEXCOORD0;
      // Calculated reflection vector used by the pixel shader
      // to perform a cube map lookup
      float3 reflectVec  : TEXCOORD1;
      // Calculated reflection scale that depends on the
      // relationship between the surface normal and
      // the eye position.
      float  reflectScale : TEXCOORD2;
   };

   VS_OUTPUT main(VertexIn_PNT IN)
   {
      VS_OUTPUT OUT = (VS_OUTPUT)0;

      // Calculate the vertex position for the view
      OUT.pos = mul(modelview,IN.pos);

      // Pass along the texture coordinates
      OUT.uv0 = IN.uv0;

      // Calculate the reflection vector used in the
      // cube map lookup
      float3 cubeVertPos = mul(cubeTrans, IN.pos.xyz);
      float3 cubeNormal = normalize( mul(cubeTrans,
                                    normalize(IN.normal)).xyz );
      float3 eyeToVert = cubeVertPos - cubeEyePos;
      OUT.reflectVec = reflect(eyeToVert, cubeNormal);

      // Power factor used to control the amount to scale the
      // reflection by.  The lower the value the less cube map
      // reflection there will be.
      float power = 0.7;

      // Calculate the amount to scale the reflection by
      float3 eyeVec = normalize( eyePos.xyz - IN.pos.xyz );
      OUT.reflectScale = saturate( pow( abs(dot( eyeVec,
                                    IN.normal.xyz )), power ) );

      // Return the output struct to the system
      return OUT;
   }
```

3. Place the following pixel shader code into a new `soldierCustomP.hlsl` file in the new `packt` directory:

```
#include "shaders/common/torque.hlsl"

// Diffuse map sampler
uniform sampler2D diffuse : register(S0);

// Cube map sampler
uniform samplerCUBE cube0 : register(S1);

// Input from vertex shader
struct PS_INPUT
{
    // Texture coordinates
    float2 uv0              : TEXCOORD0;
    // Calculated reflection vector used to perform a cube
    // map lookup
    float3 reflectVec     : TEXCOORD1;
    // Calculated reflection scale that depends on the
    // relationship between the surface normal and
    // the eye position.
    float  reflectScale   : TEXCOORD2;
};

// Output to the system
struct PS_OUTPUT
{
    float4 color    : COLOR0;
};


PS_OUTPUT main(PS_INPUT IN)
{
    PS_OUTPUT OUT = (PS_OUTPUT)0;

    // Blend between the diffuse color and the cube map
    // reflection based on the reflection scale calculated
    // by the vertex shader
    OUT.color = lerp(texCUBE( cube0, IN.reflectVec ),
                  tex2D(diffuse, IN.uv0), IN.reflectScale);

    // Perform any necessary HDR encoding using a function
    // defined in torque.hlsl
    OUT.color = hdrEncode( OUT.color );

    // Return the output struct to the system
    return OUT;
}
```

4. Open `art/shapes/actors/Soldier/materials.cs` in a text editor, such as Torsion. Comment out the entire `Mat_Soldier_Main` material.

5. Just below the commented-out material, add the following code to define the custom material:

```
/ Build out the references to the HLSL files
singleton ShaderData(SoldierCustomShaderData)
{
    DXVertexShaderFile = "shaders/common/packt/soldierCustomV.
hlsl";
    DXPixelShaderFile = "shaders/common/packt/soldierCustomP.hlsl";

    // Pixel shader version 2 is required
    pixVersion = 2.0;
};

// Our custom material to replace the standard one
singleton CustomMaterial(Mat_Soldier_Main_Custom)
{
    // Map this custom material to the soldier's body
    mapTo = "base_Soldier_Main";

    // The first sampler points to our diffuse texture.  This
    // is the same texture that is used by the standard
    // material.
    sampler["diffuse"] = "Soldier_Dif.dds";
    // The second sampler points to a cube map.
    sampler["cube0"] = "$cubemap";

    // Define the cube map that we will use.  This is
    // a standard cube map defined by the core game code.
    cubemap = DesertSkyCubemap;

    // Point to our shader data we defined above
    shader = SoldierCustomShaderData;

    // Our minimum shader version requirements
    version = 2.0;
};
```

6. The standard player `Datablock` definition defines a number of skins that the player randomly chooses between when connecting to a game. So that we will always see our new custom material, we will comment out the list of skins. Open `art/datablocks/player.cs` in a text editor and go to the bottom of the file. Comment out the `availableSkins` line as follows:

```
// available skins (see materials.cs in model folder)
//availableSkins = "base  DarkBlue  DarkGreen  LightGreen
Orange  Red  Teal  Violet  Yellow";
```

7. Now start up the `Full` template game and load the `Empty Terrain` level. Switch to the third-person by pressing the *Tab* key. You will now see the soldier with a reflection of the sky around his edges:

How it works...

Torque 3D uses the `ShaderData` class to connect vertex and pixel shaders up to a `CustomMaterial` class. Shaders are API-specific and the `ShaderData` class supports both DirectX and OpenGL shaders. However, as of the writing of this book, Torque 3D's OpenGL layer is not complete, so we're only focusing on DirectX shaders here.

In addition to pointing to the shader files, the `ShaderData` class allows control over how the shaders will be compiled. The `pixVersion` property defines the target level to which the shader should be compiled. Valid versions are `1.1`, `1.4`, `2.0`, and `3.0`. However, if the user's hardware does not support the compiled version of the shader, then the shader will not run properly.

Instead of explicitly defining the version to which to compile the shader, the `userDevicePixVersion` property may be used. When this property is set to `true`, then the maximum pixel shader version that is offered by the graphics card will be used.

With a `ShaderData` instance defined, we use a `CustomMaterial` class to connect the shader to the rendered objects. The `CustomMaterial` class inherits from the standard `Material` class and is used in the same way to map from materials to object surfaces. The Torque 3D script manual lists all of the `CustomMaterial` properties and what they do. All properties except the `sampler` array that is.

The `CustomMaterial` class's `sampler` array is used to define each of the samplers used by the pixel shader. Up to eight samplers may be defined which take the form of:

```
sampler[name] = source;
```

In the previous code, the `name` parameter is the name of the sampler as used by the pixel shader, and the `source` parameter is the data source for the sampler. Our previous example `CustomMaterial` class defines two `sampler` arrays:

```
sampler["diffuse"] = "Soldier_Dif.dds";
sampler["cube0"] = "$cubemap";
```

The first sampler is named `diffuse` and points to a texture file. This is the most common type of sampler used and is referenced using the `sampler2D` type in the pixel shader. The second sampler is named `cube0` and uses a special data source of `$cubemap` which points to the single `cubemap` property defined in the `CustomMaterial` class. Cubemap samplers are referenced using the `samplerCUBE` type in the pixel shader.

There are a number of different special sampler data sources which always begin with a dollar sign ($). The following table lists all of them:

Sampler source	Description	Type
$backbuffer	Back buffer texture.	sampler2D
$cubemap	Cubemap as defined in `CustomMaterial` class's `cubemap` property.	samplerCUBE
$dynamicCubemap	Dynamic cubemap as generated by the scene. Typically used for dynamic reflections. Requires the custom material to be on a `ShapeBase` object whose `Datablock` definition references a `ReflectorDesc` `Datablock` definition to define the dynamic reflections.	samplerCUBE
$dynamiclight	Shadow map from advanced lighting.	sampler2D
$dynamiclightmask	Lighting cookie mask from advanced lighting.	samplerCUBE
$lightmap	Light map from the scene.	sampler2D
$miscbuff	Miscellaneous texture used by some subsystems, such as the `DecalManager` class.	sampler2D
$reflectBuffer	Current planar reflection texture.	sampler2D

The final components to a custom material are the vertex and pixel shaders. These are standard HLSL shaders with reference to Torque 3D-specific structures, functions, and constants.

On the vertex shader side we can include `shaders/common/hlslStructs.h` to gain access to some predefined vertex input structures. Our example vertex shader given previously uses the `VertexIn_PNT` structure, which includes access to a vertex's position, normal, and texture coordinate values.

For a pixel shader we can include `shaders/common/torque.hlsl` to gain access to some helper functions. Our example pixel shader uses the `hdrEncode()` function on the final color output to ensure it is set up correctly if HDR rendering is enabled (the function automatically passes through the value if HDR rendering is disabled).

Pixel shaders also have access to the samplers we defined within the `CustomMaterial` class. We access the samplers in the same order they were defined in the material. For example, our `Mat_Soldier_Main_Custom CustomMaterial` class defines the following sampler properties:

```
sampler["diffuse"] = "Soldier_Dif.dds";
sampler["cube0"] = "$cubemap";
```

With the sampler sources and order defined, our pixel shader gains access to these samplers with the following code:

```
uniform sampler2D diffuse : register(S0);
uniform samplerCUBE cube0 : register(S1);
```

Finally, both vertex and pixel shaders have access to a number of Torque 3D-defined constants. These constants are used to provide data that doesn't change during the run of a material's shaders, such as the model view matrix to transform an object's vertices into the view's space. As the `CustomMaterial` class inherits from the `Material` class, there are a large number of constants that are available and that are not often used by a `CustomMaterial` class, but they may come in handy to pass data into a shader. The following is a list of all the available shader constants:

Constant name	Description	Type
accumTime	Current time from the `MaterialManager` class, in seconds.	float
alphaTestValue	The `Material` class's `alphaRef` property in the range of 0 to 1.	float
ambient	The ambient light color of the scene.	float4

Constant name	Description	Type
bumpAtlasParams	Contains the Material class's normal texture atlas data in each component: x = 1 / (Material class's cellLayout property x component) y = 1 / (Material class's cellLayout property y component) z = Material class' cellSize property in pixels w = power of 2 of Material class's cellSize property in pixels	float4
bumpAtlasTileParams	Contains the Material class's normal texture atlas index data in each component: x = Material class's cellIndex property x component y = Material class's cellIndex property y component z = 0 w = 0	float4
cubeEyePos	Cube map eye position relative to the object.	float3
cubeTrans	Object to cube map matrix (internally calculated as object to world matrix, but in a 3 x 3 format).	float3x3
detailBumpStrength	The Material class's detailNormalMapStrength property.	float
detailScale	The Material class's detailScale property.	float2
diffuseAtlasParams	Contains the Material class's diffuse texture atlas data in each component: x = 1 / (Material class's cellLayout property x component) y = 1 / (Material class's cellLayout property y component) z = Material class's cellSize property in pixels w = power of 2 of Material class's cellSize property in pixels	float4

Constant name	Description	Type
diffuseAtlasTile Params	Contains the `Material` class's diffuse texture atlas index data in each component:	`float4`
	x = `Material` class's `cellIndex` property x component	
	y = `Material` class's `cellIndex` property y component	
	z = 0	
	w = 0	
diffuseMaterialColor	The `Material` class's `diffuseColor` property.	`float4`
eyeMat	The camera transform (view to world) matrix.	`float4x4`
eyePos	The eye/camera position relative to the object's position.	`float3`
eyePosWorld	Position of the eye/camera in the world.	`float3`
fogColor	Scene's fog color.	`float4`
fogData	Contains the scene's fog data in each component:	`float3`
	x = fog density	
	y = fog density offset	
	z = fog height falloff	
inLightColor[0] – inLightColor[3]	The color of the first four lights in the scene. The value has been multiplied by the light's brightness. Each index holds the entire light's RGBA color.	`float4` array
inLightInvRadiusSq	The inverse square range of the first four lights in the scene. The actual formula is 1 / (range x range).	`float4`
inLightPos[0] – inLightPos[2]	Positions of the first four lights in the scene. The positions are packed such that all of the position x components are in the first index, all y components are in the second index, and all z components are in the third index.	`float4` array
inLightSpotAngle	Spotlight angle for the first four lights in the scene, stored in each of the four components. The actual value is the cosine of one half of the spotlight's outer cone angle, in radians. If the light is not a spotlight, then the value is -1.	`float4`

Constant name	Description	Type
`inLightSpotDir[0]` – `inLightSpotDir[2]`	Forward vector of the first four lights in the scene. The directions are packed such that all of the vector x components are in the first index, all vector y components are in the second index, and all vector z components are in the third index.	`float4` array
`inLightSpotFalloff`	Spotlight falloff for the first four lights in the scene, stored in each of the four components, in radians. If the light is not a spotlight, then the value is `F32_MAX`.	`float4`
`minnaertConstant`	The `Material` class's `minnaertConstant` property.	`float`
`modelview`	Object to view matrix.	`float4x4`
`objTrans`	Object to world matrix.	`float4x4`
`oneOverFarplane`	(1.0 / `farPlane`) stored in each component.	`float4`
`oneOverTargetSize`	1.0 / `targetSize`.	`float2`
`parallaxInfo`	The `Material` class's `parallaxScale` property.	`float`
`rtParams0` – `rtParams15`	Render target parameters for each texture stage, where each component means: x = target offset in x direction (plus a half pixel) y = target offset in y direction (plus a half pixel) z = target scale in x direction w = target scale in y direction	`float4`
`specularColor`	The `Material` class's `specular` property.	`float4`
`specularPower`	The `Material` class's `specularPower` property.	`float`
`subSurfaceParams`	Contains the `Material` class's subsurface data in each component: x, y, z = `Material` class's `subSurfaceColor` property w = `Material` class's `subSurfaceRolloff` property	`float4`
`targetSize`	Resolution of the active render target.	`float2`
`texMat`	Texture matrix that depends on the `Material` class' `animFlags` property and the various other scroll, rot, wave, and sequence properties.	`float4x4`
`vEye`	Camera forwards vector.	`float3`

Constant name	Description	Type
`viewProj`	World to view matrix.	`float4x4`
`viewToObj`	Camera to object matrix.	`float4x4`
`visibility`	Object visibility with a range from 0 (invisible) to 1 (fully visible).	`float`
`worldToCamera`	World to camera matrix.	`float4x4`
`worldToLightProj`	World to light view projection matrix for the first light in the scene (usually the sun or some other default light).	`float4x4`
`worldToObj`	World to object matrix.	`float4x4`
`worldViewOnly`	Object to camera matrix.	`float4x4`

Shader constants may be accessed within the shader in a manner that is similar to samplers. Our example vertex shader given previously makes use of the following constants as defined near the beginning of the HLSL file:

```
// Matrix to convert into view space
uniform float4x4  modelview;

// Matrix to go from object to cube map space
uniform float3x3  cubeTrans;

// Eye position relative to the cube map
uniform float3    cubeEyePos;

// Eye position relative to the object
uniform float3    eyePos;
```

There's more...

While we have covered a lot about custom materials already, there is a lot more to discuss.

Using named render targets as sampler data sources

In addition to the standard sampler data sources, there are named render targets that may also be used as sampler sources. Named render targets always begin with a hash symbol (#). There are a few standard named render targets, but render targets may also be generated as required by other systems, such as a postFX. The standard ones are as follows:

Sampler source	Description	Type
`#glowbuffer`	Buffer produced by the glow postFX	`sampler2D`
`#lightInfo`	Light info pass as generated by advanced lighting	`sampler2D`
`#prepass`	Linear depth and normal buffer generated as the first pass for advanced lighting.	`sampler2D`

When making use of the #lightInfo and #prepass render targets as sampler inputs, we need to use some special xxxUncondition() functions to unpack the data they contain. For example, we may extract the #prepass data as follows:

```
float4 prepassSample = prepassUncondition( prePassBuffer,
                                           uvScene);
float3 normal = prepassSample.rgb;
float depth = prepassSample.a;
```

In the previous code, the prePassBuffer parameter is a sampler containing the prepass buffer, and the uvScene parameter is the UV coordinates of the sample to retrieve.

The #lightInfo data is obtained in a similar way:

```
float3 lightColor;
float NL_Att;
float specular;
lightinfoUncondition( tex2D(lightInfoBuffer, uvScene),
                      lightColor, NL_Att, specular );
```

In the previous code, the lightInfoBuffer parameter is a sampler containing the lightInfo buffer, the uvScene parameter is the UV coordinates of the sample to retrieve, the lightColor parameter is the color of the sample, the NL_Att parameter is a calculated value of the dot product of the light direction and normal, multiplied by the light attenuation, and the specular parameter is the specular value of the sample.

To have access to these xxxUncondition() functions, we need to add the following include directive to our shader's HLSL file:

```
#include "shadergen:/autogenConditioners.h"
```

Single pass only

While the Material class supports multiple passes while rendering, the CustomMaterial class only supports a single pass.

Passing defines to the shader compiler using ShaderData

The ShaderData class allows us to pass in any number of HLSL defines to the shader compiler. With this feature we can re-use our shader files while still allowing us to modify a shader's data on a per ShaderData class basis. And as a defines' values are baked in at compile time, they don't have the same overhead as using a shader constant.

We use the ShaderData class's defines property to pass in a list of case-sensitive HLSL defines that are delimited by a semicolon, tab, or a newline character. For example, if we want to pass in a couple of color defines to our vertex and pixel shaders, we could do the following:

```
Singleton ShaderData(MyShaderData)
{
   // Set up shader files
   DXVertexShaderFile = ...
   DXPixelShaderFile = ...

   // Build some defines that will be passed to
   // the shader compiler
   defines = "RED_COLOR=float4(1.0, 0.0, 0.0, 0.0)" TAB
             "WHITE_COLOR=float4(1.0, 1.0, 1.0, 0.0)";

   ...
}
```

We could now reference RED_COLOR and WHITE_COLOR within our shaders and they would be replaced with the float4 values.

Working with a custom GFXStateBlockData class

The GFXStateBlockData class allows us to control the rendering states for our CustomMaterial class, such as how it will interact with the depth buffer, or the type of alpha blending to perform. While our example CustomMaterial class does not make use of it, we may create our own GFXStateBlockData instance and reference it using the CustomMaterial class's stateBlock property.

The *Torque 3D Script Manual* found at docs.garagegames.com/torque-3d/official/ content/documentation/Scripting/Torque%203D%20-%20Script%20Manual.chm has a good description of the GFXStateBlockData class's properties. If you're familiar with DirectX or OpenGL rendering states, you'll recognize what each property does right away.

See also

▸ *Building a custom material using advanced lighting*

Building a custom material using advanced lighting

The preceding *Building a custom material* recipe went into the details of creating a custom material that uses our own vertex and pixel shaders. In this recipe, we will build upon that work and add in advanced lighting and shadows.

Getting ready

We will be making TorqueScript changes in a project based on the Torque 3D `Full` template, and try them out using the `Empty Terrain` level. If you haven't already, use the Torque Project Manager (`Project Manager.exe`) to create a new project from the `Full` template. It will be found under the `My Projects` directory. Then start up your favorite script editor, such as Torsion, and let's get going!

How to do it...

In the following steps, we will be replacing the soldier's standard material with a custom material that blends the sky cube map on to polygons that are angled away from the camera. The scene's lighting will also be taken into account.

1. Create a new `shaders/common/packt` directory.

2. Place the following vertex shader code into a new `SoldierCustomAdvancedV.hlsl` file in the new `packt` directory. This shader is very similar to the one used in the previous recipe, with the changes highlighted:

```
#include "shaders/common/hlslStructs.h"

// Matrix to convert into view space
uniform float4x4  modelview;

// Matrix to go from object to cube map space
uniform float3x3  cubeTrans;

// Eye position relative to the cube map
uniform float3     cubeEyePos;

// Eye position relative to the object
uniform float3     eyePos;

// The vertex shader uses one of the input structures
// as defined in hlslStructs.h.  In this particular
// case it is the VertexIn_PNT struct.

// Output to the pixel shader
struct VS_OUTPUT
{
    // Standard position not passed to the pixel shader
    float4 pos           : POSITION;
    // Texture coordinates
    float2 uv0           : TEXCOORD0;
    // Calculated reflection vector used by the pixel shader
    // to perform a cube map lookup
```

```
    float3 reflectVec     : TEXCOORD1;
    // Calculated reflection scale that depends on the
    // relationship between the surface normal and
    // the eye position.
    float  reflectScale  : TEXCOORD2;
    // Pass the screen space position used for lighting
    // calculations
    float4 screenspacePos : TEXCOORD3;

};

VS_OUTPUT main(VertexIn_PNT IN)
{
    VS_OUTPUT OUT = (VS_OUTPUT)0;

    // Calculate the vertex position for the view
    OUT.pos = mul(modelview,IN.pos);

    // Pass along the texture coordinates
    OUT.uv0 = IN.uv0;

    // Calculate the reflection vector used in the
    // cube map lookup
    float3 cubeVertPos = mul(cubeTrans, IN.pos.xyz);
    float3 cubeNormal = normalize( mul(cubeTrans,
                               normalize(IN.normal)).xyz );
    float3 eyeToVert = cubeVertPos - cubeEyePos;
    OUT.reflectVec = reflect(eyeToVert, cubeNormal);

    // Power factor used to control the amount to scale the
    // reflection by.  The lower the value the less cube map
    // reflection there will be.
    float power = 0.7;

    // Calculate the amount to scale the reflection by
    float3 eyeVec = normalize( eyePos.xyz - IN.pos.xyz );
    OUT.reflectScale = saturate( pow( abs(dot( eyeVec,
                               IN.normal.xyz )), power ) );

    // Store the screen space position for RT lighting
    // calculations
    OUT.screenspacePos = OUT.pos;


    // Return the output struct to the system
    return OUT;
}
```

3. Place the following pixel shader code into a new `soldierCustomAdvanced.hlsl` file in the new `packt` directory. This shader is very similar to the one used in the previous recipe, with the changes highlighted:

```
#include "shadergen:/autogenConditioners.h"
#include "shaders/common/torque.hlsl"

// Diffuse map sampler
uniform sampler2D diffuse : register(S0);

// Cube map sampler
uniform samplerCUBE cube0 : register(S1);

// Advanced lighting info sampler
uniform sampler2D lightInfoBuffer : register(S2);

// Advanced lighting constants
uniform float4 rtParams2;


// Input from vertex shader
struct PS_INPUT
{
    // Texture coordinates
    float2 uv0           : TEXCOORD0;
    // Calculated reflection vector used to perform a cube map
    // lookup
    float3 reflectVec    : TEXCOORD1;
    // Calculated reflection scale that depends on the
    // relationship between the surface normal and the eye
    // position.
    float  reflectScale  : TEXCOORD2;
    // Screen space position used for lighting calculations
    float4 screenspacePos : TEXCOORD3;

};

// Output to the system
struct PS_OUTPUT
{
    float4 color    : COLOR0;
};


PS_OUTPUT main(PS_INPUT IN)
{
```

```
PS_OUTPUT OUT = (PS_OUTPUT)0;

// Blend between the diffuse color and the cube map
// reflection based on the reflection scale calculated
// by the vertex shader
OUT.color = lerp(texCUBE( cube0, IN.reflectVec ),
                          tex2D(diffuse, IN.uv0),
                          IN.reflectScale);

// Deferred RT Lighting
float2 uvScene = IN.screenspacePos.xy /
                 IN.screenspacePos.w;
uvScene = ( uvScene + 1.0 ) / 2.0;
uvScene.y = 1.0 - uvScene.y;
uvScene = ( uvScene * rtParams2.zw ) + rtParams2.xy;
float3 d_lightcolor;
float d_NL_Att;
float d_specular;
lightinfoUncondition(tex2D(lightInfoBuffer, uvScene),
                     d_lightcolor, d_NL_Att, d_specular);
OUT.color *= float4(d_lightcolor, 1.0);

// Perform any necessary HDR encoding using a function
// defined in torque.hlsl
OUT.color = hdrEncode( OUT.color );

// Return the output struct to the system
return OUT;
}
```

4. Open `art/shapes/actors/Soldier/materials.cs` in a text editor, such as Torsion. Comment out the entire `Mat_Soldier_Main` material.

5. Just below the now commented-out material, add the following code to define the custom material. This is very similar to the `CustomMaterial` class from the previous recipe, with the changes highlighted:

```
// Build out the references to the HLSL files for advanced
// lighting
singleton ShaderData(SoldierCustomAdvancedShaderData)

{
   DXVertexShaderFile = "shaders/common/packt/
soldierCustomAdvancedV.hlsl";
   DXPixelShaderFile  = "shaders/common/packt/
soldierCustomAdvancedP.hlsl";
```

```
      // Pixel shader version 2 is required
      pixVersion = 2.0;
};


// Our custom material that uses advanced lighting to replace
// the standard one
singleton CustomMaterial(Mat_Soldier_Main_Custom_Advanced)

{
   // Map this custom material to the soldier's body
   mapTo = "base_Soldier_Main";

   // The first sampler points to our diffuse texture.   This
   // is the same texture that is used by the standard
   // material.
   sampler["diffuse"] = "Soldier_Dif.dds";
   // The second sampler points to a cube map.
   sampler["cube0"] = "$cubemap";
   // The third sampler is the lighting info generated by
   // advanced lighting
   sampler["lightInfoBuffer"] = "#lightInfo";


   // Define the cube map that we will use.   This is a
   // standard cube map defined by the core game code.
   cubemap = DesertSkyCubemap;

   // Point to our shader data we defined above
   shader = SoldierCustomAdvancedShaderData;

   // Our minimum shader version requirements
   version = 2.0;
};
```

6. Perform step 6 from the previous recipe to the standard player `Datablock` definition.

7. Start up the `Full` template game and load the `Empty Terrain` level. Switch to third-person by pressing the *Tab* key. You will now see the soldier with a reflection of the sky around his edges, but this time with shadows:

How it works...

The key to having advanced lighting work with your `CustomMaterial` class is making use of the `#lightInfo` named render target as a sampler for our pixel shader. This sampler holds the per-pixel lighting properties that were produced during the lighting pass. In order to make use of this sampler, the vertex shader also needs to include the vertex screen coordinates in its output.

To calculate the lighting for the object, the pixel shader makes use of the render target parameters that are passed in using a shader constant. We use the `rtParams2` constant as our lighting info is coming from sampler `S2`.

The calculations themselves are in the `Deferred RT lighting` section of the pixel shader, which looks up the light info sample and extracts the required lighting info using the `lightinfoUncondition()` function. Our calculated diffuse value (based on the diffuse texture and cube map) is then multiplied by the extracted light color to produce the final shaded results.

There's more...

Torque 3D's rendering passes are based on the work by Wolfgang Engel, where there is a pre-pass render, a light info render, and a geometry render using the lighting texture. You can read more about the methodology in his blog:

```
http://diaryofagraphicsprogrammer.blogspot.ca/2008/03
/light-pre-pass-renderer.html
```

See also

▶ *Building a custom material*

Building a postFX

Torque 3D's postFX system allows us to create full screen shader effects using the `PostEffect` class. Examples of postFX included with Torque 3D are object glows, screen gamma correction, and camera depth of field effects. Building our own postFX is very similar to working with the `CustomMaterial` class, which also allows us to write custom shaders, but for 3D objects instead (please see the *Building a custom material* recipe).

While a discussion on writing HLSL code to produce shaders is beyond the scope of this book, this recipe demonstrates how to hook up custom vertex and pixel shaders into Torque 3D's postFX pipeline, and provides TorqueScript parameters to change the postFX rendering in real time.

Getting ready

We will be making TorqueScript changes in a project based on the Torque 3D `Full` template, and try them out using the `Empty Terrain` level. If you haven't already, use the Torque Project Manager (`Project Manager.exe`) to create a new project from the `Full` template. It will be found under the `My Projects` directory. Then start up your favorite script editor, such as Torsion, and let's get going!

How to do it...

In the following steps, we will be building a postFX that causes the scene to render with a sepia tone. There are a number of parameters that may be adjusted while the effect is enabled:

1. Create a new `shaders/common/packt` directory.

2. Place the following pixel shader code into a new `sepiaP.hlsl` file in the new `packt` directory:

```
#include "./../postFx/postFx.hlsl"
#include "./../torque.hlsl"

// Back buffer sampler
uniform sampler2D backBuffer : register( S0 );

// Constant used to calculate the intensity of the image
uniform float3 intensityConstant;

// Constant for the amount to desaturate the image by
uniform float desaturation;

// Constant for the color tone of the "paper"
uniform float3 paperTone;

// Constant for the color tone used to stain the image
uniform float3 stainTone;

// Constant describing how much of the sepia effect to apply
uniform float amount;

float4 main( PFXVertToPix IN ) : COLOR0
{
    // Obtain the color from the back buffer
    float3 color = tex2D(backBuffer, IN.uv0.xy).xyz;

    // Calculate the base tone of the image prior to the
    // stain being added
    float3 baseTone = paperTone * color;

    // Calculate the intensity of the sample based
    // on our constant
    float intensity = dot(intensityConstant, baseTone);

    // Desaturate the base tone based on our desaturation value
    float3 desaturatedColor = lerp(baseTone, intensity.xxx,
                                   desaturation);
```

```
    // Calculate the stain amount based on the intensity.
    float3 stain = lerp(stainTone, paperTone, intensity);

    // Calculate the final color based on how much we want
    // the sepia stain to be applied.
    float3 outColor = lerp(desaturatedColor, stain, amount);

    // Return the HDR encoded color in case HDR rendering
    // is enabled
    return float4( hdrEncode(outColor), 1 );
}
```

3. Place the following TorqueScript code into a new `sepiaPostFX.cs` file in the `core/scripts/client/postFX` directory:

```
// Amount to desaturate the image by
$SepiaPF::desaturation = 0.5;

// The color tone of the "paper"
$SepiaPF::paperTone = "1 0.9 0.5";

// The color tone used to stain the image
$SepiaPF::stainTone = "0.2 0.05 0";

// Used to calculate the intensity of the image
$SepiaPF::intensityConstant = "0.3 0.59 0.11";

// How much of the sepia effect to apply
$SepiaPF::amount = 1.0;

singleton ShaderData( PFX_SepiaShader )
{
    DXVertexShaderFile = "shaders/common/postFx/postFxV.hlsl";
    DXPixelShaderFile  = "shaders/common/packt/sepiaP.hlsl";
    pixVersion = 2.0;
};

singleton GFXStateBlockData( PFX_SepiaStateBlock )
{
    // Modify the default depth buffer behavior
    zDefined = true;
    // Don't perform depth reads
    zEnable = false;
    // Don't perform depth writes
    zWriteEnable = false;
```

```
      // Modify the default sampler states
      samplersDefined = true;
      // Change to clamp the texture and use point filtering
      samplerStates[0] = SamplerClampPoint;
};

singleton PostEffect( SepiaPostFX )
{
   // When will this postFX be applied
   renderTime = "PFXAfterDiffuse";
   // Priority for this postFX at the render time
   renderPriority = 0.1;
   // Enable this postFX by default
   isEnabled = true;
   // Don't apply this postFX during the reflection pass
   allowReflectPass = false;

   shader = PFX_SepiaShader;
   stateBlock = PFX_SepiaStateBlock;

   // First sampler used
   texture[0] = "$backBuffer";
   // Our render target
   target = "$backBuffer";
};

function SepiaPostFX::setShaderConsts( %this )
{
   // Copy each of the global variables into the
   // appropriate shader constant to allow for
   // run time changes.
   %this.setShaderConst( "$intensityConstant",
                         $SepiaPF::intensityConstant );
   %this.setShaderConst( "$desaturation",
                         $SepiaPF::desaturation );
   %this.setShaderConst( "$paperTone",
                         $SepiaPF::paperTone );
   %this.setShaderConst( "$stainTone",
                         $SepiaPF::stainTone );
   %this.setShaderConst( "$amount",
                         $SepiaPF::amount );
}
```

4. Now start up the `Full` template game and load the `Empty Terrain` level. Our new `SepiaPostFX` postFX class is set to start automatically, so we'll see the sepia tone immediately:

How it works...

Torque 3D uses the `ShaderData` class to connect vertex and pixel shaders up to a `PostEffect` class. Shaders are API-specific and the `ShaderData` class supports both DirectX and OpenGL shaders. However, as of the writing of this book, Torque 3D's OpenGL layer is not complete; so we're only focusing on DirectX shaders here. Please see the *Building a custom material* recipe for further discussion on the `ShaderData` class and its properties.

As most postFX do their work in the pixel shader, a default vertex shader is available. In our preceding example, we're making use of the `postFxV.hlsl` default vertex shader, which just acts as a pass through to our custom pixel shader.

Our example `SepiaPostFX` class is also making use of a custom `GFXStateBlockData` class. The `GFXStateBlockData` class allows us to control the rendering states for our postFX, such as how it will interact with the depth buffer, or the type of alpha blending to perform. The Torque 3D Script Manual found at `docs.garagegames.com/torque-3d/ official/content/documentation/Scripting/Torque%203D%20-%20Script%20 Manual.chm` has a good description of the `GFXStateBlockData` class's properties. If you're familiar with DirectX or OpenGL rendering states, then you'll recognize what each property does right away.

Our example's `GFXStateBlockData` instance indicates we want to modify how we interact with the depth buffer by setting its `zDefined` property to `true`. Setting any of the `GFXStateBlockData` class's `xxxDefined` properties to `true` indicates that we want to modify that group's behaviors. Specifically, we're turning off all depth buffer reading and writing for our postFX by setting both the `zEnabled` and `zWriteEnabled` properties to `false`.

Our `GFXStateBlockData` class example instance is also modifying the standard sampler states for our postFX. Specifically, we're setting the first sampler state (our shader is only using one sampler, the back buffer) to clamp its UV lookup and use point filtering by setting the `samplerStates[0]` property to the system-defined `SampleClampPoint` class. We could have also built our own `GFXSampleStateData` instance and passed that into our sampler property.

With the `ShaderData` and `GFXStateBlockData` classes defined, we use the `PostEffect` class to connect up the shader into the Torque 3D rendering pipeline. The first thing we need to decide is when our `PostEffect` class should render, which is determined by both the `renderTime` and `renderPriority` properties. The `renderTime` property may be one of the following:

The renderTime value	Description
PFXBeforeBin	Before a `RenderInstManager` bin
PFXAfterBin	After a `RenderInstManager` bin
PFXAfterDiffuse	After the diffuse rendering pass
PFXEndOfFrame	When the end of the frame is reached
PFXTexGenOnDemand	The `PostEffect` class is not automatically processed and only renders when requested

The PFXBeforeBin and PFXAfterBin values are special because they allow us to place the PostEffect class at a very specific point in the rendering pipeline. When either of those values is chosen, the renderBin property indicates the reference render bin. Valid renderBin values are ObjTranslucentBin, GlowBin, and EditorBin. However, the full list of render bins is available in core/scripts/client/renderManager.cs and if we wish to add a PostEffect class around one of the others bins, we just need to provide that bin with a proper name during its creation. Our example PostEffect class makes use of the PFXAfterDiffuse render time, so it doesn't need to set the renderBin property.

In addition to choosing a renderTime value, we also need to decide on the renderPriority value. The renderPriority value is a float value that determines the order of postFXs when they render at the same time. The PostEffect instances are processed in the descending order of renderPriority by the PostEffectManager when more than one has the same renderTime and/or renderBin value.

After we decide when the PostEffect class should render, we need to determine what samplers the pixel shader will use as its inputs. The PostEffect class's texture array is used to define each of the six available samplers used. Our example sepia tone PostEffect only makes use of one sampler, which is set up as follows:

```
singleton PostEffect ( SepiaPostFX )
{
    . . .
    texture[0] = "$backBuffer";
    . . .
};
```

Each texture index may point to a texture file, or to one of the following special textures that always begin with a dollar sign ($):

Sampler source	Description	Type
$backBuffer	Current back buffer texture.	sampler2D
$inTex	Any previous PostEffect class's render that uses the $outTex render target. Allows for chaining effects together.	sampler2D

In addition to these standard texture sources, there are named render targets that may also be used. Named render targets always begin with a hash symbol (#). Please see the *Building a custom material* recipe for a list of common named render targets. In addition to one of the common named render targets, we may also use a named render target that has been automatically generated by a previous PostEffect class, which we'll talk about next.

Once we have the input textures defined, we need to set up the PostEffect render target. This is the destination of the PostEffect class's rendering. The following table lists the standard PostEffect target names:

PostEffect target	Description
`$backBuffer`	Rendering goes to the current back buffer.
`$outTex`	Rendering goes to a special render target that may be used by another `PostEffect` class that follows this one, and is a member of the same render time or render bin. See the `$inTex` sampler source given previously.

In addition to one of these standard render targets, a `PostEffect` class may use an arbitrarily-named render target. A named render target always starts with the hash symbol (#) and if it does not already exist, the `PostEffect` class will create it. The size of this new named render target comes from the `PostEffect` instance's `targetSize` property, or if that is set to `0`, it comes from the size of the first texture input (which may be scaled using the `targetScale` property). Finally, if there is no texture input, then the new named render target's size comes from the current active render target, which is often the back buffer (also scaled by the `targetScale` property).

These named render targets exist so long as the `PostEffect` instance is around. This allows for another method of passing the rendering results from one `PostEffect` instance to another, even if that `PostEffect` renders during a different time or bin.

Finally, the `PostEffect` instance's shaders have access to a number of Torque 3D-defined constants, as well as shader constants specifically defined by the `PostEffect` class. These constants are used to provide data that doesn't change during at least a single render of the `PostEffect` instance, such as the world-to-view transform matrix. The following is a list of all standard shader constants that are available:

Constant name	Description	Type
`accumTime`	Current time from the `MaterialManager` class, in seconds	`float`
`ambientColor`	The ambient light color of the scene	`float3`
`camForward`	The camera's forward vector	`float3`
`deltaTime`	The frame's delta time from the `MaterialManager` class, in seconds	`float`
`eyePosWorld`	Position of the eye/camera in the world	`float3`
`fogColor`	Scene's fog color	`float4`
`fogData`	Contains the scene's fog data in each component: x = fog density y = fog density offset z = 1 / atmosphere height	`float3`
`invCameraMat`	The camera's inverse transform matrix	`float4x4`

`invNearFar`	Contains the inverse of scene's near and far plane distances from the camera in each component: x = 1 / near plane distance y = 1 / far plane distance	`float2`
`lightDirection`	The sun's forward vector	`float3`
`matPrevScreenToWorld`	Previous frame's view to world matrix	`float4x4`
`matScreenToWorld`	View-to-world matrix	`float4x4`
`matWorldToScreen`	World-to-view matrix	`float4x4`
`nearFar`	Contains the scene's near and far plane distances from the camera in each component: x = near plane distance y = far plane distance	`float2`
`oneOverTargetSize`	Results of 1 / `targetSize`	`float2`
`rtParams0 - rtParams5`	Render target parameters for each texture stage, where each component means: x = target offset in x direction (plus a half pixel) y = target offset in y direction (plus a half pixel) z = target scale in x direction w = target scale in y direction	`float4`
`screenSunPos`	The sun's position in screen space	`float2`
`targetSize`	Size of the render target	`float2`
`texSize0 - texSize5`	The size of each of the six possible input textures. Constant is not defined if the input texture is not set.	`float2`
`waterColor`	Scene's water fog color	`float4`
`waterDepthGradMax`	Depth in world units of the maximum range of the color gradient texture	`float`
`waterFogData`	Contains the scene's water fog data in each component: x = fog density y = fog density offset z = depth in world units at which full darkening will be received (`wetDepth`) w = refract color intensity scaled at `wetDepth` (`wetDarkening`)	`float4`
`waterFogPlane`	The current water plane	`float4`
`worldToScreenScale`	The world size to screen size scale	`float2`

Shader constants may be accessed within the shader by using the `uniform` keyword. For example, to access the `ambientColor` and `matWorldToScreen` constants, we would add the following to our shader:

```
uniform float3   ambientColor;
uniform float4x4 matWorldToScreen;
```

In addition to these standard shader constants, a `PostEffect` instance may define its own shader constants. These custom constants may be set from the `PostEffect` class's `setShaderConsts()` callback, which is called just prior to the `PostEffect` instance being processed. Our example sepia tone postFX sets up five custom constants whose values come from the global TorqueScript variables. Because these custom constants are refreshed each time the `PostEffect` instance renders, changing any of the sepia tone's global variables will update the effect's rendering in real time.

There's more...

While we have covered a lot about postFX's already, there is even more to discuss.

Dynamically changing a postFX's texture

Normally a `PostEffect` instance sets up all of its texture inputs at creation time. And while we always need to define which texture inputs (and thus samplers) will be in used, we can dynamically modify the input sources for these textures, such as changing the file or render target used.

Just before any textures are bound for rendering, the `PostEffect` instance's `preProcess()` callback is called. Within this callback we may use the `PostEffect` class's `setTexture()` method to modify the textures, which has a form of:

```
PostEffect.setTexture( index, filePath );
```

In the previous code, the `index` parameter is the texture input index (0 through 5) to modify, and the `filePath` parameter is the path to the new texture file. Instead of a file path, we may also use one of the special texture inputs that start with a dollar sign ($) or hash symbol (#), such as $backBuffer.

Defining shader macros

We can pass in any number of HLSL defines to the shader compiler used by the `PostEffect` instance. With this feature we can re-use our shader files while still allowing us to modify a shader's data on a per-`PostEffect` basis. Normally, we set up these defines during the `PostEffect` class's `onAdd()` callback which happens when the postFX is first created, or during the `preProcess()` callback that occurs just before rendering.

To add a shader define, we use the `PostEffect.setShaderMacro()` method, which has a form of:

```
PostEffect.setShaderMacro( defineName, value );
```

In the previous code, the `defineName` parameter is the name of the define/macro, and the `value` parameter is the optional value we wish to give to the define.

Chaining multiple postFX together

The `PostEffect` class inherits from `SimGroup`, which means that it may have children. When the parent `PostEffect` class is processed, all of its `PostEffect` children are also processed in order. This allows us to chain together multiple `PostEffect` instances to produce more complicated effects. The depth of field postFX found in `core/scripts/client/postFx/dof.cs` or the glow postFX found in `core/scripts/client/postFx/glow.cs` are good examples of this.

When chaining `PostEffect` instances together, we usually want to pass the results of one into the input of another. We may either do this using the `$outTex` and `$inTex` combination, or use custom named render targets that begin with the hash symbol (#). The Torque 3D depth of field postFX actually makes use of both methods to pass results around and is well worth a look over.

See also

▸ *Building a custom material*

6
Make That
Sound Happen

In this chapter, we will cover the following topics:

- ▶ Playing a quick 2D or 3D sound on all clients
- ▶ Using `SFXEmitter` to create networked sound effects
- ▶ Playing a sound on a `ShapeBase` object
- ▶ Playing music while a level is loading
- ▶ How to have a background sound for a level
- ▶ How to have music change according to the mood
- ▶ Triggering an event during sound playback

Introduction

To paraphrase a famous writer and director:

> *Sound is 50 percent of the experience.*

Torque 3D's sound system helps us build that second 50 percent into our games by providing us with a variety of options.

It starts by allowing for a number of different sound providers to choose from (OpenAL, DirectSound, XAudio, and FMOD) and wraps all that in a standard SFX layer, while still keeping robust access. In this chapter, we will touch the surface of what is available in Torque 3D's sound system.

Playing a quick 2D or 3D sound on all clients

Torque 3D allows the game developer to broadcast either a 2D or 3D sound event to all clients connected to a server during gameplay. This is true even during a single-player game as Torque 3D internally still has a client/server environment.

In this recipe, we will learn the TorqueScript commands to issue sound events and discover their limitations.

Getting ready

We will be using a project based on the Torque 3D's `Full` template and issuing console commands using the `Empty Terrain` level. If you haven't already, use the Torque Project Manager (`Project Manager.exe`) to create a new project from the `Full` template. It will be found under the `My Projects` directory. Then start up our new `Full` template game and load the `Empty Terrain` level.

How to do it...

In the following steps we will trigger 2D and 3D sounds that play on all clients:

1. Open the console using the tilde (~) key and enter the following at the bottom of the screen to play a 2D sound on all connected clients:

   ```
   ServerPlay2D( ThunderCrash4Sound );
   ```

   You will hear a thunder crash all around you.

2. Enter the following at the bottom of the console screen to play a 3D sound on all connected clients:

   ```
   ServerPlay3D( GrenadeExplosionSound, "50 0 240" );
   ```

   You will hear an explosion sound, some distance away.

3. Try rotating the player slightly and issuing the same `ServerPlay3D()` function again to hear the explosion sound shift in stereo space.

How it works...

Torque 3D has two standard functions that are used to broadcast either 2D or 3D sound events to all clients connected to the server.

The 2D sound function is as follows:

```
ServerPlay2D( SFXProfile );
```

Here the SFXProfile parameter is a 2D sound profile Datablock that defines the sound to play. In the previous example we make use of the ThunderCrash4Sound sound profile, which is defined in art/datablocks/environment.cs as follows:

```
datablock SFXProfile(ThunderCrash4Sound)
{
    filename = "art/sound/environment/thunder4";
    description = Audio2d;
};
```

This Datablock provides the name and path to the sound file, as well as how the sound will be played by assigning an SFXDescription instance to the description property of the profile.

The following is the 3D sound function:

```
ServerPlay3D( SFXProfile, transform );
```

Here the SFXProfile parameter is a 3D sound profile Datablock that defines the sound to play, and the transform parameter is the space-delimited position of the sound in the world. In this example we make use of the GrenadeExplosionSound sound profile, which is defined in art/datablocks/weapons/grenade.cs as follows:

```
datablock SFXProfile(GrenadeExplosionSound)
{
    filename = "art/sound/CT_fx/weapons/GRENADELAND.wav";
    description = AudioDefault3d;
    preload = true;
};
```

This Datablock is similar to the 2D one we looked at previously, but with the addition of the preload property. When set to true, this property ensures that the sound file is loaded during initialization of the game rather than during gameplay, making it immediately available for playback.

There's more...

Torque 3D makes it easy to play sounds on all connected clients. However, we need to be aware that this ease of use includes some limitations.

Limitations of ServerPlay2D

The ServerPlay2D() function sends out a 2D audio event to all clients currently connected to the server. However, if a client joins immediately after the ServerPlay2D() function is called, it will not receive the event. This means that ServerPlay2D() is best used for either short sounds, or sounds that don't need to be heard by a client that has just joined.

Please see the *Using SFXEmitter to create networked sound effects* recipe for another method of playing 2D sound effects on all clients.

Limitations of ServerPlay3D

The `ServerPlay3D()` function has the same limitations as the `ServerPlay2D()` function discussed previously. In addition, `ServerPlay3D()` uses the distance from the sound to the client's control object (usually the player) to determine if a sound event should be sent to the client.

If the distance between the sound and the client's control object is greater than the maximum distance as defined by `maxDistance` property of `SFXDescription` of the `SFXProfile` parameter, then the sound event will not be sent. This means that if the client's control object were to close in on the sound to be within the `maxDistance` while it was playing, they would not hear it (the sound event is not automatically issued to the client).

Please see the *Using SFXEmitter to create networked sound effects* recipe for another method of playing 3D sound effects on all clients.

Local client sound playing equivalent

The `ServerPlay2D()` and `ServerPlay3D()` functions only work on a server (or during a single player game). If we want to play a 2D or 3D sound only on a single client, we may use the client side `sfxPlayOnce()` function.

The `sfxPlayOnce()` function has a number of different overloads to account for playing 2D or 3D sounds, with or without a defined `SFXTrack datablock` instance. Please see the Torque 3D Script Manual found at `Documentation/Torque 3D - Script Manual.chm` for a detailed description of each of these forms.

See also

▶   *Using SFXEmitter to create networked sound effects*

Using SFXEmitter to create networked sound effects

While Torque 3D makes it easy to play single, short sound effects at any time (see the previous recipe), there are times when we need to play longer sound effects that all clients need to hear when they connect to the game server, or when they are in range (for 3D effects).

In this recipe, we will learn how to set up a sound source that will be in scope for all clients, new or old, and will automatically handle clients that come in range.

Getting ready

We will be making TorqueScript changes and working with *World Editor* in a project based on the Torque 3D's `FPS Tutorial` template. We will then try them out using the `China Town Day` level.

If you haven't already, use the Torque Project Manager (`Project Manager.exe`) to create a new project from the `FPS Tutorial` template; it can be found under the `My Projects` directory. Then start your favorite script editor, such as Torsion, and let's get going!

How to do it...

In the following steps, we will play two different sounds that all connected clients can hear at any time they are in range:

1. We will create the two sound profiles that will play during this recipe. Place the following TorqueScript code at the bottom of `art/datablocks/ambientSounds.cs`:

    ```
    datablock SFXProfile(DragonAlarm1Sound)
    {
      fileName = "art/sound/orc_death";
      description = "AudioCloseLoop3D";
      preload = true;
    };

    datablock SFXProfile(DragonAlarm2Sound)
    {
      fileName = "art/sound/CT_fx/items/TRASHCAN";
      description = "AudioCloseLoop3D";
      preload = true;
    };
    ```

2. Next we will create the commands that will be issued using console of the game. Place the following TorqueScript code at the bottom of `scripts/server/game.cs`:

    ```
    function startDragonAlarm1()
    {
        DragonAlarm.track =
          DragonAlarm1Sound;
        DragonAlarm.play();
    }

    function startDragonAlarm2()
    {
        DragonAlarm.track =
          DragonAlarm2Sound;
        DragonAlarm.play();
    }
    ```

```
function stopDragonAlarm()
{
    DragonAlarm.stop();
}
```

3. Now we will create the sound source within the game level. Start our `FPS Tutorial` game and load the `China Town Day` level.

4. Press *F11* to open *World Editor*. As we want to work with objects in the scene, the *Object Editor* should be selected (*F1* or by using the **Editors** menu).

5. Press *Alt + C* to switch to the third-person camera.

6. Fly over to the dragon statue that is above one of the doorways near the courtyard.

7. Go to the **Library** tab of *Object Editor*.

8. Click on the **Level** tab and double-click on **Environment | Sound Emitter** to place an `SFXEmitter` object into the scene. The sound emitter will show up as a black box (black to indicate that it is not currently playing a sound).

9. Select the new `SFXEmitter` object, and place it near head of the dragon statue.

10. Using the property inspector on the right-hand side, change name (look at the **name** field) of the new `SFXEmitter` object to `DragonAlarm`.

11. Also in the property inspector, uncheck `playOnAdd` property of the `SFXEmitter` object, as shown in the following screenshot:

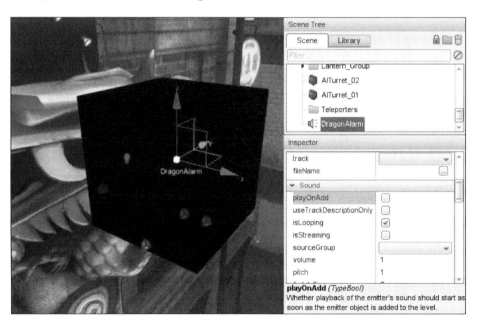

12. Save the level and press *F11* to go back to the game. Press *Alt + C* to return to the first-person camera.

13. Open the console with the tilde (~) key and enter the following command at the bottom of the screen to play our first sound:

    startDragonAlarm1();

14. Close the console with the tilde (~) key and walk around. The sound will shift between your stereo speakers as you rotate and the volume will change as you move closer or farther away from the DragonAlarm sound emitter.

15. Open the console again and enter the following command at the bottom of the screen to have the DragonAlarm sound emitter play our second sound:

    startDragonAlarm2();

16. Close the console again and walk around the level to hear volume of the 3D sound and apparent position change.

17. Finally, open the console one last time to issue the following command to stop any sound playing from the DragonAlarm sound emitter:

    stopDragonAlarm();

How it works...

The SFXEmitter scene object acts as a place to anchor sound effects within the scene. As it is a networkable scene object, its properties and current play state will automatically be sent to all players as appropriate—this includes any changes that are made to the SFXEmitter object through script.

In this example, we placed an SFXEmitter object in the scene but left most of its properties untouched. We didn't want to define what sound would play from the emitter while editing the level, and instead have left that to our TorqueScript functions.

In this example, we turned off playOnAdd property of our SFXEmitter object. This property determines if the emitter's assigned sound should start to play as soon as the level has loaded. While this doesn't affect the operation of this recipe (we are not assigning a sound to the emitter from the *World Editor*) setting this property to false makes sure that if we accidentally save the level with a sound assigned to our emitter (such as saving the level after using one of our earlier scripts) it won't accidentally start to play.

Our two example script functions, `startDragonAlarm1()` and `startDragonAlarm2()`, perform the following two objectives:

1. Assign an `SFXTrack` instance (in our case an `SFXProfile` instance, which inherits from `SFXTrack`) to the sound emitter's `track` property. This tells the sound emitter which sound to play.

2. Call the sound emitter's `play()` method to start the playing of the sound. This change in play state will be broadcast to call concerned player connections. As our chosen sound profile is set to loop, the sound will continue to play until it is specifically told to stop.

Our last script function, `stopDragonAlarm()`, calls the sound emitter's `stop()` method to stop all sounds from playing.

To change this from 3D sounds to 2D sounds that everyone will hear, all we need to do is use `SFXTrack` or `SFXProfile` instances that make use of 2D `SFXDescriptions`. When using 2D sounds it doesn't matter where the `SFXEmitter` object is placed in the scene.

There's more...

We've learned how to place an `SFXEmitter` object in the scene and trigger sound playback from TorqueScript, but there is still more to be aware of when working with sounds in Torque 3D.

Dynamically creating the sound source

In this example, we made use of an `SFXEmitter` object, which was already placed within the scene. It is also possible to create `SFXEmitter` objects while the game is running just like any other scene object:

```
New SFXEmitter(OurSoundEmitter)
{
    position = "-2.5 -6.0 7.4";
    playOnAdd = "0";
};
MissionCleanup.add(OurSoundEmitter);
```

As with any object we dynamically add to the scene, it is a good idea to add our emitter to the `MissionCleanup` group to ensure it is automatically deleted when the level ends. With `OurSoundEmitter` object now created, we can assign it a `track` instance and tell it to play (`play()`) or stop (`stop()`) at any time. And if the game doesn't need it any more, we can manually delete it with the following code:

```
OurSoundEmitter.delete();
```

Alternatively, we can just allow it to be cleaned up when the level ends.

Using a mono sound source

Most sound providers (OpenAL, DirectSound, and others) require that all sound files that are used for 3D sound effects be in a mono format. If you do use a stereo sound it could either play as a 2D sound instead, or not play at all. One exception to this rule is FMOD, which doesn't place this restriction on sound format for 3D sound effects.

Sounds not fading with distance

Sometimes, while building your game you may find that a 3D sound effect is not fading its volume based on the listener's (such as the player) distance from the `SFXEmitter` object. If this happens, the first thing to check is that the `SFXDescription` class used by track or profile of the sound has the appropriate minimum and maximum distances set.

However, even when the `SFXDescription` instance is set up properly, sometimes a lone sound effect still doesn't fade with distance. The culprit here may actually be your Windows speaker set up. By default, the **Loudness Equalization** sound effect may be enabled for your speakers. This sound effect created by Microsoft, automatically boosts the volume of quiet sounds, especially when they are the only sound playing. While this can improve the overall sound canvas of games and other sound sources, it can be frustrating when used with a single sound source we are tweaking during game development.

The **Loudness Equalization** sound effect may be disabled for your speakers from the Windows **Sound** control panel. This step alone may help you regain some sanity after a long session of trying to figure out why your finely crafted sounds are just not behaving as expected.

See also

▶ *Playing a quick 2D or 3D sound on all clients*

▶ *Triggering an event during sound playback*

Playing a sound on a ShapeBase object

All `ShapeBase` class objects are able to play up to four simultaneous sounds that track position of the object. In this recipe, we will learn how to play and stop sounds on a `ShapeBase` object.

Getting ready

We will be issuing console commands in a project based on the Torque 3D's `FPS Tutorial` template, and try them out using the `China Town Day` level. If you haven't already, use the Torque Project Manager (`Project Manager.exe`) to create a new project from the `FPS Tutorial` template; it can be found under the `My Projects` directory.

Subsequently, start the game and load the `China Town Day` level. You may want to change settings of the level just prior to playing to make sure we don't change levels while experimenting. Set the **Time Limit** to `Infinite` and uncheck the **Map Cycle** setting.

How to do it...

In the following steps, we will make a `ShapeBase` object in the level play different sound effects:

1. After the `China Town Day` level starts, run the player over to the first AI turret located in the alley off of the courtyard that is behind the yellow car—be careful as the turret will shoot!

2. Open the console with the tilde (~) key and enter the following TorqueScript command at the bottom of the screen to start playing a sound:

   ```
   AITurret_01.playAudio(0, PoliceRadioChatter);
   ```

   This causes the `PoliceRadioChatter SFXPlayList` sound to be emitted by the turret using sound playback slot `0`.

3. Now enter the following TorqueScript command into the console to start playing another sound:

   ```
   AITurret_01.playAudio(1, ElectricBuzz);
   ```

   This causes the `ElectricBuzz SFXProfile` sound to be emitted by the turret using sound playback slot `1`.

4. Now enter the following TorqueScript command into the console to stop playing our first sound:

```
AITurret_01.stopAudio(0);
```

This causes the police radio chatter to stop playing, and only leaves the electric buzz sound on the turret.

How it works...

All ShapeBase derived objects (the AITurretShape class used in this example being one of them) support up to four simultaneous sounds to be played on them. These sounds could either stop after playing once, or loop continuously, depending on which SFXDecription instance, the sound Datablock instance uses.

And just as with the SFXEmitter class mentioned in the *Using SFXEmitter to create networked sound effects* recipe, all connected clients that are in range (or later become in range) will hear the sounds.

To start playing a sound on a ShapeBase object we use the following method:

```
result = ShapeBase.playAudio( slot, SFXTrack );
```

In this method, the slot parameter is the slot index for the sound (ranges from 0 to 3), and the SFXTrack parameter is an SFXTrack derived Datablock instance that contains the details of the sound to play. In this example, we make use of an SFXPlayList Datablock instance and an SFXProfile datablock instance. The playAudio() method returns true if the sound is successfully playing on the ShapeBase object.

To stop playing a sound we use the following method:

```
result = ShapeBase.stopAudio( slot );
```

In this method, the slot parameter is the slot index of a previously playing sound. The stopAudio() method returns true so long as the provided slot index is valid.

See also

▸ *Using SFXEmitter to create networked sound effects*

Playing music while a level is loading

Waiting for a level to load on a multiplayer client can take some time, especially for large levels with a lot of content. Having music play during this downtime can help pass the time. In this recipe, we will learn how to play music while a level is loading, and how to stop the music once the level has loaded.

Getting ready

We will be making TorqueScript changes and working with the *World Editor* in a project based on the Torque 3D's `FPS Tutorial` template, and try them out using the `China Town Day` level. If you haven't already, use the Torque Project Manager (`Project Manager.exe`) to create a new project from the `FPS Tutorial` template; it can be found under the `My Projects` directory.

How to do it...

In the following steps we will set up some music to play while the level is loading:

1. Start the `FPS Tutorial` game and load the `China Town Day` level.

2. Press *F11* to open *World Editor*; make sure the *Object Editor* is active (*F1* or by using the **Editors** menu).

3. Go to the **Scene** tab of the *Object Editor* (in the **Scene Tree** window on the right-side). Click on the **MissionGroup** object at the top of the list.

4. In the property inspector scroll down to the bottom to the **Dynamic Fields** section. If there isn't already a **musicTrack** field listed here, click on the green circle with a plus in it and add a new **musicTrack** dynamic field.

5. Give the **musicTrack** dynamic field a value of `CT_music/action`.

6. Save the level and close the game.

7. Load the `scripts/client/missionDownload.cs` file in a text editor, such as Torsion, and add the following code to the `onMissionDownloadPhase1()` function, then save the file:

```
function onMissionDownloadPhase1
  (%missionName, %musicTrack)
{
  // Create the mission music sound source based on
    // the passed in music track.
  $MissionMusic = sfxPlayOnce(AudioMusicLoop2D,
    "art/sound/" @ %musicTrack);

  // Have the mission music play immediately.
  $MissionMusic.play();

  // Load the post effect presets for this mission.
  %path = "levels/" @ fileBase( %missionName )
    @ $PostFXManager::fileExtension;
  if ( isScriptFile( %path ) )
    postFXManager::loadPresetHandler( %path );
  else
```

```
PostFXManager::settingsApplyDefaultPreset();

// Close and clear the message hud (in case it's open)
if ( isObject( MessageHud ) )
  MessageHud.close();

// Reset the loading progress controls:
if ( !isObject( LoadingProgress ) )
  return;

LoadingProgress.setValue(0);
LoadingProgressTxt.setValue
  ("LOADING DATABLOCKS");
Canvas.repaint();
}
```

8. Load the `scripts/client/serverConnection.cs` file, add the following code to the `GameConnection::initialControlSet()` method, and save the file:

```
function GameConnection::
  initialControlSet(%this)
{
  echo ("*** Initial Control Object");

  // The first control object has been set by the server
  // and we are now ready to go.

  // first check if the editor is active
  if (!isToolBuild() || !Editor::
    checkActiveLoadDone())
  {
    if (Canvas.getContent() != PlayGui.getId())
      Canvas.setContent(PlayGui);
  }

  // Schedule for the mission music to stop in 5 seconds
  // (5000 miliseconds). We pass in a value of "10" to
  // the stop() method to have the music fade out over
  // 10 seconds once the 5 seconds have passed.
  $MissionMusic.schedule(5000, stop, "10");
}
```

9. Start the FPS Tutorial game and load the China Town Day level. While the level is downloading the music will play. Once the level has downloaded the music will begin to fade out five seconds later.

How it works...

Torque 3D already has a mechanism in place to pass level-specific music track information from the server to the client. On the server side, this occurs in `core/scripts/server/missionDownload.cs` within the `GameConnection::loadMission()` method:

```
function GameConnection::loadMission(%this)
{
  // Send over the information that will display the
  // server info when we learn it got there, we'll send
  // the data blocks
  %this.currentPhase = 0;
  if (%this.isAIControlled())
  {
    // Cut to the chase...
    %this.onClientEnterGame();
  }
  else
  {
    commandToClient(%this, 'MissionStartPhase1',
      $missionSequence,
      $Server::MissionFile, MissionGroup.musicTrack);

    echo("*** Sending mission load to client: " @
        $Server::MissionFile);
  }
}
```

This method sends the contents of the `MissionGroup musicTrack` dynamic property to the client as the second parameter of the `MissionStartPhase1` client command.

On the client side, the `onMissionDownloadPhase1()` function is called as a result of that client command and is also passed the music track information. However, nothing is done with it in the default Torque 3D set up. In this example, we add a 2D looping sound source that references our music track and starts it to play. The music will now continuously play while the mission is being downloaded to the client.

To stop the music once the level has loaded, we add a command to the `GameConnection::initialControlSet()` method. This method is called once the level has been loaded and the client's player object has been set up. It is here that the GUI is switched from the loading screen to the game screen. We have added a schedule to the same global variable we defined in `onMissionDownloadPhase1()` (which points to an `SFXSource` object) that will trigger `stop()` of the sound source method in five seconds. This gives some time for the rendering of the first few frames to catch up, which can cause hiccups in the client's event loop and make the volume fade out property, which we wish to apply, to stutter. We have passed in a parameter of `10` to the `stop()` method (by way of the `schedule()` method) to have the music fade out over 10 seconds before finally stopping. As `SFXSource` was created with the `sfxPlayOnce()` function, it will automatically be deleted from the game once the music has stopped.

How to have a background sound for a level

Sometimes, you want a background sound loop that just plays continuously while playing a level. It could be howling wind, heavy rain, and so on. Torque 3D makes it easy to add a 2D sound to any level, and have it start playing as soon as the level loads. In this recipe, we will learn how to add a continuously playing 2D sound to a level.

Getting ready

We will be working with the *World Editor* in a project based on the Torque 3D's FPS Tutorial template. If you haven't already, use the Torque Project Manager (Project Manager.exe) to create a new project from the FPS Tutorial template; it can be found under the My Projects directory.

How to do it...

In the following steps we will have a looping sound play continuously while playing a level:

1. Start up our FPS Tutorial game and load the China Town Mist level.
2. Press *F11* to open the *World Editor*. As we want to work with objects in the scene, the *Object Editor* should be selected (*F1* or by using the **Editors** menu).
3. Go to the **Library** tab of the *Object Editor*.
4. Click on the **Level** tab and double-click on **Environment | Sound Emitter** to place a SFXEmitter object into the scene. As we are going to use this emitter to play a 2D sound, it doesn't matter where the emitter is placed.
5. With the new SFXEmitter object selected, go to the property inspector and uncheck the emitter's is3D property.
6. Also from the property inspector, click on the . . . button beside the emitter's fileName property—this will open a window to choose a sound file. We'll use the art/sound/environment/amb.ogg sound. Choose that sound file and click on the **Open** button on the window. The amb.ogg sound should immediately load and start to play (thanks to the emitter's playOnAdd property being set).
7. Save the level and press *F11* to go back to the game. Now the amb.ogg sound will always play whenever the China Town Mist level is started.

Look at the following screenshot:

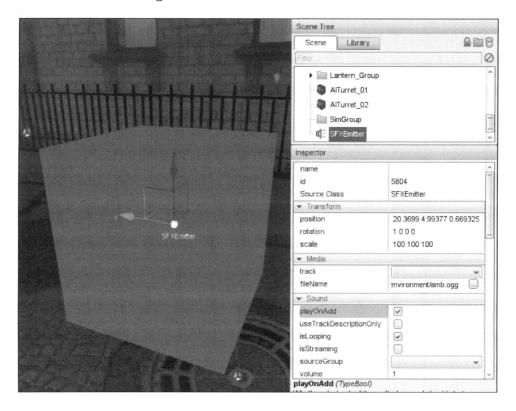

How it works...

The SFXEmitter class is used to add 2D or 3D sounds to a level. In this example, we have turned off is3D property of our SFXEmitter object, thereby making it a 2D sound emitter. When set up in this way, it doesn't matter where we place the SFXEmitter object in the scene as its position has no impact on the 2D sound.

We have also left the playOnAdd property enabled (set to true), which allows the sound emitter to begin playing as soon as the level has finished loading (rather than waiting for a script command to start the emitter playing). The isLooping property of sound emitter is also set so that our sound will play forever.

With all of these factors put together, we now have a background sound that will always play while the level is active.

How to have music change according to the mood

Torque 3D allows us to change the sounds that are playing based on various states. One example is modifying the background music of a level depending on the current mood, or to reflect a change that has occurred in the game.

In this recipe, we will learn how change the music currently being played, depending on if the player is being hurt through the use of mood states.

Getting ready

We will be making TorqueScript changes and working with the *World Editor* in a project based on the Torque 3D's FPS Tutorial template, and try them out using the China Town Dusk level.

If you haven't already, use the Torque Project Manager (Project Manager.exe) to create a new project from the FPS Tutorial template; it can be found under the My Projects directory. After that, start your favorite script editor, such as Torsion, and let's get going!

How to do it...

In the following steps, we will set up some audio mood ambiences that will be switched between, when the player is hurt:

1. We start by defining all the audio that will be used by this recipe. Open scripts/client/game.cs in a text editor and add the following code:

```
// Description we'll use for all of our mood music
singleton SFXDescription
    ( AudioMoodMusicLoop2D : AudioMusic )
{
  // The sound will loop
  isLooping       = true;

  // Stream the sound rather than load it all into memory
  isStreaming     = true;

  // Fade up the volume when the sound starts to play
  fadeInTime      = 2.0;

  // Fade down the volume when the sound stops playing
  fadeOutTime     = 2.0;
};

// Custom sound state used when the player is in explore
```

```
// mode (just walking around). Our other sound state
// (aggressive) is already defined in Torque 3D.
singleton SFXState( AudioMoodExplore )
{
  // This state belongs to the mood group
   parentGroup = AudioMood;

   // When this state is active disable all other mood states
   className = "AudioStateExclusive";
};

// Sound profile used when in the aggressive mood
singleton SFXProfile( ActionMoodMusic )
{
   filename = "art/sound/CT_music/action";
   description = AudioMoodMusicLoop2D;
};

// Sound profile used when in the explore mood
singleton SFXProfile( ActionExploreMusic )
{
  filename = "art/sound/CT_music/explore";
   description = AudioMoodMusicLoop2D;
};

// Play list that sets up the properties for each
// possible mood
singleton SFXPlayList( MoodMusicPlayList )
{
  // Want the play list to loop
  description = AudioMusicLoop2D;

  // Points to music for first track
  track[0] = ActionExploreMusic;
  // Continue to use a source that may still be playing
  replay[0] = "KeepPlaying";
  // Make the list wait until the track has finished playing
  transitionOut[0] = "Wait";
  // The mood this track is attached to
  state[0] = AudioMoodExplore;
  // Pause the sound source when switching to another state
  stateMode[0] = "PauseWhenDeactivated";

  // Points to music for second track
  track[1] = ActionMoodMusic;
  // Continue to use a source that may still be playing
  replay[1] = "KeepPlaying";
  // Make the list wait until the track has finished playing
  transitionOut[1] = "Wait";
  // The mood this track is attached to
```

```
    state[1] = AudioMoodAggressive;
    // Pause the sound source when switching to another state
    stateMode[1] = "PauseWhenDeactivated";
};

// The ambience that ties it all together and may be used
//by the LevelInfo object.
Singleton SFXAmbience( AudioAmbienceMoodMusic )
{
    soundtrack = MoodMusicPlayList;
};
```

2. Save the script file. Now start the `FPS Tutorial` game and load the `China Town Dusk` level. Press *F11* to open the *World Editor*. As we want to work with objects in the scene, the *Object Editor* should be selected (*F1* or by using the **Editors** menu).

3. Go to the **Scene** tab of the *Object Editor* and choose `theLevelInfo` object from the tree list.

4. In the **Inspector** window, scroll down to the `soundAmbience` property. Use the drop-down option to select our newly created `AudioAmbienceMoodMusic Datablock instance`.

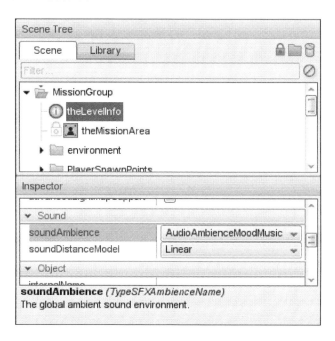

5. Save the level and quit the game.

6. Open `scripts/client/serverConnection.cs` in a text editor and add the following code, which changes the mood, to the bottom:

```
// This method changes the music based on the given mood
function GameConnection::
    changeMoodMusic(%this, %audioMood)
{
  // Make sure the requested mood is valid
  if(isObject(%audioMood))
  {
    // Only change the mood if it is not currently active
    if(!%audioMood.isActive())
    {
      echo("Changing mood to: " @ %audioMood);

      // Activate the mood
      %audioMood.activate();
    }
  }
}
```

7. In the same file, add the highlighted code to the `GameConnection::initialControlSet()` method to set the starting mood:

```
function GameConnection::initialControlSet(%this)
{
  echo ("*** Initial Control Object");

  // The first control object has been set by the server
  // and we are now ready to go.

  // first check if the editor is active
  if (!isToolBuild() || !Editor::
      checkActiveLoadDone())
  {
    if (Canvas.getContent() != PlayGui.getId())
      Canvas.setContent(PlayGui);
  }

  // Set the starting mood music to that of exploring
  %this.changeMoodMusic(AudioMoodExplore);
}
```

8. Save the file.

9. Now open `scripts/client/client.cs` and add the highlighted code to the `clientCmdSetDamageDirection()` function; this will change the mood when the player is damaged:

```
function clientCmdSetDamageDirection(%direction)
{
  eval("%ctrl = DamageHUD-->damage_" @ %direction @ ";");
  if (isObject(%ctrl))
  {
    // Show the indicator, and schedule an event to hide it again
    cancelAll(%ctrl);
    %ctrl.setVisible(true);
    %ctrl.schedule(500, setVisible, false);
  }

  // We've been damaged so change the mood
  ServerConnection.changeMoodMusic(AudioMoodAggressive);

  // Cancel any previous reset of the mood
  cancel($MissionMoodSchedule);

  // Schedule a change in the mood to happen some time
  // from now. This means that if we're not damaged
  // again (causing this schedule to cancel) then
  // we will switch to this calmer mood in 10 seconds.
  $MissionMoodSchedule = ServerConnection.schedule(10000,
                                        changeMoodMusic,
                                        AudioMoodExplore);
}
```

10. Save the file.

11. Finally, start the `FPS Tutorial` game and load the `China Town Dusk` level. Our exploration music will play in the background.

12. Run the player over to one of the turrets and get shot. While the damage flashes are happening, the aggressive music will begin to play.

13. Run away from the turret so that it stops hitting the player. Ten seconds later the music will switch to the original, exploration theme.

How it works...

The key to all of this working is the `SFXState Datablock` class that defines our moods. Torque 3D already comes with a number of these predefined classes, including the `AudioMoodAggressive Datablock` class, which we make use.

The example in this recipe also creates our custom `AudioMoodExplore Datablock` (using the `singleton` keyword as it is on the client and won't be synchronized over the network) to trigger our exploration music. A `SFXState Datablock` class may be activated or deactivated (`SFXState` is more fully explored later), and any sound class that is watching state changes, such as our `MoodMusicPlayList`, responds to these changes.

When the mission has finished loading and the player has been added to the scene, we set our initial `AudioMoodExplore` mood (done in `GameConnection::initialControlSet()`).This mood/state will cause our playlist to choose the exploration music while the player is walking around. But whenever the player is damaged and the `clientCmdSetDamageDirection()` function is called by the server to display the damage flash, we change our mood to `AudioMoodAggressive`, which causes our aggressive music to play (again due to our playlist). We also set up a `schedule()` method on the client's connection to switch back to the explore mood automatically if the player has not been damaged for at least 10 seconds.

There's more...

Let's talk some more about using the `SFXState Datablock` class.

SFXState activations are reference counted

The `SFXState Datablock` instance may be enabled or disabled in order to activate or deactivate some sound activity that is watching an `SFXState` instance. It internally increments a counter each time it is activated, and decrements that same counter each time it is deactivated. This means that if we do a number of activations on the same `SFXState` instance then we will also need to do the same number of deactivations to turn it off.

In this recipe, we first check if an `SFXState` instance is already activated before attempting to activate it again. This ensures that we never pile on the activations, which will require the same number of deactivations to counter them. We can check if an `SFXState` instance is active with the `isActive()` method as follows:

```
function GameConnection::changeMoodMusic
        (%this, %audioMood)
{
  // Make sure the requested mood is valid
  if(isObject(%audioMood))
  {
```

```
// Only change the mood if it is not currently active
if(!%audioMood.isActive())
{
  echo("Changing mood to: " @ %audioMood);

  // Activate the mood
  %audioMood.activate();
}
}
}
```

Having more than one active SFXState instance

While we usually have SFXState objects set up so that only a single one is active at a time, we may have multiple groups of SFXState objects defined, which allow for multiple active states. In fact, Torque 3D comes with two SFXState groups already set up—one for location and one for mood. This allows us to have a collection of sounds that depend on where the player is, such as outside or underwater, and another collection of sounds that depend on the current mood of the game, such as our aforementioned music. In fact, we could define our own SFXState groups for even more combinations.

See core/scripts/client/audioStates.cs for the creation of these default sound state groups and the various states themselves. Then feel free to expand on these, just as we did in this recipe.

Triggering an event during sound playback

Torque 3D allows us to set markers on the timeline of a sound that triggers a callback. In this recipe, we will learn how to set markers on a sound source and respond to their callback while a sound is playing.

Getting ready

We will be making TorqueScript changes in a project based on the Torque 3D's FPS Tutorial template, and try them out using the China Town Day level. If you haven't already, use the Torque Project Manager (Project Manager.exe) to create a new project from the FPS Tutorial template; it can be found under the My Projects directory. After that, start your favorite script editor, such as Torsion, and let's get going!

How to do it...

In the following steps we will have an explosion trigger based on a sound playing:

1. Open `scripts/client/game.cs` in a text editor, add the following TorqueScript code to the bottom of the file, and save it:

```
// This function will create an explosion one of the
// street lamps as indicated by %lampIndex.
function createLampExplosion(%lampIndex)
{
  if(%lampIndex == 0)
  {
    %pos = StreetLamp_CS_01.getPosition();
  }
  else
  {
    %pos = StreetLamp_CS_02.getPosition();
  }

  new Explosion()
  {
    dataBlock = GrenadeLauncherWaterExplosion;
    position = %pos;
  };
}

// Define the ActionMusic namespace to be used by the
// sound source. It handles doing an action when a
// sound marker callback has been called.
function ActionMusic::onMarkerPassed(%this, %markerName)
{
  // Create an explosion at the lamp for each marker
  switch$(%markerName)
  {
    case "lamp1":
        createLampExplosion(0);

    case "lamp2":
        createLampExplosion(1);
  }
}

// Starts the action music and defines markers
function startActionMusic()
{
  // Create a new sound source
  %source = sfxCreateSource( AudioMusic2D,
        "art/sound/CT_music/action" );
```

```
    // Set the source to delete when it stops playing
    sfxDeleteWhenStopped(%source);

    // Assign a class to the source to be used by the
    // marker callback
    %source.class = ActionMusic;

    // Add markers (in seconds) to trigger a callback
    %source.addMarker( "lamp1", 3.5 );
    %source.addMarker( "lamp1", 10.5 );
    %source.addMarker( "lamp2", 20.5 );
    %source.addMarker( "lamp2", 27.5 );

    // Play the music
    %source.play();
}
```

2. Start the `FPS Tutorial` game and load the `China Town Day` level. Walk to the end of the courtyard where the noodle cart is and make sure that the two lamp posts are in view.

3. Open the console with the tilde (~) key and enter the following TorqueScript code at the bottom of the screen:

   startActionMusic();

4. Close the console with the tilde (~) key and watch the four purple explosions (two at each lamp post) happen in time to the music as shown in the following image:

How it works...

The first function we wrote, `createLampExplosion()`, creates the actual explosions around the lamp posts. This function takes a lamp index (either `0` or `1`) and retrieves the position of the appropriate lamp post. It then creates a new explosion at that position using a standard explosion `datablock` instance.

> The `Explosion` class may only be used on the client. It doesn't instantiate itself across the network, nor does it allow itself to be added to the server scene graph. It is meant to be created due to some other network event.

The second function we wrote is actually a method on a custom namespace. We created the `ActionMusic` namespace specifically to be used by any sound sources we want to make use of the marker callback. By assigning the `ActionMusic` namespace to the `class` property of our sound source, it will be able to make use of the `onMarkerPassed()` method we have defined.

> Please see the *Extending a SimObject instance using the class property* recipe in *Chapter 1, TorqueScript: The Only Script You Need to Know* for an explanation on making use of the *class* property.

The `onMarkerPassed()` method takes one parameter (other than the standard `%this` parameter) that contains the name of the marker that has just been triggered. We use this name to determine which lamp post index to pass to our `createLampExplosion()` function to create the actual explosion.

Finally, we build the `startActionMusic()` function to create our sound source (a 2D one in this case so we don't need to worry about position) and assign our `ActionMusic` namespace to it. We then use the `addMarker()` method to add a number of callback markers to the sound source at specific times (in seconds) and tag each marker with a name (used by `onMarkerPassed()` to determine which lamp post to explode). Then we start the sound source to play and watch the explosions happen in time to the music. We may call `startActionMusic()` as many times as we want to continue the explosion display.

There's more...

Let's continue our discussion about sound sources and events.

Only on client

The various functions used to create sound sources may only be used on the client, and are not meant to be created on the server. This also means that adding markers to a sound source may only be done on the client. We can still trigger sounds to play on all clients from the server but we'll need to set up our own network event and response to cause it to happen.

Markers on an SFXEmitter class

The `SFXEmitter` class is used to start and stop the playing of sounds across all connected clients.

 Please see the *Using SFXEmitter to create networked sound effects* recipe for more information about the `SFXEmitter` class.

The client side of an `SFXEmitter` instance may use the `getSource()` method to retrieve the emitter's sound source and use the `addMarker()` method to add markers. This can be tricky to set up, as the client side needs to know which `SFXEmitter` to add the markers to (perhaps with a `commandToClient()` call from the server that includes ghost ID of the `SFXEmitter` object for the client once the mission has loaded), but it could be done if needed.

The appropriate namespace would also need to be put into *class* property of the `SFXEmitter` client side as that property isn't networked between `NetObject` instances. This isn't something that is commonly done on the client side, but would need to be for sound source markers to work.

Problem with looped sounds

Markers are intended to be triggered even when a sound is looping. Unfortunately, there is a bug with Torque 3D 2.0 that only has the markers trigger their callback the first time a sound plays through. The next version of Torque 3D will correct this bug and allow markers to always trigger regardless of how many times the sound loops.

See also

▶ *Extending a SimObject instance using the class property* in *Chapter 1, TorqueScript: The Only Script You Need to Know*

▶ *Using SFXEmitter to create networked sound effects*

7
Game Objects

In this chapter we will cover the following topics:

- ► Playing an animation sequence on a `TSStatic` class
- ► Playing an animation sequence on a `ShapeBase` class
- ► How to make it rain using a `Precipitation` object
- ► Using the `Lightning` object to automatically create a thunderstorm
- ► Using the `TimeOfDay` object to generate events

Introduction

A typical 3D game is made up of a number of components. We have objects that are controlled by the players, interactive objects that are controlled by the computer, and background objects that make up a game's atmosphere. All of these put together make a complete game.

Torque 3D has a large number of game objects to choose from and use. In this chapter, we will be diving into the details of some of the objects that make up a game's atmosphere, both figuratively and literally.

Playing an animation sequence on a TSStatic class

The most commonly used shape class in Torque 3D is `TSStatic`. When you place a shape file in a scene using the *Object Editor* (which is part of the *World Editor*) it is automatically turned into a `TSStatic` class object. While the `TSStatic` class doesn't do a lot other than sit in the scene, it supports some basic animation capabilities.

In this recipe, we will learn how to play an animation sequence that exists within an exported model on a `TSStatic`-based object and discover its limitations.

Getting ready

We will be using a project based on the Torque 3D's `Full` template using the `Empty Terrain` level.

If you haven't already, use the Torque Project Manager (`Project Manager.exe`) to create a new project from the `Full` template; it can be found under the `My Projects` directory. Then start our new `Full` template game and load the `Empty Terrain` level.

How to do it...

In the following steps, we will add a `TSStatic` shape to a level and have its ambient animation sequence play automatically:

1. Press *F11* to open the *World Editor*. As we want to work with objects in the scene, the *Object Editor* should be selected (by pressing *F1* or by using the **Editors** menu).

2. Go to the **Library** tab of the *Object Editor*.

3. Click on the **Meshes** tab.

4. Double-click on **teleporter** located at `art/shapes/teleporter` to add a new `teleporter` shape to the scene.

5. Use the axis gizmo to place our new `teleporter` somewhere near the ground.

6. From the **Inspector** window, find the **playAmbient** property of shape. Make sure this property is checked. The lights of the teleporter now rotate about the perimeter as this motion is part of the sequence of ambient animation of the shape:

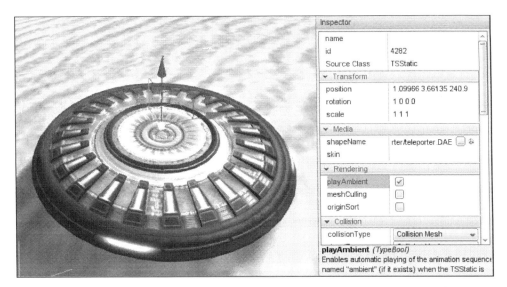

7. Save the level and press *F11* to go back into the game.

How it works...

The `playAmbient` property of `TSStatic` controls if an animation sequence named `ambient` will play on the object when it is added to the scene. For the `playAmbient` property to work, the shape file of the object must contain an animation sequence named `ambient`.

In this example, the `teleporter` object has more than an ambient animation sequence applied. It is also making use of the `Material` animation. This is why the top of the `teleporter` shape continues to animate after the `playAmbient` property is checked off. Our ambient animation sequence is only the light that rotates about the perimeter.

There's more...

If the `playAmbient` property of the `TSStatic` object is modified after the object has already been added to the scene, then the change will not take effect. This means that we cannot toggle the playing of animation of a `TSStatic` object on or off while the game is running. The `TSStatic` class is light both in terms of features and network bandwidth.

If we need finer control over animation playback of an object, we may use the `StaticShape` class. This class inherits its playback capabilities from the `ShapeBase` class, but also requires much more set up before an instance may be used in the game.

See also

▶ *Playing an animation sequence on a ShapeBase class*

Playing an animation sequence on a ShapeBase class

All classes that derive from the `ShapeBase` class (such as `StaticShape`) allow full control over the animation sequences that play on an object instance. In this recipe, we will learn how to start and stop multiple animation sequences on a `StaticShape` class.

Getting ready

We will be making TorqueScript changes, and working with the *World Editor* in a project based on the Torque 3D's `Full` template using the `Empty Terrain` level.

If you haven't already, use the Torque Project Manager (`Project Manager.exe`) to create a new project from the `Full` template. It can be found under the `My Projects` directory. After that, start your favorite script editor, such as Torsion, and let's get going!

How to do it...

In the following steps, we will change the animation sequences, which will play on a `ShapeBase` object:

1. Create a new TorqueScript text file as `art/datablocks/npcSoldier.cs` and load it into your text editor.

2. Add the following code to the file that will be used by a new `Datablock` instance, which we are about to create and save the file:

```
// Callback on the Datablock when an object using this
// datablock is added to the scene.
Function NPCSoldierData::onAdd(%this, %npc)
{
  // Start the idle animation for the NPC soldier
  %npc.playThread(0, "root");

  // Schedule the NPC soldier's celebrate animation
  //sequence
  %this.scheduleCelebration(%npc);
}

// Callback on the Datablock when a non-cyclic sequence
// has come to an end.
```

```
Function NPCSoldierData::onEndSequence
      (%this, %npc, %thread)
{
   // The NPC Soldier plays its celebration sequence on
   // thread 1
   if (%thread == 1)
   {
      // We want to destroy the thread when it ends.
      // This ensures that it won't interfere with
      // any other thread.
      %npc.destroyThread(%thread);

      // Reschedule the celebration sequence
      %this.scheduleCelebration(%npc);
   }
}

// Schedule the playing of the celebration animation
// sequence on the NPC soldier.
Function NPCSoldierData::scheduleCelebration
      (%this, %npc)
{
   // Have the celebration sequence play every 10 seconds.
   %npc.schedule(10000, playThread, 1, "Celebrate_01");
}
```

3. Start our `Full` template and load the `Empty Terrain` level.

4. Press *F11* to open the *World Editor*. We want to create a new `Datablock` so select the *Datablock Editor* (by pressing *F6* or by using the **Editors** menu).

5. Go to the **New** tab of the *Datablock Editor*.

6. Scroll down to the **StaticShapeData** entry and double-click on it to start building a new `StaticShapeData Datablock`—this will open the **Create New Datablock** dialog box, as shown in the following screenshot:

7. Name our new `Datablock` as **NPCSoldierData**, and click on the **Create** button. This will open our new `Datablock` in the **Inspector** window, below the **Datablock Library** window on the right-side of the screen.

8. Using the **Inspector** window, click on the ellipse button (**...**) beside the **shapeFile** property, to display the **Open File** dialog box.

   Use the drop-down control in the lower-right corner, and set it for **COLLADA Files (*.dae)**. Choose `art/shapes/actors/Soldier/soldier_rigged.DAE` and click on the **Open** button.

9. Set the `Datablock` object's **category** property to **NPC**. This is the category name under which the shape will show in the *Object Editor*.

10. Click on the disk icon at the top right of the **Inspector** window to save our new `Datablock`. The `Datablock` will automatically be saved to `art/datablocks/managedDatablocks.cs`.

11. We now want to add a new shape based on the `Datablock` instance we just created. Select the *Object Editor* by pressing *F1*, or by using the **Editors** menu.

12. Go to the **Library** tab of the *Object Editor*, and choose the **Scripted** tab that is just underneath.

13. Double-click on the **NPC** folder icon. If this folder icon is not displayed, we may need to force a refresh of the list. We can do this by clicking on the **Meshes** tab and then back to the **Scripted** tab.

14. Double-click on the **NPCSoldierData** entry to create a new `StaticShape` class based on our new `Datablock`.

15. Use the axis gizmo to place the character on the ground.

16. The soldier NPC continuously plays its `root` animation sequence. Every ten seconds it plays its `celebrate` animation sequence, and then goes back to the `root` sequence.

How it works...

All classes derived from ShapeBase require that we define a Datablock instance to describe the object we wish to create. In this recipe, we use a StaticShape class object to represent a soldier NPC in the world. This makes our NPC non-interactive, such as a guard that is just standing there. For our NPC, we have created the NPCSoldierData Datablock instance using the _Datablock Editor_, and filled in the information of the shape file.

Each Datablock class (we are using StaticShapeData here) has a number of predefined callbacks that are made on the server. We are making use of the onAdd() (called when an object instance is added to the scene) and the onEndSequence() (called when a non-cyclic animation sequence has ended) callbacks. We may also write our own methods for a Datablock instance, such as the scheduleCelebration() method that we have built for our example. All the playing, stopping, and scheduling of animation sequences of the object is done within these methods.

Any ShapeBase-derived object supports up to four different animation sequences to play at once. Each sequence is layered on the previous one and they all take advantage of the blend modes and sequence priority settings of Torque's object animation system. In order to start playing an animation sequence on a ShapeBase object we use the following method:

```
result = ShapeBase.playThread( slot, sequenceName );
```

In this method, the slot parameter is the slot index for the animation sequence (ranges from 0 to 3), and the sequenceName parameter is the name of the animation sequence contained within the shape file.

In this example, we start the root sequence right away on slot 0 when the object is added to the scene using this method. The playThread() method returns true if the sequence is found on the shape and is successfully assigned to a slot.

> Torque 3D calls each animation sequence that plays on an object a **thread**. This is named after the TSThread class, which is used internally. For our purposes here, we can think of slot number and thread number as the same thing, and each of the animation methods that we'll see in this recipe, will have the word *Thread* in them.

To stop an animation sequence from playing we use the following method:

```
result = ShapeBase.stopThread( slot );
```

In this method, the slot parameter is the slot index for the animation sequence to stop playing. We don't make use of the stopThread() method in our example, as we have let our Celebrate_01 sequence to run at the end and our root sequence runs continuously in cycles.

Something to be aware of with the stopThread() method is that it doesn't actually remove the animation sequence from the object. This means that the sequence will still affect how the object looks. In order to completely remove an animation sequence from an object, we use the following method:

```
result = ShapeBase.destroyThread( slot );
```

In this method, the slot parameter is the slot index for the animation sequence to remove from the object. This method returns true if the given slot has not already been destroyed.

We use the destroyThread() method during the onEndSequence() callback to remove the celebration animation sequence from the object. If we didn't do this, the last frame of the celebration sequence would remain on the object. As this sequence has the same priority defined in the shape file as the root sequence, and it sits one layer above the root sequence in slot 1, we would no longer see the root sequence play. It would be as if the NPC is frozen in place.

There's more...

Let's continue our discussion of playing animation sequences on `ShapeBase` objects.

Pausing an animation sequence playback

We use the following method to pause a playing animation sequence:

```
result = ShapeBase.pauseThread( slot );
```

In this method, the `slot` parameter is the slot index of the animations sequence (ranges from `0` to `3`) to pause; pausing a sequence immediately stops it from advancing.

The difference between pausing and stopping a playing animation sequence is in how it continues if the `playThread()` method is called on the slot. A paused sequence will continue from where it was paused, while a stopped sequence will start over from the beginning.

Jumping to a location in timeline of an animation sequence

It is possible to jump to a particular spot in timeline of an animation sequence by using the following method:

```
result = ShapeBase.setThreadPosition( slot, position );
```

In this method, the `slot` parameter is the slot index of the animation sequence, and the `position` parameter is the location on timeline of the animation sequence, normalized to a range of `0.0` to `1.0`. For example, passing in a `position` parameter of `0.5` starts the animation sequence half way through its timeline.

We can force a sequence's starting play back position by first calling `playThread()` and then `setThreadPosition()`. We could also pause a playing sequence with `pauseThread()`, modify its timeline position with `setThreadPosition()`, and then continue playing the sequence by calling `playThread()` with only the slot index passed-in.

Changing playback direction and speed of a sequence

In order to change direction of an animation sequence from forward to backward (reverse its direction) we use the following method:

```
result = ShapeBase.setThreadDir( slot, direction);
```

In this method, the `slot` parameter is the index of the animation sequence, and the `direction` parameter is `true` to play forward and `false` to play backward.

In order to change the playback speed of a sequence we use the following method:

```
result = ShapeBase.setThreadTimeScale( slot, scale );
```

In this method, the `slot` parameter is the index of the animation sequence, and the `scale` parameter is the new time scale for the sequence. For example, setting `scale` to `2.0` will double the playback speed, while a value of `0.5` will play the sequence at half speed.

Both of these methods may be called at anytime on a valid animation sequence slot.

See also

▸ *Playing an animation sequence on a TSStatic class*

How to make it rain using a Precipitation object

Torque 3D makes it easy to add precipitation to a level, such as rain, snow, or volcanic ash. In this recipe, we will add basic rain to a level and go through all of the more advanced options.

Getting ready

We will be using a project based on the Torque 3D's `FPS Tutorial` template using the `China Town Mist` level. If you haven't already, use the Torque Project Manager (`Project Manager.exe`) to create a new project from the `FPS Tutorial` template. It can be found under the `My Projects` directory. Then start our new `FPS Tutorial` template game and load the `China Town Mist` level.

How to do it...

In the following steps we will add a `Precipitation` object to the level and make it rain:

1. Press *F11* to open the *World Editor*. As we want to work with objects in the scene, the *Object Editor* should be selected (by pressing *F1* or by using the **Editors** menu).

2. Go to the **Library** tab of the *Object Editor*.

3. Click on the **Level** tab.

4. Double-click on the **Environment** folder.

5. Double-click on the **Precipitation** item to add a new one to the scene—this will open the **Create Object: Precipitation** dialog box.

6. In the **Object Name** field of dialog box enter `Rain`.

7. Click on the **Precipitation data** drop-down menu of dialog box, and select the **HeavyRain** `Datablock` option, as shown in the following screenshot:

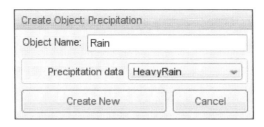

8. Click on **Create New** button of the dialog box to create the new `Precipitation` object instance and add it to the scene.

9. The default size of the rain is too large. So from the **Inspector** window on the right-hand side, set both the **dropSize** and **splashSize** properties to a value of `0.1`.

10. Increase the number of rain drops by setting the **numDrops** property to a value of `3000`.

11. Reduce the radius of the rain drops around the player by setting the **boxWidth** property to `50`.

12. Decrease the starting height of the rain drops, above the player, by setting the **boxHeight** property to `10`.

13. These settings give a heavy rain shower around the player when outside, while allowing the player to stay dry inside.

How it works...

The `Precipitation` class creates a volume of precipitation based on both the supplied `Datablock` instance and properties of the object. The `PrecipitationData` `Datablock` instance is used to define drop and splash texture of the precipitation, as well as any background sound used by the precipitation. In this example, we are using the standard `HeavyRain` `Datablock` instance and its sound profile; these are found at `art/datablocks/environment.cs`.

```
// -------------------------------------------------------
// Rain
// -------------------------------------------------------

datablock SFXProfile(HeavyRainSound)
{
  filename = "art/sound/environment/amb";
  description = AudioLoop2d;
};

datablock PrecipitationData(HeavyRain)
{
  soundProfile = "HeavyRainSound";

  dropTexture =
    "art/environment/precipitation/rain";
  splashTexture =
    "art/environment/precipitation/water_splash";
};
```

With these two `Datablock` objects, we have falling rain that splashes when it hits objects, and thunder and bird sounds playing in the background.

The primary use of the `Precipitation` object is to simulate precipitation falling over the entire level. However, it would be too costly to have it actually occur over an entire level, so only the volume around the camera is rendered. The size of this volume is controlled by the `boxWidth` and `boxHeight` properties, which need to be tuned for each level to maintain the illusion of precipitation everywhere. As the precipitation volume is only rendered around the location of camera, the starting position of the `Precipitation` object is not important.

Within the volume, the precipitation is created, falls downwards, and is recycled. The amount of precipitation is controlled by the `numDrops` property. Increasing the number of drops allowed to exist at any given time gives a sense of a larger storm, but at a rendering and collision detection (if the `doCollision` property is checked) cost on the client. It is also possible to increase the density of falling drops by decreasing the precipitation volume.

It is important to keep boxHeight property of the precipitation volume at least as high as the tallest structure a player may enter; otherwise, precipitation may start within the building rather than colliding with its exterior.

In addition to overall density of the precipitation, the Precipitation class allows us to control how fast the precipitation falls. This is done with the minSpeed and maxSpeed properties. These two properties provide a random range of speeds for each drop to allow for a variety. In this example, we didn't modify the default values, which have a minSpeed value of 1.5 and a maxSpeed value of 2.0. These default values work well for falling rain.

The final set of properties that we will discuss here are those that control the visual size of each individual drops. The dropSize property is the world size of each individual drop. In this example, we have set dropSize to 0.1 as the default value of 0.5 gives too large of a rain drop.

The splashSize property is the world size of each splash that occurs when a drop hits something. These splashes only occur if the precipitation is allowed to collide with the scene by setting the doCollision property to true. In this example, we have set the splashSize to 0.1, as that seems fitting for our chosen rain drop size.

There's more...

Let's continue the discussion of the Precipitation class.

Sprite sheet for drops and splashes

The texture image provided for the precipitation drops and splashes may contain more than one individual image. In both cases, the sprite sheet may be used either to animate the drop or splash over its lifetime, or to randomly select one of the sprite sheet images to display for the entire drop or splash lifetime. The following screenshot shows the drop (on the left-hand side) and splash (on the right-hand side) sprite sheets that come with the FPS Tutorial level:

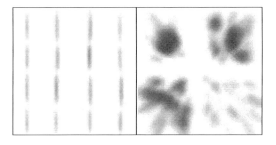

We need to tell Torque 3D how many images are within each sprite sheet. In the aforementioned example of a drop sprite sheet, there are four rows and columns. In the splash sheet there are two rows and columns. We place this information into the `dropsPerSide` and `splashesPerSide` properties of the `PrecipitationData` `Datablock` object as 4 and 2, respectively.

The `Precipitation` class determines how these sprite sheets are used. If the `dropAnimateMS` property is set to 0, then drops will randomly select one of the images in the drop sprite sheet for usage. If the `dropAnimateMS` property is greater than zero, then each drop cycles through the frames in the drop sprite sheet (left- to right-hand side, top to bottom) at the rate given by the property in milliseconds.

For splashes, the `animateSplashes` property determines how the splash sprite sheet is used. When `animateSplashes` is `false`, the splash randomly selects one of the images in the splash sprite sheet for usage. When `animateSplashes` is `true`, the splash will cycle through the frames in the splash sprite sheet at the rate given by the `splashMS` property, in milliseconds.

Using a shader for drops and splashes

Unless it is explicitly defined by the `PrecipitationData` `Datablock` object, the `Precipitation` class doesn't use a shader to draw either the drops or the splashes. This makes for straightforward, but basic precipitation.

With the addition of a shader to our `PrecipitationData` `Datablock` object, we gain access to the more advanced properties of the `Precipitation` class; plus we may do whatever we want within the shader (psychedelic rain?). Fortunately, Torque 3D comes with a precipitation shader, which we may use once we have set it up.

The first step is to create a `ShaderData` instance that points to the shaders themselves. Open `scripts/client/shaders.cs` in a text editor, add the following code snippet to the end, and save it:

```
singleton ShaderData( HeavyRainShaderData )
{
  DXVertexShaderFile   =
        "shaders/common/precipV.hlsl";
  DXPixelShaderFile    =
        "shaders/common/precipP.hlsl";

  OGLVertexShaderFile =
        "shaders/common/gl/precipV.glsl";
  OGLPixelShaderFile   =
        "shaders/common/gl/precipP.glsl";

  pixVersion = 2.0;
};
```

Now start the `FPS Tutorial` game, which we used in this example, and load the `China Town Mist` level. Open the *World Editor* by pressing *F11* and switch to the *Datablock Editor* by pressing *F6*.

Now in the **Datablock Library** window, click on the **Existing** tab. Scroll down to the **PrecipitationData** item, and click on the **HeavyRain** `datablock` instance to open it within the **Datablock** window.

The two properties we will modify are **dropShader** and **splashShader**. Enter `HeavyRainShaderData` into both these text fields to connect our `ShaderData` instance. Finally, click on the disk icon at the top-right to save our **HeavyRain** `datablock` instance. We have now set up our precipitation to use the shader.

Now go back to the *Object Editor* by pressing *F1*, and choose our **Rain** object from the **Scene Tree** window. The precipitation shader we are using accepts the various advanced rendering properties of the `Precipitation` class, such as **fadeDist**, **fadeDistEnd**, **useLighting**, and **glowIntensity**. These are under the **Rendering** section of the **Inspector** window.

If we set **fadeDist** to `20` and **fadeDistEnd** to `50`, our rain will render at full intensity up until 20 meters from the camera, and then fade to complete transparency at 50 meters (chosen to match our **boxWidth**). This can give a pleasing effect, especially when used with fog. Finally, we will activate the **useLighting** property by clicking on it. This forces the rain to respect the local lighting conditions and gives the rain a more subtle appearance, as shown in the following screenshot:

Precipitation at a fixed location

While it is common to use the `Precipitation` class to simulate precipitation falling over an entire level, it is also possible to have precipitation at a fixed location. By setting the **followCam** property to `false`, the `Precipitation` object will remain at the location it is placed in the level and not follow the camera around. Using multiple `Precipitation` objects in this way is more costly to process compared to the default method of using the class.

Modifying precipitation over time

The `Precipitation` class has a couple of TorqueScript methods that may be used on the server to modify the intensity of a storm. The first is the `modifyStorm()` method, which has the following form:

```
Precipitation.modifyStorm( percentage, seconds );
```

In this method, the `percentage` parameter is the new percentage of `numDrops` property of the `Precipitation` object expressed as a range of 0 to 1; and the `seconds` parameter is the length of time over which to make the change. Passing in a `seconds` parameter value of 0, causes the change in the `numDrops` property to occur instantly.

The second method is `setTurbulence()`, which is as follows:

```
Precipitation.setTurbulence( max, speed, seconds );
```

In this method, the `max` parameter is the new `maxTurbulence` value of the `Precipitation` object, the `speed` parameter is the new `turbulenceSpeed` value, and the `seconds` parameter is the length of time over which to make the change. Setting the `max` parameter to 0 disables all turbulence.

Turbulence causes drops of a `Precipitation` object to spiral as they fall. The `maxTurbulence` property is the radius at which the drop spirals, while the `turbulenceSpeed` property controls how fast the drops spirals. Rain usually doesn't make use of turbulence, whereas gently falling snowflakes may spiral as they come down.

In order for the turbulence properties to have an effect, `useTurbulence` property of the `Precipitation` object must be set to `true`.

Global control of Precipitation drop density

The `$pref::precipitationDensity` TorqueScript global variable controls the density of all `Precipitation` objects. It ranges from 0 to 1, and its default value is 1. This global variable may be used to adjust the amount of precipitation to account for a user's computer processing power, for example.

See also

▶ *Using the Lightning object to automatically create a thunderstorm*

Using the Lightning object to automatically create a thunderstorm

With or without precipitation (please see the *How to make it rain using a Precipitation object* recipe) Torque 3D allows us to create a thunder storm with lighting in our game's level.

In this recipe, we will learn how to set up automatic lightning strikes, along with strikes at specific locations. Who says lightning never strikes twice!

Getting ready

We will be using a project based on the Torque 3D's `FPS Tutorial` template using the `China Town Mist` level. If you haven't already, use the Torque Project Manager (`Project Manager.exe`) to create a new project from the `FPS Tutorial` template. It can be found under the `My Projects` directory. Then start our new `FPS Tutorial` template game and load the `China Town Mist` level.

In order to help with the ambience, you may first want to apply the rain effects from the *How to make it rain using a Precipitation object* recipe.

How to do it...

In the following steps, we will add a `Lightning` object to the level to cause a thunderstorm:

1. Press *F11* to open the *World Editor*. As we want to work with objects in the scene, the *Object Editor* should be selected (by pressing *F1* or by using the **Editors** menu).
2. Go to the **Library** tab of the *Object Editor*.
3. Click on the **Level** tab.
4. Double-click on the **Environment** folder.
5. Double-click on the **Lightning** item to add a new one to the scene—this will open the **Create Object: Lightning** dialog window.
6. In the dialog's **Object Name** field enter `Storm`.

7. Click on **Data block** drop-down menu of the dialog box, and select the **DefaultStorm** `Datablock` option as shown in the next screenshot:

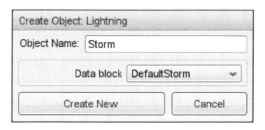

8. Click on **Create New** button of the dialog box to create the new `Lightning` object instance and add it to the scene.

9. Using the axis gizmo, drag our new `Storm` object to somewhere within the China Town courtyard, in order to center it within the level's geometry.

10. The width of the default lightning bolts is too large, especially when a bolt strikes nearby. Using the **Inspector** window on the right-hand side, set **strikeWidth** property of the `Storm` object to be `1`.

The remaining default settings provide a continuous thunderstorm with lightning striking all around the level, as shown in the following screenshot:

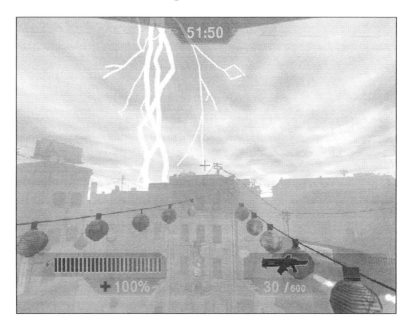

How it works...

The `Lightning` class creates lightning strikes within its boundaries, and plays a thunder sound effect during each strike. The `LightningData` `Datablock` instance defines the thunder sounds to be used, as well as any textures for the lightning. In this example, we are using the standard `DefaultStorm` `Datablock` instance, and the sound profiles it is pointing to; these are found in `art/datablocks/environment.cs`:

```
// ----------------------------------------------------------
// Lightning
// ----------------------------------------------------------

// When setting up thunder sounds for lightning it should be
// known that:
// - strikeSound is a 3d sound
// - thunderSounds[n] are 2d sounds

datablock SFXProfile(ThunderCrash1Sound)
{
   filename = "art/sound/environment/thunder1";
   description = Audio2d;
};

datablock SFXProfile(ThunderCrash2Sound)
{
   filename = "art/sound/environment/thunder2";
   description = Audio2d;
};

datablock SFXProfile(ThunderCrash3Sound)
{
   filename = "art/sound/environment/thunder3";
   description = Audio2d;
};

datablock SFXProfile(ThunderCrash4Sound)
{
   filename = "art/sound/environment/thunder4";
   description = Audio2d;
};


datablock LightningData(DefaultStorm)
{
   thunderSounds[0]  = ThunderCrash1Sound;
   thunderSounds[1]  = ThunderCrash2Sound;
   thunderSounds[2]  = ThunderCrash3Sound;
   thunderSounds[3]  = ThunderCrash4Sound;
};
```

The thunderSounds array property on a LightningData Datablock instance can define up to eight 2D sound effect profiles that are chosen at random for each lightning strike. The LightningData Datablock instance also supports the strikeSound property, which points to a 3D sound profile that is played when the lightning strikes and damages an object. The strikeSound property is not defined by the DefaultStorm Datablock.

The lightning strikes may either be untextured (rendered in the color property of the Lightning class instance) or covered in a texture. The strikeTextures array property of LightningData object defines up to eight image files that are randomly chosen for each strike. This lightning texture is stretched across the surface of the individual segments of the lightning bolts, and is not defined by the DefaultStorm Datablock instance.

When our Lightning class object is added to the level, it automatically starts to produce lightning strikes. The strikesPerMinute controls how often these strikes occur, which defaults to 12 per minute. These strikes occur randomly within the bounds of the Lightning object, and the width of the primary lightning bolt is set with the strikeWidth property. The color of the bolts is defined by the color property (which blends with any texture as defined in the Datablock class).

Following a strike, a lightning bolt begins to fade. Before the bolt fades completely, it transitions to the color defined by the fadeColor property. This allows the lightning bolt to fade, for example, from white to blue.

There's more...

Let's continue our discussion of the Lightning class.

Striking a player or vehicle

When a lightning bolt strikes, there is a chance that it will damage a player or a vehicle. The radius around the lightning bolt that is searched is defined by strikeRadius property of the Lightning class. If a player or vehicle is found within that radius, then it is checked for a hit. The chanceToHitTarget property, which ranges from 0 to 1, determines the chance that the object will be damaged. If more than one object is to be damaged by a lightning bolt, then only the object closest to the sky will actually be damaged.

When an object is damaged a callback is made on the Lightning object itself. This callback is as follows:

```
Lightning::applyDamage( this, hitPosition, hitNormal,
                        hitObject )
```

Here, the this parameter points back to the Lightning object in the scene, the hitPosition parameter is where the object has been hit in world space, the hitNormal parameter is the normal of the hit point (which always points up), and the hitObject parameter is SceneObject that has been hit. It is then up to the callback to determine what to do with the hit object.

Manual lightning strikes

The `Lightning` class allows us to manually trigger lightning strikes on all clients from the server. Often, this is used when `strikesPerMinute` property of a `Lightning` object is set to `0` (disabling automatic strikes) but it can also be used to supplement the automated lightning bolts at any time. The method to manually trigger strikes is as follows:

```
Lightning.strikeRandomPoint();
```

Internally, this is the exact same method used each time an automated strike is triggered and has the same effects, including the possibility of damaging players and vehicles.

The `Lightning` class also has a method to manually trigger lightning strikes that won't damage objects, which is as follows:

```
Lightning.warningFlashes();
```

Unfortunately, while it does produce lightning bolts and sounds, it doesn't correctly choose random lightning bolt locations. All the lightning bolts end up in the same place. This will be corrected in the next version of Torque 3D.

See also

▶ *How to make it rain using a Precipitation object*

Using the TimeOfDay object to generate events

Torque 3D allows us to set up an automatic day/night cycle for our game's level, which will control either a `Sun` instance or position of the sun in the sky of a `ScatterSky` object. We may also create events that are triggered at specific times of the day.

In this recipe, we will set up a `TimeOfDay` object and use it to control the sun and lighting of a `ScatterSky` object, as well as trigger an event at a particular time.

Getting ready

We will be using a project based on the Torque 3D's `Full` template using the `Empty Terrain` level. If you haven't already, use the Torque Project Manager (`Project Manager.exe`) to create a new project from the `Full` template. It can be found under the `My Projects` directory. Subsequently, start our new `Full` template game and load the `Empty Terrain` level.

How to do it...

In the following steps, we will add a `TimeOfDay` object to the level and have some events be triggered by it:

1. Press *F11* to open the *World Editor*. As we want to work with objects in the scene, the *Object Editor* should be selected (by pressing *F1* or by using the **Editors** menu).

2. Go to the **Library** tab of the *Object Editor*.

3. Click on the **Level** tab.

4. Double-click on the **Level** folder.

5. Double-click on the **Time of Day** item in the list to add the class to the scene—this will open the **Create Object: TimeOfDay** dialog window.

6. In **Object Name** field of the dialog box enter `DayCycle`, as shown in the following screenshot:

7. Click on the **Create New** button of the dialog box to create the new `TimeOfDay` object instance, and add it to the scene.

8. The `ScatterSky` object, which is already in the scene, will automatically pick up on the new `TimeOfDay` instance and transition the scene to night. Over the course of two minutes the sky will go to day and back to night. The sun will traverse the sky.

9. We will now create the object that will be manipulated by the `TimeOfDay` events, which we will set up later. Go to the **Library** tab of the Object Editor.

10. Click on the **Level** tab.

11. Double-click on the **Environment** folder.

12. Double-click on the **Precipitation** item to add a new one to the scene—this will open the **Create Object: Precipitation** dialog window.

13. In **Object Name** field of the dialog box enter `Rain`.

14. Click on **Precipitation data** drop-down menu of the dialog box, and select the **HeavyRain** `Datablock` instance, as shown in the following screenshot:

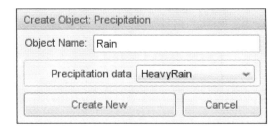

15. Click on the **Create New** button of the dialog box to create the new `Precipitation` object instance and add it to the scene.

16. See the *How to make rain using a Precipitation object* recipe for setting up the rest of the `Rain` object. In order to make it look nice, also add the shader referenced in that recipe, and put a check mark in the **useLighting** property.

17. Save the level from the **File** menu and quit Torque 3D.

18. Open `scripts/server/gameCore.cs` in a text editor such as Torsion and add the following TorqueScript code to the `GameCore::onMissionLoaded()` method:

```
function GameCore::onMissionLoaded(%game)
{
   //echo (%game @"\c4 -> "@ %game.class @
   //      " -> GameCore::onMissionLoaded");

   //set up the game and game variables
   %game.initGameVars(%game);

   $Game::Duration = %game.duration;
   $Game::EndGameScore = %game.endgameScore;
   $Game::EndGamePause = %game.endgamePause;

   if(isObject(Rain))
   {
      // Stop rain from falling when the mission first starts
      // up. Time of Day events will trigger the rain.
      Rain.modifyStorm(0, 0);
   }

   if(isObject(DayCycle))
   {
      // Set up our two time of day events to start and stop
      // the rain. These are given in a normalized sun
      // elevation where 0=sunrise, 90=zenith, 180=sunset,
      // 270=nadir, all in degrees.
```

```
        // This event happens at sunrise. This will start the
        // rain. The second parameter is the ID of this event.
        DayCycle.addTimeOfDayEvent(0.0, 1);

        // This event happens half-way between sunrise and noon.
        //  This will stop the rain.
        DayCycle.addTimeOfDayEvent(45.0, 2);
    }

    physicsStartSimulation("server");
    %game.startGame();
}
```

19. At the end of the same file, add the following method:

```
// This method is called for every time of day event
function DayCycle::onTimeEvent
        (%this, %id, %currentTime,
        %currentElevation)
{
    // Determine what to do based on the event's ID
    switch(%id)
    {
        case 1:
            // Start the rain. We will ramp up to full
            // in 5 seconds.
            echo("Here comes the rain!");
            Rain.modifyStorm(1.0, 5.0);

        case 2:
            // Stop the rain. We will slowly turn off the
            // shower over 15 seconds.
            echo("Rain shower is over.");
            Rain.modifyStorm(0.0, 15.0);
    }
}
```

20. Save the file.

21. Start our `Full` template again and load the `Empty Terrain` level. Wait through a full day/night cycle, wherein there will be a morning rain that will taper off before noon:

How it works...

The `TimeOfDay` class may be added to any level where we wish to control the apparent time of day. Two other classes may be used (although, not at the same time) to change a level's lighting, according to the time of day: `Sun` and `ScatterSky`.

In our example, we make use of the `ScatterSky` object that is already a part of `Empty Terrain` level of the `Full` template. It not only moves the sun, but also adjusts colors of the sky according to the time of day. All of this happens internally, and there is nothing more we need to set up.

There are three properties that control how long a day is. The `dayLength` property of `TimeOfDay` class is the number of real-time seconds an entire day lasts. By default this is set to `120` seconds. The `dayScale` and `nightScale` properties control the relative lengths of the day and night over the virtual 24-hour period. This allows us to have a longer day than night to simulate summer time, for example. By default, `dayScale` is `1.0`, while `nightScale` is `1.5`. This means that the night goes by 50 percent faster than the day.

Moving to the TorqueScript changes in our example, we modified the `GameCore::onMissionLoaded()` method, which is called after the level has loaded. Our first new code block immediately turns off precipitation of our `Rain` object using the `modifyStorm()` method. We disable the precipitation because we want to control it from the timed events. Please see the *How to make it rain using a Precipitation object* recipe for more information about controlling the amount of precipitation.

The second code block, which we have added, creates two events on our `DayCycle` object—one at sunrise and one half-way until noon. The method we use to add events is as follows:

```
TimeOfDay.addTimeOfDayEvent( elevation, id );
```

In this method, `elevation` is the normalized sun elevation (rather than the actual sun elevation) at which to trigger the event, with a range of 0 to 360, and `id` is a unique identifier for this event. In our example, we create one event at 0 degrees and the other event at 45 degrees, or half-way between sunrise and noon.

Finally, we have created the time of day event callback itself for our `DayCycle` object. This method is called each time the sun reaches an elevation that matches a defined event. This callback is passed through the event's unique identifier, the time of the event (with a range of 0 to 1), and the elevation of the event (with a range of 0 to 360). In our example, we either start or stop the rainstorm according to the ID passed to the callback.

There's more...

Let's continue our discussion of the `TimeOfDay` object and its interaction with other objects.

Setting up the ScatterSky class for night

The `ScatterSky` class supports an optional night sky cube map that may be used with a `TimeOfDay` object. In order to use the cube map instead of the colored sky, set the `useNightCubemap` property to `true`, and pass-in a cube map material to the `nightCubemap` property, such as the `nightCubemap` material.

The `ScatterSky` class also supports an optional moon object, which may be displayed in the sky. In order to activate the moon, set the `moonEnabled` property to `true`, and the `moonMat` property to a material such as `Moon_Glow_Mat`. Activating the moon does not activate the night sky cube map, and they may be used independently. The actual location of the moon in the sky is controlled by the `moonAzimuth` and `moonElevation` properties of `ScatterSky` class, and its size in the sky is controlled by the `moonScale` property.

Manually modifying the time of day

In this recipe, we made use of the automatic change of the time of day. However, it is also possible to manually control the time of day from TorqueScript. In order to do so, we'll either want to first set the `play` property of our `DayCycle` object to `false`, or call its `setPlay()` method with a value of `false`.

With the automated time of day now disabled, we may use one of two server-side methods to manually set the time. The first method is as follows:

```
TimeOfDay.setTimeOfDay( time );
```

In this method, the `time` parameter is the time of day with a range of `0.0` to `1.0`. A value of `0` is sunrise and `0.5` is sunset. Using this method causes the time and sun to immediately change.

The second method allows us to adjust the time of day over a number of real-time seconds:

```
TimeOfDay.animate( elevation, degreesPerSecond );
```

In this method, the `elevation` parameter is the normalized elevation of the sun in the sky with a range of `0` to `360` degrees, and the `degreesPerSecond` parameter is how fast, in real time, the game time should change. This method allows us to smoothly change from one time to another.

When using the `animate()` method, the `onAnimateStart()` callback is called when the sun first starts to animate, and the `onAnimateDone()` callback is called when the sun reaches its destination. These callbacks are as follows:

```
TimeOfDay::onAnimateStart( this )
TimeOfDay::onAnimateDone( this )
```

Here, the `this` parameter points back to the `TimeOfDay` object in the scene. No other parameters are passed into these callbacks.

See also

 ▸ *How to make it rain using a Precipitation object*

8
Multiplayer Servers

In this chapter, we will cover the following topics:

- ▸ How to start a dedicated server
- ▸ What ports are needed to be open or forwarded for a multiplayer server
- ▸ Passing arbitrary parameters from the client to the server
- ▸ How to become an admin on a server
- ▸ Kicking and banning people from the server
- ▸ Stopping a server from restarting when the last player leaves
- ▸ Accessing the server connection from the client
- ▸ How to access all client connections from the server
- ▸ Broadcasting a message to all clients and having it displayed in the center of the screen

Introduction

Torque 3D is inherently a multiplayer game engine and its networking code is known to be one of the best in the industry. This multiplayer heritage even comes through while making a single player game. Behind the scenes there is still a client and a server, although there are shortcuts in place so no actual external networking takes place.

When setting up a multiplayer game, we need to make it available to the outside world. We also need to be able to manage the players that connect to our game server. In this chapter, we will discover how to start and allow others to connect to our game server, as well as how to administer it.

How to start a dedicated server

A Torque 3D multiplayer game may be started in one of three modes—client only (requires a server to play a game), dedicated server (clients connect to it to play a game), and client/server combined (also used in single player games). In this recipe, we will learn how to start a Torque 3D game as a dedicated server and allow a client to connect.

Getting ready

We will be using a project based on the Torque 3D's `Full` template, using the `Empty Terrain` level. If you haven't already, use the Torque Project Manager (`Project Manager.exe`) to create a new project from the `Full` template. Give this project a name of `MyGame`; it will be found under the `My Projects` directory.

How to do it...

In the following steps, we will demonstrate how to start a Torque 3D game as a dedicated server:

1. Start a Windows command prompt. You can find it by going to the Windows **Start** menu and choosing **All Programs | Accessories | Command Prompt**.

2. Using the command prompt, change to the directory that contains our game's executable `MyGame.exe`. This path should be: `My Projects/MyGame/game/`.

3. Start the dedicated server by entering the following at the command prompt:

   MyGame.exe -dedicated -mission "levels/Empty Terrain.mis"

4. The server is now ready and waiting for the first client to connect:

How it works...

Passing the -dedicated command-line parameter to the executable causes it to start without any graphics or sound. Without an interface to choose the level to load, we also need to include the -mission command-line parameter. This parameter is of the following form, where the <mission path> parameter is the relative path to the level to load:

```
-mission <mission path>
```

If there are any spaces in the mission's path, then it must be surrounded by quotes.

Once the game server has started and loaded the level, it will attempt to connect to the master server and wait for the first client to connect.

There's more...

Let's continue our discussion of dedicated servers.

The -game parameter

The optional -game parameter is used to pass along a mod directory to use with the game. A mod directory contains a main.cs file, which executes other TorqueScript files as necessary, and provides custom functionality for a game.

Often, the -game parameter is used to allow the players to modify a game's functionality when running their own server, but we can also use it to change the game at startup.

The -level parameter

We don't want to confuse the -level parameter with the -mission parameter we used in this recipe. The -level parameter is used by single player games to automatically start the game with a particular mission without having to go through the main menu screen. The loadMainMenu() function in scripts/client/init.cs makes use of the mission path passed using the -level parameter.

Shutting down a dedicated server

To cleanly shut down a dedicated game server, we enter the following command at the server's command prompt:

```
% quit();
```

The quit() function disconnects any users, deletes all of the level's objects, and exports any server preferences.

See also

▸ *What ports are needed to be open or forwarded for a multiplayer server*

What ports are needed to be open or forwarded for a multiplayer server

When running a multiplayer game server (either dedicated or hosting as a client/server), we need to ensure that clients can connect as they may be blocked by a router on the network. This requires knowing which network ports should be open, or forwarded to the server.

In this recipe, we will learn which ports Torque 3D uses by default, and how to change them to suit your game.

How to do it...

On your router, forward or open UDP ports `28000` through `28009` to your game server. This is required for both a dedicated server as well as a Torque 3D client hosting a game.

How it works...

Torque 3D uses UDP to communicate between the server and connected clients. When the server starts, one of its first tasks is to bind to a UDP port and listen for packets. The UDP port used is defined by the `$Pref::Server::Port` global variable as set in `core/scripts/server/defaults.cs`, and defaults to `28000`.

However, it is possible that this port has already been taken by another program on the computer. Rather than fail, Torque 3D goes through a range of ports. The `portInit()` function in `scripts/server/server.cs` as called during `createServer()` tries ten ports in order, for a default range of `28000` to `28009`. If none of these ports end up being free, then the server's network connection will finally fail.

When it comes to making sure that your Torque 3D game server can reach out to the Internet, you'll need to ensure that UDP ports `28000` to `28009` are either being forwarded to your server, or otherwise made available.

There's more...

Let's continue our discussion about Torque 3D UDP ports.

Changing the port used by the game server

While the Torque 3D default UDP port is `28000`, it is possible to have it use a different port. In order to change the port used, modify the `$Pref::Server::Port` global variable in `core/scripts/server/defaults.cs`.

However, as the port is stored in a preference variable, it may be cached between launches of the game server. In order to ensure that any changes to the `defaults.cs` file are made, be sure to also run the `DeletePrefs.bat` file by double-clicking on it—this will delete all preferences, and allow the defaults to again take effect.

Master server considerations

When a Torque 3D game is set to host the game (or it is running as a dedicated server), it attempts to contact a **master server** to pass along information about the game. The master server keeps a list of all the available game servers, and passes this information onto any client that requests for it. This allows a client to connect to a game server without needing to know its IP address ahead of time.

By default, the master server is defined by the `$Pref::Master[0]` global variable and is set to:

```
$pref::Master[0] = "2:master.garagegames.com:28002";
```

This is the GarageGames' master server, and should only be used for testing our game. When it comes to releasing a multiplayer game, we should set up our own master server. There are a number of different master servers available in the **Resources** section of the GarageGames website.

The previous default setup uses UDP port `28002` to communicate with the master server. We will need to make sure that our game server is allowed to send outbound traffic over this port from our network.

The `$Pref::Master` global variable is actually an array and we may set up more than one master server, in case one of them goes offline. When more than one master server is defined, a Torque 3D game server will attempt to communicate with all of them by sending its **heartbeat** information. For example, we could define three possible master servers in the following format:

```
$pref::Master[0] = "2:master1.mygame.com:28002";
$pref::Master[1] = "2:master2.mygame.com:28002";
$pref::Master[2] = "2:master3.mygame.com:28002";
```

Each master server could have its own custom port to communicate over. In that case, we would need to make sure that the Torque 3D game server may send outbound UDP traffic to each of them.

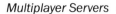

In addition to defining the name (or IP address) and port for each master server, the $Pref::Master global array also defines a region to search within. In our previous examples, this is the 2: field just before the server name, where 2 is the region number. Most games do not make use of the region number and just use the default value of 2, which is defined by the $Pref::Server::RegionMask global variable.

If we did define master servers in different regions, then we may use the $Pref::Server::RegionMask global variable to limit our broadcast to only those regions. A region could be anything we want it to be, such as a geographical region, to keep players within the same region playing on the same Torque 3D game servers.

Playing over a LAN

In addition to playing multiplayer games over the Internet, Torque 3D allows for games over the local area network (LAN). When searching for LAN games, Torque 3D uses the $Pref::Net::Port global variable to broadcast over (no IP address is used as the request goes over the whole LAN subnet). The default port number is 28000, and needs to match the port number that the game server uses.

Passing arbitrary parameters from the client to the server

Sometimes, a game client needs to pass along information to the server when it connects. This information could be the player's name, or what the player looks like.

In this recipe, we will learn how to send any data we require from the client to the server when the client first connects.

Getting ready

We will be making TorqueScript changes in a project based on the Torque 3D's Full template, using the Empty Terrain level. If you haven't already, use the Torque Project Manager (Project Manager.exe) to create a new project from the Full template; it can be found under the My Projects directory. After that, start your favorite script editor, such as Torsion, and let's get going!

How to do it...

In the following steps, we will pass some game-specific parameters from the client to the server when the client first connects:

1. Open the `scripts/client/game.cs` file in your text editor, add the following code to the top of the file, and save it:

```
$Player::ServerParam1 = 100;
$Player::ServerParam2 = "Red";
$Player::ServerParam3 = $Player::ServerParam1 + 10;
```

2. Open the `core/scripts/server/server.cs` file and change the following line within the `createAndConnectToLocalServer()` function—be sure to save the file:

```
function createAndConnectToLocalServer
        ( %serverType, %level )
{
  if( !createServer( %serverType, %level ) )
    return false;

  %conn = new GameConnection( ServerConnection );
  RootGroup.add( ServerConnection );

  %conn.setConnectArgs( $pref::Player::Name,
                        $Player::ServerParam1,
                        $Player::ServerParam2,
                        $Player::ServerParam3 );

  %conn.setJoinPassword( $Client::Password );

  %result = %conn.connectLocal();
  if( %result !$= "" )
  {
      %conn.delete();
      destroyServer();

      return false;
  }

  return true;
}
```

3. Open the `core/scripts/client/missionDownload.cs` file, change the following line within the `connect()` function, and then save the file:

```
function connect(%server)
{
   %conn = new GameConnection(ServerConnection);
   RootGroup.add(ServerConnection);
   %conn.setConnectArgs($pref::Player::Name,
                        $Player::ServerParam1,
                        $Player::ServerParam2,
                        $Player::ServerParam3);

   %conn.setJoinPassword($Client::Password);
   %conn.connect(%server);
}
```

4. Open the `art/gui/joinServerDlg.gui` file and change the following line within the `join()` method. Save the file after you have made the change.

```
function JoinServerDlg::join(%this)
{
   cancelServerQuery();
   %index = JS_serverList.getSelectedId();

   // The server info index is stored in the row along with the
   // rest of displayed info.

   if( setServerInfo( %index ) )
   {
     Canvas.setContent("LoadingGui");
     LoadingProgress.setValue(1);
     LoadingProgressTxt.setValue
            ("WAITING FOR SERVER");
     Canvas.repaint();

     %conn = new GameConnection(ServerConnection);
     %conn.setConnectArgs($pref::Player::Name,
                          $Player::ServerParam1,
                          $Player::ServerParam2,
                          $Player::ServerParam3);

     %conn.setJoinPassword($Client::Password);
     %conn.connect($ServerInfo::Address);
   }
}
```

5. Open the `scripts/server/gameCore.cs` file and make the following changes; save the file when done:

```
function GameConnection::onConnect(%client,
          %name, %param1, %param2, %param3)

{
  // Send down the connection error info, the client
  // is responsible for displaying this message if a
  // connection error occurs.
  messageClient(%client, 'MsgConnectionError',"
                ",$Pref::Server::ConnectionError);

  // Send mission information to the client
  sendLoadInfoToClient(%client);

  // Simulated client lag for testing...
  // %client.setSimulatedNetParams(0.1, 30);

  // Get the client's unique id:
  // %authInfo = %client.getAuthInfo();
  // %client.guid = getField(%authInfo, 3);
  %client.guid = 0;
  addToServerGuidList(%client.guid);

  // Set admin status
  if (%client.getAddress() $= "local")
  {
    %client.isAdmin = true;
    %client.isSuperAdmin = true;
  }
  else
  {
    %client.isAdmin = false;
    %client.isSuperAdmin = false;
  }

  // Save client preferences on the connection object for
  // later use.
  %client.gender = "Male";
  %client.armor = "Light";
  %client.race = "Human";
  %client.setPlayerName(%name);
  %client.team = "";
  %client.score = 0;
```

```
    %client.kills = 0;
    %client.deaths = 0;

    //
    echo("CADD: "@ %client @" "@ %client.getAddress());

    // Add our custom paramteres
    %client.param1 = %param1;
    %client.param2 = %param2;
    %client.param3 = %param3;
    echo("  p1: " @ %client.param1);
    echo("  p2: " @ %client.param2);
    echo("  p3: " @ %client.param3);


    // If the mission is running, go ahead download it to
    // the client
    if ($missionRunning)
    {
      client.loadMission();
    }
    else if ($Server::LoadFailMsg !$= "")
    {
      messageClient(%client, 'MsgLoadFailed',
                  $Server::LoadFailMsg);
    }
    $Server::PlayerCount++;
}
```

6. Start our `Full` template and load the `Empty Terrain` level.

7. Press the tilde (~) key to open the console. Scroll through the console until you find the client parameter output. These are the parameters that the server received from the (local) client:

```
Game -> activatePackages
*** Mission loaded
Connect request from:
Connection established 4282
CADD: 4283 local
  p1: 100
  p2: Red
  p3: 110
*** Sending mission load to client: levels/Empty Terrain.mis
Mapping string: ServerMessage to index: 0
```

How it works...

On the client side, we have defined the following three global variables:

```
$Player::ServerParam1 = 100;
$Player::ServerParam2 = "Red";
$Player::ServerParam3 = $Player::ServerParam1 + 10;
```

These variables represent information that the client wishes to pass along to the server. They could be options that the player has chosen, or could come from some other source (such as a separate client-side login system that includes a username and login token).

When the time comes to pass on these client-side parameters, we make use of the `GameConnection` class's `setConnectArgs()` method. This method has the following form:

```
GameConnection.setConnectArgs( p1, p2, p3, …, p16 );
```

In this method, `p1` through `p16` are the up to 16 possible parameters that are accepted. Searching through the Torque 3D TorqueScript files for the `Full` template, we will find that this method is already being called in three different locations. Each location is used depending on how we are connecting to a game server.

The first location we have modified is the `createAndConnectToLocalServer()` function in `core/scripts/server/server.cs`. This function is called when we start a Torque 3D game in either a single player mode, or when hosting a multiplayer game without using a dedicated server.

The second location we have modified is the `connect()` function in `core/scripts/client/missionDownload.cs`. This is a helper function that is used to connect directly with a game server when the server's IP address is known. It can be used to quickly connect to a known server by entering this command from the console, for example.

The third and final location we have modified is `JoinServerDlg::join()` method in `art/gui/joinServerDlg.gui`. This method is called when the user has chosen a game server to play on from the **Join Server** window.

In all three cases, we change the `GameConnection` object's `setConnectArgs()` method call to include our client-side parameters:

```
%conn.setConnectArgs($pref::Player::Name,
                     $Player::ServerParam1,
                     $Player::ServerParam2,
                     $Player::ServerParam3);
```

As you may see, a client-side parameter was already being sent to the server. The `$pref::Player::Name` global variable is set when the user modifies the **Player Name** field on the **Join Server** window, and is used on the server as the player's name above their head. We have added our three parameters to this method call for a total of four client-side parameters being sent to the server. The `setConnectArgs()` method allows up to 16 parameters to be set.

That takes care of the client side. On the server, these parameters are passed to the `GameConnection` object's `onConnect()` method. In this example, we have modified this method found in `scripts/server/gameCore.cs` to now read as the following:

```
function GameConnection::onConnect
             (%client, %name, %param1,
             %param2, %param3)
{
   ...
}
```

The `%name` parameter was already there and receives the value of the client-side `$pref::Player::Name` global variable. The `%param1`, `%param2`, and `%param3` parameters were added by us and receive each of our own client-side global variables. We may do whatever we want with the parameters. In our example, we just store them on the `GameConnection` as dynamic properties and print them out to the console. As with anything that comes from the client, it would likely be a good idea to validate their values and not accept them outright.

How to become an admin on a server

Torque 3D supports one or more players having special administrative powers on a multiplayer server. A Torque 3D game server doesn't define what these powers are by default, but does provide a framework we may use for our own games.

In this recipe, we will learn how to make a player an administrator and what this title means on the server.

Getting ready

We will be making TorqueScript changes in a project based on the Torque 3D's `Full` template using the `Empty Terrain` level. If you haven't already, use the Torque Project Manager (`Project Manager.exe`) to create a new project from the `Full` template. Give this project a name of `MyGame`. It will be found under the `My Projects` directory. After that, start your favorite script editor, such as Torsion, and let's get going!

How to do it...

In the following steps, we will allow a player to connect as an administrator to a dedicated server:

1. Open `core/scripts/server/defaults.cs`, and modify `$Pref::Server::AdminPassword` to have a custom password. Save the file after making this change:

   ```
   // If the password is set, clients must provide it in order
   // to connect to the server
   $Pref::Server::Password = "";

   // Password for admin clients
   $Pref::Server::AdminPassword = "MyPassword";

   // Misc server settings.
   $Pref::Server::MaxPlayers = 64;
   $Pref::Server::TimeLimit = 20;      // In minutes
   $Pref::Server::KickBanTime = 300;   // specified in seconds
   $Pref::Server::BanTime = 1800;      // specified in seconds
   $Pref::Server::FloodProtectionEnabled = 1;
   $Pref::Server::MaxChatLen = 120;
   ```

2. We need to delete any preferences that may have been saved if the game had been previously run. Double-click on the `My Projects/MyGame/DeletePrefs.bat` batch file to delete all preferences files.

3. Start a Windows command prompt. You can find it by going to the Windows **Start** menu, and choosing **All Programs** | **Accessories** | **Command Prompt**.

4. Using the command prompt, change to the directory that contains our game's executable `MyGame.exe`. This path should be: `My Projects/MyGame/game/`.

5. Start a dedicated server by entering the following command at the command prompt:

   MyGame.exe -dedicated -mission "levels/Empty Terrain.mis"

6. The server is now ready and waiting for the first client to connect.

7. Now start our game's GUI by double-clicking on the `My Projects/MyGame/game/MyGame` icon.

8. Click on the **Join** button to open the **Join Server** window.

9. Click on the **Query LAN** button to search for local game servers. One server should be found—this will be our dedicated server.

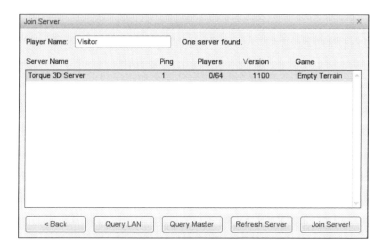

10. Select the server in the list and click on the **Join Server!** button to connect with the game server.

11. Once the game has loaded, press the tilde (~) key to open the console. Enter the following command at the bottom of the screen and press *Enter*:

    ```
    SAD("MyPassword");
    ```

12. Close the console with the tilde (~) key. At the top of the screen in the chat area, we will find that we have become an admin (**Visitor** is the default name if we don't modify it from the **Join Server** window before connecting):

> Ryder selected.
> Lurker Grenade Launcher selected.
> Lurker selected.
> Visitor has become Admin by force.

How it works...

When a client connects to a game server, it is determined if they are an administrator or not. This is done within the GameConnection::onConnect() method found in scripts/server/gameCore.cs. A player is automatically made an administrator only if they are the one hosting the game.

In order to become an administrator remotely, we must first define the administrator password. By default this is blank, which doesn't allow for any remote administrators. In this recipe, we set our administrator password to be MyPassword. Now any client that knows our password may become an administrator.

In order to become a remote administrator, a client uses the `SAD()` function found in `scripts/client/client.cs`, which has the following form:

```
SAD( password );
```

In this function, the `password` parameter is the administrator password that is sent to the server. The easiest way of issuing this command is through the console. If you have disabled the console for your game, then you will need to provide some other way for the player to become an administrator (such as with a custom GUI). In this recipe, we just use the console. When a player becomes an administrator, all other players are notified in the chat box.

Becoming an administrator doesn't confer any real abilities to the player, by default. It is up to your game to define the powers that an administrator should have. Some examples are helping players that are stuck on world geometry, kicking or banning players, and manually changing the game level being played.

There's more...

Let's continue our discussion of game server administrators.

Different types of administrators

When a player becomes a game server administrator their `GameConnection` object's `isAdmin` and `isSuperAdmin` properties are set to `true`. This implies that there are two different types of game administrators available in Torque 3D; although in practice all administrators are set to both types by default.

If we wanted to have our game support two distinct administrator types, we could require that two different commands need to be issued to the server. The first step is to define a separate password for the super admin by adding the following line to `core/scripts/server/defaults.cs`:

```
$Pref::Server::SuperAdminPassword = "MySuperPassword";
```

After making this change, we should run `My Projects/MyGame/DeletePrefs.bat` to make sure we will overwrite any previous settings.

The next step is to remove the `isSuperAdmin` property from being set to `true` for a regular administrator player. Modify the `serverCmdSAD()` function in `core/scripts/server/commands.cs` to comment out the `isSuperAdmin` property for the `GameConnection`:

```
function serverCmdSAD( %client, %password )
{
  if( %password !$= "" &&
      %password $= $Pref::Server::AdminPassword)
  {
    %client.isAdmin = true;
```

```
    // %client.isSuperAdmin = true;

    %name = getTaggedString( %client.playerName );
    MessageAll( 'MsgAdminForce', "\c2" @ %name @
        " has become Admin by force.", %client );
    }
}
```

Just underneath this function, we will add a new function that will be called when the player attempts to become a super administrator:

```
function serverCmdSSAD( %client, %password )
{
  if( %password !$= "" &&
      %password $= $Pref::Server::SuperAdminPassword)
  {
    // Super admins are also regular admins
    %client.isAdmin = true;
    %client.isSuperAdmin = true;
    %name = getTaggedString( %client.playerName );
    MessageAll( 'MsgAdminForce', "\c2" @ %name @
        " has become Super Admin by force.", %client );
  }
}
```

Finally, we need to add the function to the client to attempt to become a super administrator. In `scripts/client/client.cs`, add the following code just underneath the existing `SAD()` function:

```
// Attempt to become a super admin
function SSAD(%password)
{
  if (%password !$= "")
    commandToServer('SSAD', %password);
}
```

Now when connected to a multiplayer server as a client, we would enter the following command in the console, to become a super administrator:

SSAD("MySuperPassword");

Currently in Torque 3D, the only ability that a super administrator has over a regular administrator is they may set the admin password by issuing the `SADSetPassword()` function as defined in `scripts/client/client.cs`. Any other special super administrator abilities would have to be defined by our own game.

Administrator password is server wide

We need to keep in mind that the administrator password is for the whole server. Anyone that knows this password could become an administrator. If one of our administrators passes along this password to another player, there is not a lot that could be done about it other than changing the server's password.

A more complete system would be to have administrator access tied to user accounts. This allows for some accountability (a log could be kept of what each administrator does) and puts the password on each user account rather than on the whole server. The implementation of such a system is beyond the scope this recipe, but it should be kept in mind when creating a feature-rich, public game server.

Kicking and banning people from the server

Sometimes a player in our multiplayer game doesn't play by the rules, and hence, needs to be temporarily kicked from the game. Sometimes, a player may do this repeatedly and needs to be banned from the game.

In this recipe, we will learn how to kick or ban a player from our game's server.

Getting ready

We will be using a project based on the Torque 3D's `Full` template using the `Empty Terrain` level. If you haven't already, use the Torque Project Manager (`Project Manager.exe`) to create a new project from the `Full` template. Give this project a name of `MyGame`; it will be found under the `My Projects` directory.

How to do it...

In the following steps, we will demonstrate how to kick a player from a game server:

1. Start a Windows command prompt. You can find it by going to the Windows **Start** menu, and choosing **All Programs | Accessories | Command Prompt**.

2. Using the command prompt, change to the directory that contains our game's executable `MyGame.exe`. This path should be: `My Projects/MyGame/game/`.

3. Start a dedicated server by entering the following command at the command prompt:

   MyGame.exe -dedicated -mission "levels/Empty Terrain.mis"

4. The server is now ready and waiting for the first client to connect.

5. Now start our game's GUI by double-clicking on the `My Projects/MyGame/game/MyGame` icon.

6. Click on the **Join** button to open the **Join Server** window.

7. Click on the **Query LAN** button to search for local game servers. One server, which will be our dedicated server, should be found:

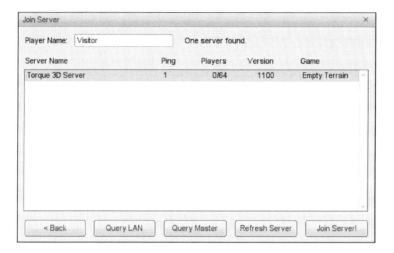

8. Select the server in the list, and click on the **Join Server!** button to connect with the game server. Allow the game to load.

9. Go back to the dedicated server window, enter the following command at the window's command prompt and press *Enter*:

```
% foreach(%c in ClientGroup)
        {echo(%c.getId() SPC
        getTaggedString(%c.playerName));}
```

10. A number followed by the player's name will be displayed in the dedicated server window. In our example, the `GameConnection` ID is `1888` and the player's name is `Visitor`. In order to kick this player off of the server, enter the following command into the dedicated server's command prompt, and press *Enter*:

    ```
    % kick(1888);
    ```

11. The connected client will immediately be disconnected from the dedicated server and the player will receive the following message:

How it works...

Torque 3D supports two methods of disconnecting a player from a game server—a kick and a ban. The difference between these two methods is the length of time until the disconnected player is allowed to join the game again. The kick and ban times are defined by global variables as defined in `core/scripts/server/defaults.cs`:

```
$Pref::Server::KickBanTime = 300; // specified in seconds
$Pref::Server::BanTime = 1800;    // specified in seconds
```

In order to kick a player from a server, we issue the following command from the server's console:

```
kick( clientID );
```

In this command, the `clientID` parameter is the `SimObject` ID of the player's connection object. A kicked player is not allowed to rejoin the game for five minutes by default. In order to ban a player from a server, we issue the following command:

```
ban( clientID );
```

In this command, the `clientID` parameter is also the `SimObject` ID of the player's connection object. A banned player is not allowed to rejoin a game for 30 minutes, by default.

Unfortunately, tracking down a player's `GameConnection` ID is not obvious as this is only known by the server. It is more likely that we know the player's name. In order to get a list of player names and connection IDs, we wrote a quick TorqueScript command on the server:

```
foreach(%c in ClientGroup){
        echo(%c.getId() SPC getTaggedString
        (%c.playerName));}
```

This produces a table of connection IDs followed by the player's names. The `getTaggedString()` function is used to retrieve the player's name as the `playerName` property is just an index into the networked string table.

When a player is either kicked or banned, their IP address is added to a list found in `scripts/server/banlist.cs`. For example, our kicking of the connected client added the following line to the `banlist.cs` file when the dedicated server was shut down:

```
BanList::addAbsolute(0, "IP:192.168.1.2:*", 1350335572);
```

When the server is started up again, the `banlist.cs` file is executed and any IP addresses that still have time remaining cannot connect to the game server until the time runs out.

There's more...

Let's extend the default kick and ban handling in Torque 3D.

Kicking or banning a player by name

Kicking or banning a player by their connection ID is not as handy as doing it by their name. Add the following two functions to the end of `core/scripts/server/kickban.cs`:

```
// Kick a player using their name
function kickByName(%name)
{
  foreach(%client in ClientGroup)
  {
    // Use nameBase here as playerName has some hidden color
    // codes added to it.
    if(%client.nameBase $= %name)
    {
      kick(%client.getId());
      return;
    }
  }
}

// Ban a player using their name
function banByName(%name)
```

```
{
  foreach(%client in ClientGroup)
  {
    // Use nameBase here as playerName has some hidden color
    // codes added to it.
    if(%client.nameBase $= %name)
    {
      ban(%client.getId());
      return;
    }
  }
}
```

Now, on the dedicated server we may issue the following command to kick our user rather than having to discover their GameConnection ID:

```
% kickByName("Visitor");
```

Remotely kicking or banning a player

So far, all of the kick and ban commands have been issued on the server itself. It would be handy to be able to kick or ban someone as a remote administrator player.

Begin by adding the two functions that kick or ban a player using their name as described earlier. Now, add the following code to the end of scripts/server/commands.cs:

```
// Called by client to kick a player by name
function serverCmdKickByName(%client, %name)
{
  // Make sure that the request has come from an admin
  if(!%client.isAdmin)
    return;

  // Kick the player by their name
  kickByName(%name);
}

// Called by client to ban a player by name
function serverCmdBanByName(%client, %name)
{
  // Make sure that the request has come from an admin
  if(!%client.isAdmin)
    return;

  // Ban the player by their name
  banByName(%name);
}
```

These two functions may be called by the client over the network to kick or ban a player by name. They first ensure that the player is an admin before allowing their request.

We will add the following functions on the client side to call the preceding code in `scripts/client/client.cs`:

```
// Kick a player by their name
// (Admin only)
function kickPlayer(%name)
{
   commandToServer('KickByName', %name);
}

// Ban a player by their name
// (Admin only)
function banPlayer(%name)
{
   commandToServer('BanByName', %name);
}
```

With this code in place, and a player that has been set up as an administrator (see the *How to become an admin on a server* recipe), we may kick a player from the server by entering the following command into the client's console:

```
% kickPlayer("Visitor");
```

If the client issuing the command is not an administrator, then nothing will happen.

See also

▶   *How to become an admin on a server*

Stopping a server from restarting when the last player leaves

When the last player on a Torque 3D dedicated server disconnects, the server automatically restarts itself—this includes reloading the current level. However, we may want the server to remain in its current state, especially if it represents a persistent world.

In this recipe, we will learn how to stop a dedicated server from restarting when the last of its players leave.

Getting ready

We will be making TorqueScript changes in a project based on the Torque 3D's `Full` template using the `Empty Terrain` level. If you haven't already, use the Torque Project Manager (`Project Manager.exe`) to create a new project from the `Full` template. Give this project a name of `MyGame`; it will be found under the `My Projects` directory. After that, start your favorite script editor, such as Torsion, and let's get going!

How to do it...

In the following steps, we will prevent a game server from restarting itself when the last client disconnects from it.

1. Open `scripts/server/defaults.cs` and add the following global variable:

   ```
   // First we execute the core default preferences.
   exec( "core/scripts/server/defaults.cs" );

   // Now add your own game specific server preferences as
   // well as any overloaded core defaults here.
   $Pref::Server::RestartWhenEmpty = false;
   ```

2. Save the file.

3. We need to delete any preferences that may have been saved if the game had been previously run. Double-click the `My Projects/MyGame/DeletePrefs.bat` batch file to delete all preferences files.

4. Open `core/scripts/server/clientConnection.cs`, modify the `GameConnection` class' `onDrop()` method as follows, and then save the file:

   ```
   function GameConnection::onDrop(%client, %reason)
   {
     %client.onClientLeaveGame();

     removeFromServerGuidList( %client.guid );
     messageAllExcept(%client, -1, 'MsgClientDrop',
             '\c1%1 has left the game.',
             %client.playerName,%client);

     removeTaggedString(%client.playerName);
     echo("CDROP: " @ %client @ "
         " @ %client.getAddress());
     $Server::PlayerCount--;
   ```

```
        // Reset the server if everyone has left the game
        if ( $Pref::Server::RestartWhenEmpty &&
            $Server::PlayerCount == 0 && $Server::Dedicated)
            schedule(0, 0, "resetServerDefaults");
    }
```

5. Start a dedicated server (see the *How to start a dedicated server* recipe). Now when the last player disconnects from the server, the server will not restart itself.

How it works...

We defined a new global variable, `$Pref::Server::RestartWhenEmpty`, to control if a dedicated server should restart when the last player disconnects. This allows us to keep the default behavior of restarting, if required. We then modified the `GameConnection` object's `onDrop()` method to check this variable before restarting the game server when the last player disconnects.

See also

▶   *How to start a dedicated server*

Accessing the server connection from the client

While writing gameplay code for the client, it is important to be able to access the `GameConnection` class instance to the server. In this recipe, we will learn how to access the server connection class on the client.

How to do it...

In Torque 3D there are three different locations that the connection from the client to the server may be made. In each case the code looks as follows:

```
    %conn = new GameConnection(ServerConnection);
```

In this code, the `GameConnection` instance is given a name of `ServerConnection`. It is through this name that we may work with the connection to the server on the client. For example, to access the object currently being controlled by the client, which is typically the `Player` class, we may do the following:

```
    %object = ServerConnection.getControlObject();
    if(%object.isInNamespaceHierarchy("Player"))
    {
        // Do something with the player instance
```

```
}
else
{
   // Work with another control object class, such as
   // a vehicle
}
```

See also

▸ *How to access all client connections from the server*

How to access all client connections from the server

During a game, we often need to work with all the connected clients at once, such as sending out a game update. In this recipe, we will learn how to go through the list of all the connected clients and do something with them.

How to do it...

The `ClientGroup` collection is a `SimGroup` collection that stores each of the client's `GameConnection` instances on the server. The easiest method of stepping through this group and working with each connection instance is through the TorqueScript `foreach()` operator:

```
// Step through each client in the ClientGroup on the server
foreach(%client in ClientGroup)
{
   // Play a thunder clap sound on the client.  The play2D()
   // method sends a network sound event to the client
   // for the sound to be played locally.
   %client.play2D(ThunderCrash1Sound);
}
```

How it works...

The preceding code uses the `foreach()` function to retrieve each client in the `ClientGroup` list, and does some work on it. In this example, we call the `GameConnection` `play2d()` function to tell the connected client to play the given sound effect.

See also

> ▸ *Accessing the server connection from the client*
>
> ▸ *Iterating on objects in a SimSet or SimGroup collection*, in *Chapter 1, TorqueScript: the Only Script You Need to Know*

Broadcasting a message to all clients and having it displayed in the center of the screen

During the course of a game, it may be necessary to inform all the clients about an event or share an important piece of information. Torque 3D allows the server to send out a message to all clients that will be displayed in the center of the screen for a specified length of time.

In this recipe, we will learn about the commands used to display a message in the center of the screen on all the connected clients.

How to do it...

From the server's console, enter the following command:

```
% centerPrintAll ("The server will be coming down in 5 minutes.
Please log out.", 30, 1);
```

All connected clients will see the given message in the center of their screen for 30 seconds, as shown in the following screenshot:.

How it works...

The `centerPrintAll()` function is used on the server to send a message, will be displayed in the center of their screen, to all clients. This function is as follows:

```
centerPrintAll( message, time, lines );
```

In this function, the `message` parameter is the text that will be displayed on clients' screen, the `time` parameter is the number of seconds to display the message, and the `lines` parameter is the number of lines the message will take up on the screen and ranges from 1 to 3. This last parameter controls the length of the text control, which displays the message.

There's more...

Let's continue the discussion of sending messages to clients.

Manually clearing the center print message

Sometimes, we may not want to wait for the current message displayed in the center of each client's screen to time out. In this case, we want to manually clear the message from each client. In order to do so, we use the `clearCenterPrintAll()` function, which is as follows:

```
clearCenterPrintAll();
```

This function will immediately clear the center print message from all clients.

Individual client version of center print

In addition to sending a message to all connected clients, it is possible to target a single client connection to send a center print message to. In order to send a message to a single client we use the following code, where the `client` parameter is the `SimObject` ID of the client's `GameConnection` instance:

```
centerPrint( client, message, time, lines );
```

All the other parameters are the same as for the `centerPrintAll()` function.

In order to clear a center print message from a single client, we use the following function:

```
clearCenterPrint( client );
```

9

Importance of Networking

In this chapter, we will cover the following topics:

- ▶ Sending a network event from the client to the server
- ▶ Sending a network event from the server to the client
- ▶ Connecting as a TCP client
- ▶ Setting up a TCP server
- ▶ Connecting as an HTTP client
- ▶ Using an RSS feed for game news, message of the day, or other client messages
- ▶ How to activate, deactivate, and use Telnet for console access

Introduction

Communicating between a Torque 3D game and an external network service could provide leader board support, news to be displayed within the game client, or a login service provider. And if we are building a multiplayer game, then game-specific communication between the client and server is a must.

Fortunately, Torque 3D provides the tools for both internal client/server network communication as well as external network service communication. In this chapter, we will discover how to set up Torque 3D for both types of network communication through various examples.

Sending a network event from the client to the server

Over the course of a networked game, it is often necessary to send an event from the client to the server. This event may also contain data for the server to process. In this recipe, we will learn how to send a network event from the client to the server, and how to have the server process this custom event.

Getting ready

We will be using a project based on the Torque 3D's `Full` template, using the `Empty Terrain` level. If you haven't already, use the Torque Project Manager (`Project Manager.exe`) to create a new project from the `Full` template; it will be found under the `My Projects` directory.

How to do it...

In the following steps, we will send a command from the client to the server to kill the player:

1. Start our `Full` template.
2. Once the main menu is displayed, click on the **Play** button. This will open the **Choose Level** window.
3. Choose the `Empty Terrain` level and click on the **Go!** button.
4. When the game has loaded, press *Tab* to go into third-person camera mode.
5. Press the tilde (~) key, to open the console.
6. Type the following command into the console and press *Enter*:

   ```
   commandToServer('suicide');
   ```

7. The player will instantly fall over and die.

How it works...

We use the `commandToServer()` TorqueScript function to issue a command from the client to the server along with an arbitrary list of parameters. It has the following form:

```
commandToServer( command, parameters... );
```

In this function, the `command` parameter is the name of the command to be executed on the server, and the `parameters` parameter is actually zero or more arbitrary parameters (up to a maximum of 20) that are passed along to the server.

It is important to note that the command parameter must be enclosed by *single quotes* and not double quotes. Using single quotes tells TorqueScript to convert the text string into a network string tag that will be passed to the server. Network strings only send the actual text once, and from then on pass along the numeric tag instead. This saves on network bandwidth, especially for commands that are used many times.

On the server side, we would create a TorqueScript function whose name matches the `command` parameter used earlier, but with a `serverCmd` prefix added to it. Following our `suicide` command used by our earlier example, here is the TorqueScript function that is called on the server (found in `scripts/server/commands.cs`):

```
function serverCmdSuicide(%client)
{
  if (isObject(%client.player))
      %client.player.kill("Suicide");
}
```

The `serverCmdSuicide()` function is a standard one included with Torque 3D and responds to our `suicide` command sent by the client. All callbacks that respond to a client command have their first parameter point to the calling client's `NetConnection` class instance. This is the `%client` parameter in the preceding function.

If the `commandToServer()` call on the client included any other parameters beyond the `command` parameter, they would follow the `%client` parameter on the server side. For example, if the client issues the following command to the server:

```
commandToServer('myCommand', %arg1, %arg2, %arg3);
```

We would create the following callback function on the server:

```
function serverCmdMyCommand(%client,
            %param1, %param2, %param3)
{
  // Work with the three parameters from the client here
  ...
}
```

In this function, the `%client` parameter points to the calling client's `NetConnection` instance; and the `%param1`, `%param2`, and `%param3` parameters will contain the values `%arg1`, `%arg2`, and `%arg3` parameters, from the client side, respectively.

There's more...

Let's continue our discussion about sending commands from the client to the server.

Packed network strings

You may be concerned that sending text strings from the client to the server may use up too much network bandwidth. Fortunately, Torque 3D automatically packs text strings using Huffman Coding based on a precomputed table, sorted by letter frequency in the English language. You may read more about Huffman Coding on Wikipedia: http://en.wikipedia.org/wiki/Huffman_coding.

Beyond being aware that text strings are automatically packed and unpacked over the network, there is nothing special that we need to do to take advantage of it.

Packed empty strings

If an empty string is passed along as a `commandToServer()` parameter, it is automatically packed down to a zero integer made up of two bits. In Torque 3D networking, every bit counts!

Packed network integers

If a parameter passed to `commandToServer()` starts with a minus sign or a number, the parameter is tested to determine if it is an integer. If it is found to be an integer, then the parameter is sent using the minimum number of bits required to represent the integer, rather than using a full 32 bits each time. As most numbers used by a game tend to be fairly small, this can add up to a large number of saved bits each time a command is sent.

The point at which there is no longer a bit saving is with integers greater than or equal to 32768. Integers beyond this range actually incur a 2-bit penalty as a part of the checking for smaller numbers.

Handling floating point numbers

Unfortunately, floating point numbers are not packed and are sent as full text strings. If your network bandwidth budget is tight, it may be worthwhile to keep this in mind and try to keep all numbers sent using `commandToServer()` as integers, if possible.

See also

▸ *Sending a network event from the server to the client*

Sending a network event from the server to the client

Over the course of a networked game, it is often necessary to send an event from the server to the client. This event may also contain data for the client to process. In this recipe, we will learn how to send a network event from the server to the client, and how to have the client process this custom event.

Getting ready

We will be making TorqueScript changes in a project based on the Torque 3D's `Full` template, using the `Empty Terrain` level. If you haven't already, use the Torque Project Manager (`Project Manager.exe`) to create a new project from the `Full` template; it will be found under the `My Projects` directory. After that, start up your favorite script editor, such as Torsion, and let's get going!

How to do it...

In the following steps, we will send a command from the server to all the connected clients that will pop up a message dialog and display our custom message:

1. Open the `scripts/server/game.cs` file in your text editor, add the following code to the bottom of the file, and save:

```
// Open a message box on all clients containing this message
function clientMessage(%message)
{
  // Iterate through each connected client
  foreach(%client in ClientGroup)
  {
    // Issue the MessageBox command on the client and
    // pass the message as a parameter.
    commandToClient(%client, 'MessageBox', %message);
  }
}
```

2. Open the `scripts/client/client.cs` file in your text editor, add the following code to the bottom of the file, and save:

```
function clientCmdMessageBox(%message)
{
  // Display the message to the user
  MessageBoxOK("Server Message", %message);
}
```

3. Start our `Full` template.

4. Once the main menu is displayed, click on the **Play** button. This will open the **Choose Level** window.

5. Choose the `Empty Terrain` level, and click on the **Go!** button.

6. When the game has loaded, press the tilde (~) key to open the console.

7. Type in the following command into the console and press *Enter*:

```
clientMessage("Hello from the server!");
```

8. A message box dialog, as shown in the following screenshot, will open on all connected clients (we are currently the only one) and display the text from our command:

How it works...

In our example, we have created two new functions. On the server side, our `clientMessage()` function accepts a text message as its first parameter and then uses the `commandToClient()` function to send that message to each of the connected clients. The syntax of the `commandToClient()` function is as follows:

```
commandToClient( client, command, parameters... );
```

In this function, the `client` parameter is a client's `NetConnection` instance to send the command to, the `command` parameter is the name of the command to execute on the client, and the `parameters` parameter is actually zero or more arbitrary parameters (up to a maximum of 20) that are passed along to the client.

In our example, we send our custom `MessageBox` command to each client.

> It is important to note that the command parameter must be enclosed by *single quotes* and not double quotes. Using single quotes tells TorqueScript to convert the text string into a network string tag that will be passed to the client. Network strings only send the actual text once, and from then on pass along the tag instead. This saves on network bandwidth, especially for commands that are used many times.

On the client side, we have created a function whose name matches the command being sent by the server, but with a `clientCmd` prefix added to it. Our final function name on the client side then ends up being `clientCmdMessageBox()`. Our client-side function takes a single parameter that contains the message from the server (the first and only command parameter passed into `commandToClient()`).

If the `commandToClient()` call on the server included any other command parameters, they would all follow, in order, on the client side. For example, if the server issues the following command to a client:

commandToClient(%client, 'MyCommand', %arg1, %arg2, %arg3);

We would create the following callback function on the client:

```
Function clientCmdMyCommand(%param1, %param2, %param3)
{
   // Do some work with the three parameters from the
   // server here
   ...
}
```

In this function, the `%param1`, `%param2`, and `%param3` parameters will contain the values `%arg1`, `%arg2`, `%arg3` parameters, from the server side, respectively.

There's more...

There are some details about the `commandToClient()` function that will help you understand how the parameters are packed before being sent over the network. For more information about parameter packing, please see the *Sending a network event from the client to the server* recipe. These details are same for both the `commandToClient()` and `commandToServer()` functions.

See also

▶ *Sending a network event from the client to the server*

Connecting as a TCP client

Communicating with other network-based services is important for some game types, to retrieve or store external data. In this recipe, we will learn how to have Torque 3D connect with a TCP server and communicate with it.

Getting ready

We will be using a project based on the Torque 3D's `Full` template, using the `Empty Terrain` level. If you haven't already, use the Torque Project Manager (`Project Manager.exe`) to create a new project from the `Full` template; it will be found under the `My Projects` directory. After that, start up your favorite script editor, such as Torsion, and let's get going!

How to do it...

In the following steps, we will build an object that will handle communications with an external server:

1. Open the `scripts/server/game.cs` file in your text editor, add the following code to the bottom of the file, and save:

```
// Callback: Cannot resolve name
function TimeCheck::onDNSFailed(%this)
{
   echo("TimeCheck: DNS Failed");
}

// Callback: Connection to service has failed
function TimeCheck::onConnectFailed(%this)
{
   echo("TimeCheck: Connection Failed");
}

// Callback: Have resolved name
function TimeCheck::onDNSResolved(%this)
{
   echo("TimeCheck: DNS Resolved");
}

// Callback: Connected to service
function TimeCheck::onConnected(%this)
{
   echo("TimeCheck: Connected");
}

// Callback: Disconnected from service
function TimeCheck::onDisconnect(%this)
{
   echo("TimeCheck: Disconnected");
}
```

```
// Callback: Received line from service
function TimeCheck::onLine(%this, %line)
{
   echo("TimeCheck: Response: " @ %line);
}

// Start the connection to the time service
function TimeCheck::start(%this)
{
   // Connect with a NIST internet time service server
   // on port 13.  This provides the text based Daytime
   // Protocol on connection and does not require we
   // send anything.
   // See http://www.nist.gov/pml/div688/grp40/its.cfm
   // for more information about the protocol used.
   %this.connect("time.nist.gov:13");
}
```

2. Start our `Full` template.

3. Once the main menu is displayed, press the tilde (~) key to open the console. Type the following two commands into the console and press *Enter*:

   new TCPObject(TimeCheck);

   TimeCheck.start();

4. The following output will be displayed in the console, if the connection is successful:

```
TimeCheck: DNS Resolved
TimeCheck: Connected                                          Exit
TimeCheck: Response:
TimeCheck: Response: 56230 12-10-30 06:28:25 06 0 0 312.2 UTC(NIST) *
TimeCheck: Disconnected
```

5. The response line contains the information from the time service, and then the time server automatically disconnects.

How it works...

The `TCPObject` class allows for communications between Torque 3D and a server using the TCP/IP protocol. The easiest way of using this class is to define a number of callback functions against a new namespace. In this example, we chose the `TimeCheck` name, and gave our new `TCPObject` instance that name.

A `TCPObject` is intended to be used with text-based protocols. Whenever a newline character is reached (\n in C++), the buffer contents up to that point are sent to the `onLine()` callback method; this callback has the following syntax:

```
TCPObject::onLine( this, line )
```

In this function, the `this` parameter is the `TCPObject` instance, and the `line` parameter contains the string buffer contents up to, but not including, the newline character. If the connection to the server is dropped and there is still data in the `TCPObject` instances' buffer, then `onLine()` is called with the remaining contents just before the `onDisconnect()` callback is called.

The `TCPObject` class also supports text lines that contain a carriage return character (`\r` in C++) just before the newline. In this case, the carriage return is removed before the buffer contents are sent to the `onLine()` callback.

In this example, the time server providing the **daytime protocol** does not require that we send anything in order to receive a response. We just connect to the time server, it sends the data, and then immediately disconnects us.

There's more...

Let's continue our discussion of the `TCPObject` class and setting up a TCP client.

Sending data to a server

Our previous example didn't require that we send any data to a server. However, this usually is not the case, and we often want two-way communications with a server. Once we have connected to a server, we may use the `send()` method to send data to it. This method has the following syntax, where the `data` parameter is the text data we wish to send to the server:

```
TCPObject.send( data );
```

Connecting and disconnecting

In our previous example, we connect to a time service but are automatically disconnected once the server has finished sending its time data. In order to connect with a TCP/IP server, we use the following method:

```
TCPObject.connect( address );
```

In this method, the `address` parameter is the full address and port we wish to connect with. In our previous example, we connect to the `time.nist.gov` address (which is resolved to an IP address via a DNS lookup) and port `13`.

We may disconnect from a server at any time with the following method:

```
TCPObject.disconnect();
```

If any data is left in the `TCPObject` instances' buffer, it is immediately sent to the `onLine()` callback.

Success callbacks

The `TCPObject` instance has a number of callbacks that are used to notify us of success in connecting with a server. We will list them here in the order in which they are called:

▸ `TCPObject::onDNSResolved()`: This is called when a named address has successfully been looked up in the DNS and converted to an IP address. A DNS lookup is required to convert a text-based IP address (such as `www.garagegames.com`) into a numerical version that the computer may use (such as `192.168.1.1`).

▸ `TCPObject::onConnected()`: This is called when we have successfully connected with the requested server.

▸ `TCPObject::onDisconnect()`: This is called when we have been disconnected from the server. This may also be considered a failure if we were not expecting to be disconnected.

Failure callbacks

The `TCPObject` instance has a number of callbacks that are used to notify us of a failure when attempting to connect with a server. We will list them here:

▸ `TCPObject::onDNSFailed()`: This is called when a named address may not be resolved by the DNS. Possible reasons for this include not being able to reach a DNS server, or the given textual IP address does not exist.

▸ `TCPObject::onConnectFailed()`: This is called when an attempted connection has failed for some reason. Possible reasons include the server being down, or the wrong IP address was given and there is nothing on the other end.

See also

▸ _Setting up a TCP server_
▸ _Connecting as an HTTP client_

Setting up a TCP server

Allowing other network-based services to communicate with Torque 3D is important for some game types to pass external data to the game server. In this recipe, we will learn how to have Torque 3D act as a server and listen for connections.

Getting ready

We will be using a project based on the Torque 3D's `Full` template, using the `Empty Terrain` level. If you haven't already, use the Torque Project Manager (`Project Manager.exe`) to create a new project from the `Full` template; it will be found under the `My Projects` directory. After that, start your favorite script editor, such as Torsion, and let's get going!

How to do it...

In the following steps, we will build an object that will listen for external network connections on a particular TCP port and act as an echo server:

1. Open the `scripts/server/game.cs` file in your text editor, add the following code to the bottom of the file, and save:

```
function EchoServiceListener::
    onConnectionRequest(%this, %address, %ID)
{
  echo("EchoServiceListener received
      connection request: "
      @ %address @ " [" @ %ID @ "]");

  // Create the echo service for this connection
  // The first parameter to the constructor is the SimObject
  // name.  We don't want one so we define it as empty.  The
  // second parameter is unique to TCPObject and is the ID
  // of this connection request.  It is used to connect this
  // object to the TCP socket.
  %es = new TCPObject("", %ID)
  {
    // Make use of the EchoService defined methods
    class = "EchoService";

    // Store this address in case we need it later
    fromAddress = %address;
  };

  // Add our EchoService object to a SimSet so we may track
  // all echo connections.  All TCPObjects are automatically
  // added to the TCPGroup SimGroup.
  if (!isObject(EchoServiceSet))
  {
    new SimSet(EchoServiceSet);
  }
  EchoServiceSet.add(%es);
}

function startEchoListener(%this)
```

```
{
  // Create the echo service listener
  new TCPObject(EchoServiceListener);

  // Listen on port 4000 for any TCP/IP connection
  EchoServiceListener.listen(4000);
}

function EchoService::onDisconnect(%this)
{
  echo("EchoService disconnected from " @
        %this.fromAddress);

  // Delete this object on the next tick, which will
  // clear this object from the EchoServiceSet.
  %this.schedule(0, delete);
}

function EchoService::onLine(%this, %line)
{
  echo("Received [" @ %this.fromAddress @ "]:
        " @ %line);

  // Echo it back with a carriage return and newline added
  %echoLine = %line @ "\r\n";
  %this.send(%echoLine);
}
```

2. Start our `Full` template.

3. Once the main menu is displayed, press the tilde (~) key to open the console. Type the following command into the console and press *Enter*:

   `startEchoListener();`

   Our game server is now waiting for a connection on port `4000`. We will use a Telnet client to connect to our echo server. Using a Telnet client makes it easy to send text data across a network connection.

4. Start up a Windows command prompt. You can find it by going to the Windows **Start** menu and choosing **All Programs | Accessories | Command Prompt**.

5. At the command prompt, type the following command to connect with our echo server:

   `telnet 127.0.0.1 4000`

You may not have access to the Telnet client on your Windows computer as Microsoft does not install it, by default. In order to install the Telnet client on your computer, go to the Windows **Start** menu and choose **Help and Support**. In the search box at the top of the window, enter `telnet`. You may now go to the **Telnet: frequently asked questions** section to find out how to install the Telnet client on your machines

6. When the Telnet client successfully connects to our Torque 3D echo server, the command window's contents will be cleared. Torque 3D's console will show that a connection has been made, including the origin's address and port.

7. You may now enter some text and every time you press Enter, your text will be echoed back to you. Torque 3D's console will also echo the text that has been received.

8. In order to disconnect from the echo server, press *Ctrl +]* and type `quit`. This will close the Telnet client's connection. As shown in the following screenshot, Torque 3D's console will indicate that the connection has been dropped:

```
EchoServiceListener received connection request: IP:127.0.0.1:51036 [1188]
Received [IP:127.0.0.1:51036]: Hello?
Received [IP:127.0.0.1:51036]: Anyone there?
Received [IP:127.0.0.1:51036]: Bye!
EchoService disconnected from IP:127.0.0.1:51036
```

How it works...

A TCP server is set up in two stages. The first stage is a listener on a given port. In this example, the `startEchoListener()` function sets up the `TCPObject` `EchoServiceListener` instance to listen on port `4000`. The `TCPObject` class uses the `listen()` method to attach itself to a given port, and has the following syntax, where the `port` parameter is the TCP/IP port to listen on:

```
TCPObject.listen( port );
```

You may need to modify your computer's firewall settings before being able to accept connections on a TCP/IP port we are listening to. If you wish to connect from a computer that is outside of your local network, then you may also need to modify your network router's settings to allow access to our port.

With the port listener established, a `TCPObject` instance's `onConnectionRequest()` callback is called whenever a connection is attempted on the requested port. This callback has the following syntax:

```
TCPObject::onConnectionRequest( this, address, ID )
```

In this callback, the `this` parameter is the `TCPObject` instance, the `address` parameter is the IP address and port that is making the request, and the `ID` parameter is an internal ID for this connection.

We now enter the second stage of setting up a TCP server by creating a new `TCPObject` instance that will handle the data from the connection. In this example, we create the `EchoService` namespace (the same name as our `TCPObject` instance) to handle the `onLine()` and `onDisconnect()` callbacks. Please see the *Connecting as a TCP client* recipe for more information about these callbacks.

There's more...

Let's continue our discussion of the `TCPObject` class and setting up a TCP server.

Handling more than one connection

Setting up a TCP server using the `TCPObject` automatically allows for more than one connection on a particular port. In order to test this out, use a second Telnet client with our earlier example at the same time the first Telnet client is connected. The Torque 3D console will display separate connect and disconnect messages, along with any text received from each IP address.

We could even modify the `EchoService::onLine()` method to echo all received text to all connected clients:

```
function EchoService::onLine(%this, %line)
{
  echo("Received [" @ %this.fromAddress @ "]: " @ %line);

  // Echo to all clients with a carriage return and
  // newline added
  %echoLine = %line @ "\r\n";
  foreach(%client in EchoServiceSet)
  {
    %client.send(%echoLine);
  }
}
```

Dropping a connection

We may use the `TCPObject.disconnect()` method at any time to drop an active connection. The syntax of this method is as follows:

```
TCPObject.disconnect();
```

For example, if we wanted to drop all currently active echo service connections, we could do the following:

```
foreach(%client in EchoServiceSet)
{
  %client.disconnect();
}
```

It is important to note that disconnecting a `TCPObject` instance does not delete the actual object from memory. All `TCPObject` instances are automatically added to a `TCPGroup` `SimGroup` collection and will be deleted when the game is shut down; so we don't need to worry about memory leaks.

But if we wanted to both disconnect all currently active echo server connections as well as delete the echo service instances from memory (to keep things tidy and not confuse ourselves with the number of `TCPObject` instances hanging around), we could do the following:

```
while(EchoServiceSet.getCount() > 0)
{
  %client = EchoServiceSet.getObject(0);
  %client.delete();
}
```

Deleting a `TCPObject` instance will automatically disconnect it from the other end.

See also

▸ *Connecting as a TCP client*

Connecting as an HTTP client

Communicating with an HTTP server can be quite useful for a game. An HTTP server could provide a login service or storage for a game's high scores.

In this recipe, we will learn how to have Torque 3D retrieve data from an HTTP service that returns our external network IP address.

Getting ready

We will be making TorqueScript changes in a project based on the Torque 3D's `Full` template, using the `Empty Terrain` level. If you haven't already, use the Torque Project Manager (`Project Manager.exe`) to create a new project from the `Full` template; it will be found under the `My Projects` directory. After that, start your favorite script editor, such as Torsion, and let's get going!

How to do it...

In the following steps, we will connect with an HTTP server that will give us our network IP address:

1. Open the `scripts/server/game.cs` file in your text editor, add the following code to the bottom of the file, and save:

```
// Callback: Cannot resolve name
function IPCheck::onDNSFailed(%this)
{
  echo("IPCheck: DNS Failed");
}

// Callback: Connection to service has failed
function IPCheck::onConnectFailed(%this)
{
  echo("IPCheck: Connection Failed");
}

// Callback: Have resolved name
function IPCheck::onDNSResolved(%this)
{
  echo("IPCheck: DNS Resolved");
}

// Callback: Connected to service
function IPCheck::onConnected(%this)
{
  echo("IPCheck: Connected");

  // Clear out our buffer
  %this.buffer = "";

  // Track that the buffer has just been cleared
  %this.freshBuffer = true;
}

// Callback: Disconnected from service
function IPCheck::onDisconnect(%this)
{
  echo("IP Check Results:");
  echo(%this.buffer);
}
```

```
// Callback: Received line from service
function IPCheck::onLine(%this, %line)
{
  // Store this line in our buffer
  if(%this.freshBuffer)
  {
    %this.freshBuffer = false;

    // Just copy in the line directly when working with
    // a freshly cleared buffer
    %this.buffer = %line;
  }
  else
  {
    // Append the line to the buffer using a newline
    // separator
    %this.buffer = %this.buffer NL %line;
  }
}
```

2. Start our `Full` template.

3. Once the main menu is displayed, press the tilde (~) key to open the console. Type the following two commands into the console and press *Enter*:

   `new HTTPObject(IPCheck);`

   `IPCheck.get("checkip.dyndns.org:80", "", "");`

   The following will be displayed in the console if the connection is successful:

```
==>IPCheck.get("checkip.dyndns.org:80", "", "");            Exit
IPCheck: DNS Resolved
IPCheck: Connected
IP Check Results:
HTTP/1.1 200 OK
Content-Type: text/html
Server: DynDNS-CheckIP/1.0
Connection: close
Cache-Control: no-cache
Pragma: no-cache
Content-Length: 103

<html><head><title>Current IP Check</title></head><body>Current IP Address: 65.92.76.37</body></html>
```

The response contains our external-facing IP address as seen by the Internet. Our `IPCheck` object automatically disconnects from the server once the GET request has been completed, but it is not deleted and is ready for another GET request.

How it works...

The `HTTPObject` class allows for communications between Torque 3D and a server using HTTP. An `HTTPObject` instance uses a number of callbacks to work with the HTTP connection. The `HTTPObject` class is a subclass of `TCPObject`; so all the same callbacks apply. Please see the *Connecting as a TCP client* recipe for more information.

In our example, we chose the name `IPCheck` for our `HTTPObject` instance. So we use that same namespace for all of our callbacks.

The primary method of working with a `HTTPObject` class is through the `get()` method, which has the following syntax:

```
HTTPObject.get( address, path, query );
```

In this method, the `address` parameter is the full address and port we wish to connect with, the `path` parameter is the path on the HTTP server we will connect to, and the `query` parameter is the query string we wish to send to the server (normally the text following a question mark when this is written out in a URL).

When the `get()` method is called, `HTTPObject` attempts to connect with the HTTP server on the requested path, and send the query string. In this example, just issuing a request to the server itself without any path or query string is sufficient; so those two parameters are empty strings. The `HTTPObject` instance then waits for a response from the server and finally disconnects from it.

As each line of data is received from the HTTP server, it is processed in our `onLine()` callback. The use of this callback is discussed in detail in the *Connecting as a TCP client* recipe. In this example, we just store the received line in a buffer for later use.

Once our GET request is completed and we disconnect from the HTTP server, we process the results. In our example, we just print the received HTTP header and body to the console.

There's more...

Let's continue our discussion of the `HTTPObject` class.

Separating the HTTP header and body

The response we receive from the `HTTPObject` class includes both the HTTP header as well as the body of the response. Often, we are not too concerned with the HTTP header, and just want to work with the body of the response.

The standard HTTP message structure (from `http://www.w3.org/Protocols/rfc2616/ rfc2616-sec4.html`) always has a blank line that separates the body from the header. By stepping through the response from the HTTP server and looking for an empty line, we can easily determine the body of the message. The following function takes the lines from an HTTP server's message and returns only the body:

```
// Takes a HTTP message and returns only the body
function getHTPPMessageBody(%msg)
{
  %body = "";
  %foundBody = false;

  %count = getRecordCount(%msg);
  for(%i=0; %i<%count; %i++)
  {
    %line = getRecord(%msg, %i);
    if(%foundBody)
    {
      if(strlen(%body) == 0)
      {
        // First line of the body
        %body = %line;
      }
      else
      {
        // Append the line to the body with a
        // newline separator
        %body = %body NL %line;
      }
    }
    else if(strlen(%line) == 0)
    {
      // Found the empty line indicating the start of
      // the body.
      %foundBody = true;
    }
  }

  return %body;
}
```

Processing an XML response

XML is a common format used with an HTTP server's response. In this recipe, when retrieving our external IP address, the message body is in an HTML format, but we can still treat it as if it is XML.

We could use Torque 3D's `SimXMLDocument` class to process the message body's elements. The `SimXMLDocument` class's `parse()` method would be used to process our XML data.

 Please see the `SimXMLDocument` class reference in `Torque 3D - Script Manual.chm` found in the Torque 3D `Documentation` directory for a complete list of methods for working with XML data. Also see the *Using a RSS feed for game news, message of the day or other client messages* recipe for an example of using the `SimXMLDocument` class.

See also

- ▸ *Connecting as a TCP client*
- ▸ *Using an RSS feed for game news, message of the day, or other client messages*

Using an RSS feed for game news, message of the day, or other client messages

One or more **RSS (Rich Site Summary)** feeds can be quite useful for a game. They could provide game news directly to the game client, a message of the day published to the chat window, or a summary of the current leader board.

An RSS feed is essentially a stream of data in an XML format, supplied by an HTTP server that we may parse for our own needs. In this recipe, we will learn how to retrieve an RSS feed from a server and parse its results. Our example will be the community blog feed from the `GarageGames.com` site.

Getting ready

We will be making TorqueScript changes in a project based on the Torque 3D's `Full` template, using the `Empty Terrain` level. If you haven't already, use the Torque Project Manager (`Project Manager.exe`) to create a new project from the `Full` template; it will be found under the `My Projects` directory. After that, start your favorite script editor, such as Torsion, and let's get going!

How to do it...

In the following steps, we will set up an object to handle communications with an RSS server and output the results to the console:

1. Open the `scripts/client/game.cs` file in your text editor, add the following to the bottom of the file and save:

```
// Callback: Cannot resolve name
function RSSFeed::onDNSFailed(%this)
{
  echo("RSSFeed: DNS Failed");
  %this.status = "DNS Failed";
}

// Callback: Connection to service has failed
function RSSFeed::onConnectFailed(%this)
{
  echo("RSSFeed: Connection Failed");
  %this.status = "Connect Failed";
}

// Callback: Have resolved name
function RSSFeed::onDNSResolved(%this)
{
  echo("RSSFeed: DNS Resolved");
  %this.status = "DNS Resolved";
}

// Callback: Connected to service
function RSSFeed::onConnected(%this)
{
  echo("RSSFeed: Connected");
  %this.status = "Connected";

  // Ask for the RSS feed.  We will build this out as
  // a HTTP GET request.
  %this.send("GET " @ %this.path @
      " HTTP/1.1\r\nHost: www.garagegames.com\r\n\r\n");
}

// Callback: Disconnected from service
function RSSFeed::onDisconnect(%this)
{
  echo("RSSFeed: Disconnected");
  %this.status = "Disconnected";

  // Parse our XML buffer that holds the RSS feed
  %this.xml.parse(%this.xmlBuffer);
}
```

```
// Callback: Received line from service
function RSSFeed::onLine(%this, %line)
{
  //echo("RSSFeed: Response: " @ %line);

  if(%this.haveXML)
  {
    // Store this line in our xml buffer
    %this.xmlBuffer = %this.xmlBuffer @ %line;

    // If this is the end of the RSS feed then stop
    // storing the results in the XML buffer following
    // this line.  This stops any extra characters from
    // being placed in our buffer.
    if(strstr(%line, "</rss>") >= 0)
    {
      %this.haveXML = false;
    }
  }
  else
  {
    if(strstr(%line, "<?xml") >= 0)
    {
      // We've found the XML header so start storing
      // it in our buffer
      %this.haveXML = true;
      %this.xmlBuffer = %line;
    }
  }
}
```

This sets up the standard callbacks used by a `TCPObject` instance.

2. In the same file as used earlier, add the following code and save:

```
// Contact the server and get the blogs feed
function RSSFeed::getBlogsFeed(%this)
{
  %this.status = "Startup";

  // Prepare the SimXMLDocument to process the feed
  if(isObject(%this.xml))
  {
    // Delete the previous object
    %this.xml.delete();
  }
  %this.xml = new SimXMLDocument();

  // Indicate that we've not yet received the XML body
  // from the server.  We only buffer the XML portion of
```

```
      // the server's response.
      %this.haveXML = false;

      // Clear our buffer to hold the XML reponse
      %this.xmlBuffer = "";

      // Indicate that we want to get the community blog feed
      %this.path = "/feeds/rss/blogs";

      // Connect to the GarageGames web site and retrieve
      // the community blog feed
      %this.connect("www.garagegames.com:80");
   }

   // Output the list of retrieved blog titles to the console
   function RSSFeed::getBlogTitles(%this)
   {
      echo("Blog Titles:");

      // Enter the <rss /> tag
      %ok = %this.xml.pushChildElement(0);
      if(!%ok)
      {
         echo("<rss /> tag error");
         return;
      }

      %ok = %this.xml.pushFirstChildElement("channel");
      if(!%ok)
      {
         echo("<channel /> tag error");
         return;
      }

      %ok = %this.xml.pushFirstChildElement("item");
      if(!%ok)
      {
         echo("<item /> tag error");
         return;
      }

      while(%ok)
      {
         // Get the title
         if(%this.xml.pushFirstChildElement("title"))
         {
            echo("   " @ %this.xml.getText());

            // Go back to the item element
            %this.xml.popElement();
```

```
      }

         %ok = %this.xml.nextSiblingElement("item");
      }

      echo("Done.");
   }
```

This sets up the methods to retrieve and parse the returned RSS data.

3. Start our `Full` template.

4. Once the main menu is displayed, press the tilde (~) key to open the console. Type the following two commands into the console and press *Enter*:

   new TCPObject(RSSFeed);

   RSSFeed.getBlogsFeed();

5. At this point, we have obtained a list of the most recent community blogs on the `garagegames.com` site. Enter the following command:

   RSSFeed.getBlogTitles();

6. A list of the most recent blog titles from the `garagegames.com` site will be displayed in the console:

```
==>new TCPObject(RSSFeed);                                                  Join
4152
==>RSSFeed.getBlogsFeed();
RSSFeed: DNS Resolved
RSSFeed: Connected
RSSFeed: Disconnected
==>RSSFeed.getBlogTitles();
Blog Titles:                                                              Options
   ProBones 8,000 BVH Pak. The Worlds Largest Mocap Library
   Announcing the Open Source Torque 3D Project Manager
   11 Dias a Ixtlan: Dia 8
   GarageGames at DevLearn
   ESRB Introduces No-Cost Rating Service for Games and Apps
   My First Blog: Painting My Worlds Green                                   Exit
   11 Dias a Ixtlan: Tiempo Perdido
   Character WIP - Star-date 2012 28 10
   Procedural Terrain networked
   Journal Entry #2 - The Ground Beneath My Fingers
   Temple Pack 1 - Preview 2
   Game Design - The character or the player, an informal poll
   My latest project: Assassin's Creed 3: Liberation
   Are we there yet?
   Journal Entry #1 - The Ground Beneath My Feet
   Get Your Own Copy of DotNetTorque Now!
   SFX Library - Merchants, Enemies, And Townsfolk
   TGE 1.4.2 - Could it be a significant asset for GarageGames?
   Announcing the New Torque 3D Steering Committee!
   DNT Coming this week, $99
Done.
```

How it works...

We are making use of the `TCPObject` class to send an HTTP GET request to a web server. We could have used `HTTPObject` instead, but this example shows how to form your own HTTP request, which could be extended to other request types that are not supported by `HTTPObject`.

 Please see the *Connecting as a HTTP client* recipe if you are interested in using the `HTTPObject` instead.

We begin by defining a number of callbacks to be used by our `RSSFeed` namespace and `TCPObject` instance. The details of these callbacks and how to use them may be found in the *Connecting as a TCP client* recipe.

We start our work by calling the `getBlogsFeed()` method on the `RSSFeed` object. This method starts by creating a new `SimXMLDocument` object that will be used to parse the XML data from the RSS feed. The `SimXMLDocument` class may be used to process XML data from a file or directly from a text buffer. In our case, we will be passing it a text buffer later on.

The `getBlogsFeed()` method then clears out the text buffer, which we will be using to store the XML data before passing it along to our `SimXMLDocument` object. Finally, it defines the path to the blogs feed on the web server (so we may retrieve other feeds down the road in an additional method) and then attempts to connect to the `garagegames.com` server.

If the connection with the web server is successful, the `RSSFeed` object's `onConnected()` callback is called. In this callback, we use the `TCPObject` instance's `send()` method to pass our HTTP GET request to the server.

The web server then responds to our request and we process this response within the `RSSFeed` object's `onLine()` callback. Within this callback, we look for the standard XML header before we store the results in our text buffer. This allows us to skip the supplied HTTP header, so only valid XML data will be passed to our `SimXMLDocument` object.

Once the entire response has been sent, the web server drops our connection. This is handled by the `RSSFeed` object's `onDisconnect()` callback. Within this callback, we parse our XML text buffer with our `SimXMLDocument` object. We are now ready to do something with the data.

In our example, we want to output the blog titles received from the RSS feed to the console. We perform this action with the `getBlogTitles()` method. This method uses various `SimXMLDocument` methods to move through the XML hierarchy to obtain the data we are interested in.

Please see the `SimXMLDocument` class reference in `Torque 3D - Script Manual.chm` found in the Torque 3D `Documentation` directory for a complete list of methods for working with XML data.

Rather than output the blog titles to the console, we could have placed them in a multiline GUI control, and presented them to the user. The same methodology could be used with a game's news items, or perhaps a leader board. Using an RSS feed for this data allows for it to be consumed by multiple types of clients, such as a page on a website, or a player's RSS reader on their computer.

See also

▸ *Connecting as a TCP client*

▸ *Connecting as a HTTP client*

How to activate, deactivate, and use Telnet for console access

Torque 3D's console is useful for debugging your game, as well as for altering a running game. While the console is available from both the client and the dedicated server's windows, sometimes we need to access the console remotely. This can be especially useful when a dedicated server has been started as either a Windows service or scheduled task, and there is no window available to interact with.

For these circumstances, Torque 3D provides an internal Telnet server that may be used for remote console access. In this recipe, we will learn how to set up and activate console access through Telnet.

Getting ready

We will be using a project based on the Torque 3D's `Full` template, using the `Empty Terrain` level. If you haven't already, use the Torque Project Manager (`Project Manager.exe`) to create a new project from the `Full` template; it will be found under the `My Projects` directory.

How to do it...

In the following steps, we will activate Torque 3D's Telnet console and connect to it to issue some commands:

1. Start our `Full` template.

2. Once the main menu is displayed, press the tilde (~) key to open the console. Type the following command into the console and press *Enter*:

    ```
    telnetSetParameters(4000, "", "");
    ```

    Our game is now listening for a connection on port `4000`.

3. We will now use the Windows Telnet client to connect to our game. Start a Windows command prompt. You can find it by going to the Windows **Start** menu and choosing **All Programs | Accessories | Command Prompt**.

     You may need to modify your computer's firewall settings before being able to accept connections on a TCP/IP port we are listening to. If you wish to connect from a computer that is outside of your local network, then you may also need to modify your network router's settings to allow access to our port.

4. At the command prompt, type the following command to connect with our game:

    ```
    telnet 127.0.0.1 4000
    ```

     You may not have access to the Telnet client on your Windows computer as Microsoft does not install it by default. In order to install the Telnet client on your computer, go to the Windows **Start** menu and choose **Help and Support**. In the search box at the top of the window, type `telnet`. You may now go to the **Telnet: frequently asked questions** section to find out how to install the Telnet client on your machine.

5. When the Telnet client successfully connects to our game, the command window's contents will be cleared. We will then be asked to enter in a password—just press *Enter* as we have not defined one.

6. Type in the following command and press *Enter*. This will return the number of seconds that Torque 3D has been running:

    ```
    echo(getSimTime() / 1000);
    ```

7. Type in the following command, and press *Enter* to shut down our game and close our Telnet session:

```
quit();
```

How it works...

The `telnetSetParameters()` TorqueScript function is used to activate and deactivate Telnet access to the console. Its syntax is as follows:

```
telnetSetParameters( port, adminPassword, readPassword, [echo]);
```

In this function, the `port` parameter is the TCP/IP port that will be listened to for a connection, the `adminPassword` parameter is the optional password used to provide full console access, the `readPassword` parameter is the optional password used to provide read-only access to the console, and the `echo` parameter is an optional parameter that indicates if all text entry should be echoed back to the Telnet client (it is `false` by default).

In this example, we left both the `adminPassword` and `readPassword` as empty strings. This means that the Telnet client user only needs to press return at the **Enter Password** prompt to gain full read and write access to the console. Normally, we would want to provide a value for at least the `adminPassword` parameter in order to protect access to the game. If you also want to make sure that no one may read the console without proper access, then also provide something for the `readPassword` parameter when using the `telnetSetParameters()` function.

While we didn't manually disconnect ourselves from the running game (the `quit()` function we issued shuts the whole game down and automatically disconnected us) normally, we would want to cleanly disconnect from the game when we are done using the console. In order to do so, press *Ctrl +]* from within the Windows Telnet client and type `quit`. This will return us to the Windows command prompt, and Torque 3D will return to waiting for another remote connection.

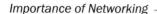

Let's continue our discussion of remote console access.

Disabling remote console access once it has been enabled

By default, Torque 3D starts with remote access to the console in a disabled state. We use the `telnetSetParameters()` function to enable this access by passing in a valid TCP/IP port number and values for the passwords. If we wish to later disable remote access to the console, we again use the `telnetSetParameters()` function but with the `port` parameter set to `0`. This will close any open listening socket and prevent remote access to the game's console.

Telnet is not secure

Something to keep in mind is that using Telnet over the Internet is not a secure connection. Everything, including the password entered, is sent as clear text. This doesn't stop it from being useful, especially if only used on the same machine that the game is running on (to access a dedicated server without a console window).

But if Internet access to the console is required for maintaining your game, then you may want to look into using a secure point-to-point connection such as VPN, or devise a custom solution for your game.

10
Miscellaneous Gameplay Features

In this chapter, we will cover the following topics:

- How to have a sprinting player use up energy
- Enabling and disabling air control
- How to jump jet
- Adjusting the fire spread of a weapon
- Changing the number of shots fired from a weapon
- Making a weapon use energy rather than ammo
- Finding objects in range
- Using the message producer/consumer system

Introduction

Torque 3D is a complete game engine. It supports graphics, sound, user input, networking, and gameplay. **Gameplay** are the rules for your game that make it unique. These are the challenges the player must overcome.

In this chapter we will be looking at various parts of Torque 3D that help you expand on the gameplay rules that are already available, and help you build your own.

How to have a sprinting player use up energy

Torque 3D's `Player` class has three main modes of movement over land: sprinting, running, and crouching. Some are designed to allow a player to sprint as much as they want, but perhaps with other limitations while sprinting. This is the default method of sprinting in the Torque 3D templates. Other game designs allow the player to sprint only for short bursts before the player becomes "tired". In this recipe, we will learn how to set up the `Player` class such that sprinting uses up a pool of energy that slowly recharges over time; and when that energy is depleted, the player is no longer able to sprint.

How to do it...

We are about to modify a `PlayerData Datablock` instance so that sprint uses up the player's energy as follows:

1. Open your player's `Datablock` in a text editor, such as Torsion. The Torque 3D templates have the `DefaultPlayerData Datablock` template in `art/datablocks/player.cs`.

2. Find the sprinting section of the `Datablock` instance and make the following changes:

   ```
   sprintForce = 4320;
   sprintEnergyDrain = 0.6; // Sprinting now drains energy
   minSprintEnergy = 10;    // Minimum energy to sprint
   maxSprintForwardSpeed = 14;
   maxSprintBackwardSpeed = 8;
   maxSprintSideSpeed = 6;
   sprintStrafeScale = 0.25;
   sprintYawScale = 0.05;
   sprintPitchScale = 0.05;
   sprintCanJump = true;
   ```

3. Start up the game and have the player sprint. Sprinting should now be possible for about 5.5 seconds before the player falls back to a run.

4. If the player stops sprinting for about 7.5 seconds, their energy will be fully recharged and they will be able to sprint again.

How it works...

The `maxEnergy` property on the `PlayerData Datablock` instance determines the maximum amount of energy a player has. All of Torque 3D's templates set it to a value of `60`. This energy may be used for a number of different activities (such as jet jumping), and even certain weapons may draw from it.

By setting the `sprintEnergyDrain` property on the `PlayerData Datablock` instance to a value greater than zero, the player's energy will be drained every tick (about one-thirty-second of a second) by that amount. When the player's energy reaches zero they may no longer sprint, and revert back to running.

Using our previous example, we have a value for the `sprintEnergyDrain` property of `0.6` units per tick. This works out to 19.2 units per second. Given that our `DefaultPlayerData` `maxEnergy` property is `60` units, we should run out of sprint energy in 3.125 seconds. However, we were able to sprint for about 5.5 seconds in our example before running out of energy. Why is this?

A second `PlayerData` property affects energy use over time: `rechargeRate`. This property determines how much energy is restored to the player per tick, and is set to `0.256` units in `DefaultPlayerData`. When we take both the `sprintEnergyDrain` and `recharcheRate` properties into account, we end up with an effective rate of (0.6 – 0.256) 0.344 units drained per tick while sprinting. Assuming the player begins with the maximum amount of energy allowed by `DefaultPlayerData`, this works out to be (60 units / (0.344 units per tick * 32 ticks per second)) 5.45 seconds.

The final `PlayerData` property that affects sprinting is `minSprintEnergy`. This property determines the minimum player energy level required before being able to sprint. When this property is greater than zero, it means that a player may continue to sprint until their energy is zero, but cannot sprint again until they have regained a `minSprintEnergy` amount of energy.

There's more...

Let's continue our discussion of player sprinting and energy use.

Balance energy drain versus recharge rate

With everything set up as described previously, every tick the player is sprinting his energy pool will be reduced by the value of `sprintEnergyDrain` property of `PlayerData`, and increased by the value of the `rechargeRate` property. This means that in order for the player's energy to actually drain, his `sprintEnergyDrain` property must be greater than his `rechargeRate` property.

As a player's energy may be used for other game play elements (such as jet jumping or weapons fire), sometimes we may forget this relationship while tuning the `rechargeRate` property, and end up breaking a player's ability to sprint (or make them sprint far too long).

Modifying other sprint limitations

The way the `DefaultPlayerData Datablock` instance is set up in all of Torque 3D's templates, there are already limitations placed on sprinting without making use of an energy drain. This includes not being able to rotate the player as fast as when running, and limited strafing ability. Making sprinting rely on the amount of energy a player has is often enough of a limitation, and the other default limitations may be removed or reduced. In the end it depends on the type of game we are making.

To change how much the player is allowed to rotate while sprinting, we modify the `sprintYawScale` and `sprintPitchScale` properties of the `PlayerData` property. These two properties represent the fraction of rotation allowed while sprinting compared with running and default to `0.05` each.

To change how much the player is allowed to strafe while sprinting, we modify the `sprintStrafeScale` property of the `PlayerData` property. This property is the fraction of the amount of strafing movement allowed while running and defaults to `0.25`.

Disabling sprint

During a game we may want to disable a player's sprinting ability. Perhaps they are too injured, or are carrying too heavy a load. To allow or disallow sprinting for a specific player we call the following `Player` class method on the server:

```
Player.allowSprinting( allow );
```

In the previous code, the `allow` parameter is set to `true` to allow a player the ability to sprint, and to `false` to not allow a player to sprint at all.

This method is used by the standard weapon mounting system in `scripts/server/weapon.cs` to disable sprinting. If the `ShapeBaseImageData Datablock` instance for the weapon has a dynamic property of `sprintDisallowed` set to `true`, the player may not sprint while holding that weapon. The `DeployableTurretImage Datablock` instance makes use of this by not allowing the player to sprint while holding a turret.

Enabling and disabling air control

Air control is a fictitious force used by a number of games that allows a player to control their trajectory while falling or jumping in the air. Instead of just falling or jumping and hoping for the best, this allows the player to change course as necessary and trades realism for playability. We can find this type of control in first-person shooters, platformers, and adventure games. In this recipe we will learn how to enable or disable air control for a player, as well as limit its effect while in use.

How to do it...

We are about to modify a `PlayerData Datablock` instance to enable complete air control as follows:

1. Open your player's `Datablock` in a text editor, such as Torsion. The Torque 3D templates have the `DefaultPlayerData Datablock` instance in `art/datablocks/player.cs`.

2. Find the section of the `Datablock` instance that contains the `airControl` property and make the following change:

   ```
   jumpForce = "747";
   jumpEnergyDrain = 0;
   minJumpEnergy = 0;
   jumpDelay = "15";
   // Set to maximum air control
   airControl = 1.0;
   ```

3. Start up the game and jump the player off of a building or a sand dune. While in the air press one of the standard movement keys: *W*, *A*, *S*, and *D*.

We now have full trajectory control of the player while they are in the air as if they were running.

How it works...

If the player is not in contact with any surface and is not swimming, the `airControl` property of `PlayerData` is multiplied against the player's direction of requested travel. This multiplication only happens along the world's XY plane and does not affect vertical motion.

Setting the `airControl` property of `PlayerData` to a value of `0` will disable all air control. Setting the `airControl` property to a value greater than `1` will cause the player to move faster in the air than they can run.

How to jump jet

In game terms, a **jump jet** is often a backpack, a helicopter hat, or a similar device that a player wears, that provides them a short thrust upwards and often uses up a limited energy source. This allows a player to reach a height they normally could not, jump a canyon, or otherwise get out of danger or reach a reward. In this recipe we will learn how to allow a player to jump jet.

Getting ready

We will be making TorqueScript changes in a project based on the Torque 3D `Full` template using the `Empty Terrain` level. If you haven't already, use the Torque Project Manager (`Project Manager.exe`) to create a new project from the `Full` template. It will be found under the `My Projects` directory. Then start up your favorite script editor, such as Torsion, and let's get going!

How to do it...

We are going to modify the player's `Datablock` instance to allow for jump jetting and adjust how the user triggers the jump jet as follows:

1. Open the `art/datablocks/player.cs` file in your text editor.

2. Find the `DefaultPlayerData Datablock` instance and just below the section on jumping and air control, add the following code:

   ```
   // Jump jet
   jetJumpForce = 500;
   jetJumpEnergyDrain = 3;
   jetMinJumpEnergy = 10;
   ```

3. Open `scripts/main.cs` and make the following addition to the `onStart()` function:

   ```
   function onStart()
   {
       // Change the jump jet trigger to match a regular jump
       $player::jumpJetTrigger = 2;

       // The core does initialization which requires some of
       // the preferences to loaded... so do that first.
       exec( "./client/defaults.cs" );
       exec( "./server/defaults.cs" );

       Parent::onStart();
       echo("\n--------- Initializing Directory: scripts
   ```

```
                --------");

        // Load the scripts that start it all...
        exec("./client/init.cs");
        exec("./server/init.cs");

        // Init the physics plugin.
        physicsInit();

        // Start up the audio system.
        sfxStartup();

        // Server gets loaded for all sessions, since clients
        // can host in-game servers.
        initServer();

        // Start up in either client, or dedicated server mode
        if ($Server::Dedicated)
            initDedicated();
        else
            initClient();
    }
```

4. Start our `Full` template game and load the `Empty Terrain` level.

5. Hold down the Space bar to cause the player to fly straight up for a few seconds. The player will then fall back to the ground. Once the player has regained enough energy it will be possible to jump jet again.

How it works...

The only property that is required to be set for jump jetting to work is the `jetJumpForce` property of the `PlayerData Datablock` instance. This property determines the amount of continuous force applied on the player object to have them flying up in the air. It takes some trial and error to determine what force works best.

Other `Datablock` properties that are useful to set are `jetJumpEnergyDrain` and `jetMinJumpEnergy`. These two `PlayerData` properties make jet jumping use up a player's energy. When the energy runs out, the player may no longer jump jet until enough energy has recharged. The `jetJumpEnergyDrain` property is how much energy per tick is drained from the player's energy pool, and the `jetMinJumpEnergy` property is the minimum amount of energy the player needs in their energy pool before they can jump jet again. Please see the *How to have a sprinting player use up energy* recipe for more information on managing a player's energy use.

Another change we made in our previous example is to define which move input trigger number will cause the player to jump jet. This is defined using the global `$player::jumpJetTrigger` variable. By default, this is set to trigger 1, which is usually the same as the right mouse button. However, all of the Torque 3D templates make use of the right mouse button for view zooming (as defined in `scripts/client/default.bind.cs`).

In our previous example, we modified the global `$player::jumpJetTrigger` variable to use trigger 2, which is usually the same as for regular jumping as defined in `scripts/client/default.bind.cs`:

```
function jump(%val)
{
    // Touch move trigger 2
    $mvTriggerCount2++;
}
moveMap.bind( keyboard, space, jump );
```

This means that we now have jump jetting working off of the same key binding as regular jumping, which is the Space bar. Now holding down the Space bar will cause the player to jump jet, unless they do not have enough energy to do so. Without enough energy, the player will just do a regular jump with their legs.

There's more...

Let's continue our discussion of using a jump jet.

Jump jet animation sequence

If the shape used by the `Player` object has a *Jet* animation sequence defined, it will play while the player is jump jetting. This sequence will play instead of all other action sequences. The hierarchy or order of action sequences that the `Player` class uses to determine which action sequence to play is as follows:

1. Jump jetting
2. Falling
3. Swimming
4. Running (known internally as the **stand pose**)
5. Crouching
6. Prone
7. Sprinting

Disabling jump jetting

During a game we may no longer want to allow a player to jump jet. Perhaps they have run out of fuel or they have removed the device that allowed them to jump jet. To allow or disallow jump jetting for a specific player, we call the following `Player` class method on the server:

```
Player.allowJetJumping( allow );
```

In the previous code, the `allow` parameter is set to `true` to allow a player to jump jet, and to `false` for not allowing him to jump jet at all.

More control over the jump jet

The `PlayerData Datablock` instance has some additional properties to fine tune a player's jump jet capability. The first is the `jetMaxJumpSpeed` property. This property determines the maximum vertical speed at which the player may use their jump jet. If the player is moving upwards faster than this, then they may not engage their jump jet.

The second is the `jetMinJumpSpeed` property. This property is the minimum vertical speed of the player before a speed multiplier is applied. If the player's vertical speed is between `jetMinJumpSpeed` and `jetMaxJumpSpeed`, the applied jump jet speed is scaled up by a relative amount. This helps ensure that the jump jet will always make the player move faster than their current speed, even if the player's current vertical speed is the result of some other event (such as being thrown by an explosion).

See also

> ▸ *How to have a sprinting player use up energy*

Adjusting the fire spread of a weapon

Some ranged weapons (those that fire a projectile) are more accurate than others. Of the weapons included in the Torque 3D templates, the pistol is very accurate while the assault rifle has some bullet trajectory drift. This is known as **projectile spread**. In this recipe we will learn how to set up projectile spread of a projectile weapon.

How to do it...

Start by making sure the `ShapeBaseImageData Datablock` instance of your projectile weapon has its `class` property set to `WeaponImage`. This gives the weapon access to Torque 3D's standard weapon handling methods.

The next step is to add the `projectileSpread` dynamic property to your weapon's `Datablock` instance and give it a value greater than zero to introduce some spread. The *Lurker* weapon included with the Torque 3D templates is set up as follows:

```
datablock ShapeBaseImageData (LurkerWeaponImage)
{
    // Add the WeaponImage namespace as a parent, WeaponImage
    // namespace provides some hooks into the inventory system.
    class = "WeaponImage";

    ...

    projectileSpread = "0.005";

    ...
};
```

How it works...

When a `ShapeBaseImageData` weapon is fired its `onFire()` method is called. The `WeaponImage` namespace already handles most cases, so it is a convenient class to have our `ShapeBaseImageData` inherit from.

The `WeaponImage::onFire()` method supports the idea of a projectile spread, which is set using the dynamic `projectileSpread` property on the `ShapeBaseImageData` `Datablock` instance. When `projectileSpread` is greater than zero, drift of a projectile is calculated as a random point within a unit circle (a value of zero keeps the projectile on a perfect path at the center of this drift circle). The `projectileSpread` property is then used as a multiplier against the calculated spread to give the final trajectory for the projectile. The actual spread calculation looks like the following:

```
if (%this.projectileSpread)
{
    // We'll need to "skew" this projectile a little bit.
    // We start by getting the straight ahead aiming point
    // of the gun
    %vec = %obj.getMuzzleVector(%slot);

    // Then we'll create a spread matrix by randomly generating
    // x, y, and z points in a circle
    %matrix = "";
    for(%j = 0; %j < 3; %j++)
        %matrix = %matrix @ (getRandom() - 0.5) * 2 * 3.1415926
                  * %this.projectileSpread @ " ";
    %mat = MatrixCreateFromEuler(%matrix);
```

```
        // Which we'll use to alter the projectile's initial
        // vector with
        %muzzleVector = MatrixMulVector(%mat, %vec);
    }
    else
    {
        // Weapon projectile doesn't have a spread factor so
        // we fire it using the straight ahead aiming point of
        // the gun
        %muzzleVector = %obj.getMuzzleVector(%slot);
    }
```

Changing the number of shots fired from a weapon

Some ranged weapons fire more than one projectile at once. A shotgun is a good example of this. In this recipe, we will learn how to set up a projectile weapon to fire multiple projectiles at once.

How to do it...

Start by making sure the `ShapeBaseImageData Datablock` instance of your projectile weapon has its `class` property set to `WeaponImage`. This gives the weapon access to Torque 3D's standard weapon handling methods.

The next step is to add the `projectileNum` dynamic property to `Datablock` of your weapon and give it a value greater than 1. This property represents the number of projectiles fired per shot.

How it works...

When a `ShapeBaseImageData` weapon is fired its `onFire()` method is called. The `WeaponImage` namespace already handles most cases so it is a convenient class to have our `ShapeBaseImageData` inherit from.

The `WeaponImage::onFire()` method supports the idea of multiple projectiles per shot, which is set up using the dynamic `projectileNum` property on the `ShapeBaseImageData` `Datablock`. The value of `projectileNum` is the number of projectiles fired per shot.

When using a weapon that fires multiple projectiles, we usually also set a projectile spread as described in the *Adjusting the fire spread of a weapon* recipe. Without some spread set, all of the projectiles would have the same trajectory down the center. The following image shows a shotgun from the *GarageGames Soldier Weapons Art Pack* after firing a single shot against a wall in the `FPS Tutorial` template. The shotgun has its `projectileNum` property set to `5`, and its `projectileSpread` property set to `0.02`.

See also

▸ *Adjusting the fire spread of a weapon*

Making a weapon use energy rather than ammo

All of the weapons that are included in the Torque 3D templates are ammunition-based. However, Torque 3D allows a weapon to instead draw from the player's energy pool and fire until that rechargeable pool is depleted. In this recipe, we will learn how to set up a weapon to make use of a player's energy pool.

Getting ready

We will be making TorqueScript changes in a project based on the Torque 3D `Full` template using the `Empty Terrain` level. If you haven't already, use the Torque Project Manager (`Project Manager.exe`) to create a new project from the `Full` template. It will be found under the `My Projects` directory. Then start up your favorite script editor, such as Torsion, and let's get going!

How to do it...

We are going to modify `Datablock` of the Lurker weapon to switch it over to use energy rather than ammunition. We will also need to modify the standard weapon scripts to take energy into account. This is done as follows:

1. Open the `art/datablocks/weapons/Lurker.cs` file in your text editor.

2. Find the `LurkerWeaponImage Datablock` instance and just below the `class` property being set, add the following code:

    ```
    . . .
        // Add the WeaponImage namespace as a parent, WeaponImage
        // namespace provides some hooks into the inventory system.
        class = "WeaponImage";
        className = "WeaponImage";

        // Set up the weapon to use energy
        usesEnergy = true;
        minEnergy = 20;
    . . .
    ```

3. Find the weapon's state `7` (named `NoAmmo`) and make the following changes:

    ```
    . . .
        // No ammo in the weapon, just idle until something
        // shows up. Play the dry fire sound if the trigger is
        // pulled.
        stateName[7]                      = "NoAmmo";
        stateTransitionGeneric0In[7]      = "SprintEnter";
        stateTransitionOnMotion[7]        = "NoAmmoMotion";
        // Change the transition state from ReloadClip to Ready
        stateTransitionOnAmmo[7]          = "Ready";
        stateTimeoutValue[7]              = 0.1;
        // Comment out this script call as we don't use clips
        //stateScript[7]                    = "onClipEmpty";
        stateSequence[7]                  = "idle";
        stateScaleAnimation[7]            = false;
        stateScaleAnimationFP[7]          = false;
        // Comment out this state transition to stay here
        //until
        // we have enough energy, even if the user attempts
        // to fire the weapon.
        //stateTransitionOnTriggerDown[7]  = "DryFire";
    . . .
    ```

4. Save the file.

5. Open `scripts/server/weapon.cs` in a text editor and make the following change to the `WeaponImage::onFire()` method to check if the weapon uses energy:

```
function WeaponImage::onFire(%this, %obj, %slot)
{
    //echo("\c4WeaponImage::onFire( "@%this.getName()@",
           "@%obj.client.nameBase@", "@%slot@" )");

    // Make sure we have valid data
    if (!isObject(%this.projectile))
    {
        error("WeaponImage::onFire() - Invalid projectile
               datablock");
        return;
    }

    // Decrement inventory ammo. The image's ammo state is
    // updated automatically by the ammo inventory hooks.
    // If the weapon uses energy then don't make any
    // ammo changes.
    if ( !%this.infiniteAmmo && !%this.usesEnergy )
        %obj.decInventory(%this.ammo, 1);

    // Get the player's velocity, we'll then add it to that of
    // the projectile
    %objectVelocity = %obj.getVelocity();
    . . .



}
```

6. Save the file.

7. Start our `Full` template game and load the `Empty Terrain` level.

8. Start firing the **Lurker** assault rifle. The weapon will continue to fire until the player runs out of energy. When enough energy has recharged in the player's energy pool, the weapon will fire again.

How it works...

To make a `ShapeBaseImageData` weapon draw from the mounted object's (usually the player) energy pool instead of ammunition, we set its `usesEnergy` property to `true`.

With this property set, we also need to determine how much energy the weapon will drain from the energy pool. This is done by setting `stateEnergyDrain[]` property of any weapon state to a value greater than zero. In our previous example, we set `stateEnergyDrain[5]` property of the `Fire` state to `30.0` units per second. So long as the weapon is in this state, energy will be drained.

Another important `ShapeBaseImageData` property is `minEnergy`, which is set to a value of `20` in the previous example. Any time the player's energy pool drops below this value while using an energy-based weapon, the state machine of that weapon will be considered out of ammunition. In our example this triggers the `NoAmmo` state. We modified the regular `NoAmmo` state of the Lurker to just transition back to the `Ready` state when enough energy becomes available rather than attempt to reload a clip (which didn't make sense for an energy-based weapon).

The final change we made was to the standard `WeaponImage::onFire()` method. This method is not aware of energy-based weapons. To make it work with our modified Lurker, we added an energy check and left the ammunition counts alone if we're using energy.

For more information on working with the `Player` class's energy pool, please see the *How to have a sprinting player use up energy* recipe. This includes information on how to set the size of the energy pool, and how to set its recharge rate.

See also

▶   *How to have a sprinting player use up energy*

Finding objects in range

Over the course of a game we often need to know what objects are around a particular point in space. Some examples are to determine the number of bad guys immediately around the player, to find the number of zombies near a grenade explosion, or to discover the number of skeletons to throw back from a Gust of Wind spell. In this recipe, we will learn how to perform a radial search of Torque 3D's scene graph for objects of interest.

How to do it...

The following code snippet performs a search for all the `ShapeBase` objects within five meters of a given position in the world:

```
echo("Starting search...");

%worldPos = "0 0 241";
initContainerRadiusSearch(%worldPos, 5,
                    $TypeMasks::ShapeBaseObjectType);
```

```
%obj = containerSearchNext();
while(%obj != 0)
{
    echo("Found object: " @ %obj.getId());

    %obj = containerSearchNext();
}


echo("Finished search.");
```

The console output will look similar to the following screenshot:

```
Starting search...
Found object: 4279
Found object: 4290
Found object: 4289
Finished search.
```

How it works...

The `initContainerRadiusSearch()` function is used to start looking for objects of a particular type within a given volume in the scene. This function has the following form:

```
initContainerRadiusSearch( position, radius, types,
                           [clientSide] );
```

In the previous code, the `position` parameter is the origin of the search in the world, the `radius` parameter is the search radius from the given position, the `types` parameter is a type mask representing the types of objects to look for, and the optional `clientSide` parameter is `true` if the search should be performed using the client-side scene graph, or `false` if the search is done with the server-side scene graph. The `clientSide` parameter defaults to `false`, so our previous example is using the server-side scene graph for its search.

The types of objects that may be searched for are listed in the *Clicking on an object in the scene (client-side)* recipe in *Chapter 4, Camera and Mouse Controls*, and we may combine multiple `TypeMasks` instances together when performing a search. For example, to search for both `Player` and `Corpse` objects you would combine the `TypeMasks` instances like the following:

```
%types = $TypeMasks::PlayerObjectType |
         $TypeMasks::CorpseObjectType;
```

The `initContainerRadiusSearch()` function does not actually return any objects found. To retrieve any found objects from the search we use the `containerSearchNext()` function, which has the following form:

```
%obj = containerSearchNext(  [clientSide] );
```

In the previous code, the optional `clientSide` parameter is `true` if this is a client-side scene graph search and `false` if this is a server-side scene graph search. This parameter should match that used with the `initContainerRadiusSearch()` function. If an object has been found, it is returned by `containerSearchNext()`. If there are no more objects found within the search volume, a zero is returned.

There's more...

Let's continue our discussion about scene graph searching.

Obtaining the distance to a found object

If an object was found using the `containerSearchNext()` function, the following function is a shortcut to obtain that object's distance from the search's origin:

```
%distance = containerSearchCurrDist( [clientSide] );
```

In the previous code, the optional `clientSide` parameter is the same as discussed with `containerSearchNext()` earlier. The `containerSearchCurrDist()` function returns the distance from the search origin to the origin of world bounds of the found object (which may not be the same as the actual position of the object in the world).

Obtaining the distance to the closest point to a found object

If an object was found using the `containerSearchNext()` function, the following function is a shortcut to obtain that distance of the object from its closest point to the origin of search:

```
%distance = containerSearchCurrRadiusDist( [clientSide] );
```

In the previous code, the optional `clientSide` parameter is the same as discussed with `containerSearchNext()` earlier. The `containerSearchCurrRadiusDist()` function returns the distance from the search origin to the closest side of the world aligned bounds of the found object.

Searching for all objects of a particular type

If we are interested in finding all objects of a given `TypeMasks` instance regardless of where they are in the world, we may use the following function:

```
initContainerTypeSearch( types, [clientSide] );
```

In the previous code, both the `types` and optional `clientSide` parameters are the same as for the `initContainerRadiusSearch()` function described previously. After calling the `initContainerTypeSearch()` function, we use the same `containerNextSearch()` function to step through the internal list of objects.

A very quick search test

Sometimes we just wish to know if there are any objects of a particular type within a search volume without worrying about the objects themselves. In this case we may use the following function:

```
%isEmpty = containerBoxEmpty( types, position, xRadius,
                              yRadius, zRadius,
                              [clientSide] );
```

In the previous code, the `types`, `position`, and optional `clientSide` parameters are the same as for the `initContainerRadiusSearch()` function described previously. The `containerBoxEmpty()` function uses a world aligned box for its search algorithm, rather than a sphere of the other functions. The `xRadius`, `yRadius`, and `zRadius` parameters are the half lengths of each side of the search box, with the search box centered over the given `position` parameter.

If there are *no* objects of the requested type within the defined world aligned box, this function returns `true`. Otherwise, if any objects of the requested type have been found, this function returns `false`.

Performing a ray cast search of the scene graph

In addition to the container type searches discussed in the previous section, we often need to know if a ray that is cast from a particular spot in the world, and out to a particular direction, hits any objects. This could be for a line of sight test, or to check for a collision, for example.

To perform a ray cast we may use the `containerRayCast()` function. This function is discussed in detail, in the *Clicking on an object in the scene (client-side)* and *Clicking on an object in the scene (server-side)* recipes in *Chapter 4, Camera and Mouse Controls*.

See also

  ▸   *Clicking on an object in the scene (client-side)* in *Chapter 4, Camera and Mouse Controls*

Using the message producer/ consumer system

Most games generate events that require some form of action. For example, a player has entered an area and an alarm should sound, or a pig has run out of food and the farmer needs to refill the trough. Rather than hardcode these actions to each event, it is preferred that objects listen for the event messages they are interested in and then act accordingly. This decouples the whole process and makes it much easier to add and remove event message responders. In this recipe, we will learn how to generate an event message and have objects listen for that message.

Getting ready

We will be making TorqueScript changes and working with the *World Editor* in a project based on the Torque 3D `FPS Tutorial` template, and try them out using the `China Town Day` level. If you haven't already, use the Torque Project Manager (`Project Manager.exe`) to create a new project from the `FPS Tutorial` template. It will be found under the `My Projects` directory. Then start our new `FPS Tutorial` game and load the `China Town Day` level.

How to do it...

We are going to create a trigger volume that broadcasts an event message when the player enters it, and a couple of particle effects that will respond to the message. We will then test everything out by having the player run through the trigger volume.

1. Press *F11* to open the *World Editor*. As we want to work with objects in the scene, the *Object Editor* should be selected (*F1* or by using the **Editors** menu).

2. Go to the **Library** tab of the *Object Editor*.

3. Click on the **Level** tab.

4. Double-click on **Level | Trigger** to add a new `Trigger` class instance to the scene.

5. Use the axis gizmo to move the trigger object between the yellow car and the open, ornamental gates in the level. Scale the trigger to fill the space as shown in the following screenshot:

6. From the *property inspector* find the trigger's **name** property and enter a name of PlayerTrigger.

7. Go to the **Scene** tab of the *Object Editor*. Click on the folder icon to the right-hand side of the tabs to add a new SimGroup object to the scene tree.

8. Right-click on this new SimGroup object and choose the **Rename** operation. Give the object a name of TriggerEffectGroup and press *Enter*.

9. We want our next two objects to be created as children of the `TriggerEffectGroup` group. Right-click on the group again and choose the **Add New Objects Here** operation. The folder icon for the group will change from gray to yellow.

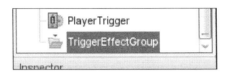

10. We will create our first particle effect. Go to the **Library** tab of the *Object Editor*. Click on the **Level** tab under it.

11. Double-click on **Environment | Particle Emitter** to add a new `ParticleEmitterNode` instance to the scene. This will open the **Create Object: ParticleEmitterNode** dialog box.

12. In the **Object Name** field of the dialog box enter `TriggerEffect1`.

13. Click on the **datablock** drop-down menu of dialog box and select the `DefaultEmitterNodeData Datablock` instance.

14. Click on the **Particle data** drop-down menu of dialog box and select the `RocketDebrisTrailEmitter Datablock` instance. Please refer to the following screenshot:

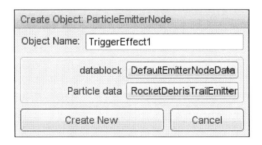

15. Click on the **Create New** button of dialog box to create the new `ParticleEmitterNode` object instance and add it to the scene under the `TriggerEffectGroup` group.

16. Use the axis gizmo to place this particle emitter just above the manhole cover that is beside the yellow car as shown in the next screenshot:

17. From the *property inspector* find the emitter's `class` property, enter a value of `TriggerEffectClass` and press *Enter*.

18. We don't want the emitter to be on right now, so find the emitter's `active` property in the *property inspector* and make sure it is unchecked.

19. We will create our second particle effect. Go back to the **Level** tab in the *Object Editor* and double-click on **Environment | Particle Emitter** to add a new `ParticleEmitterNode` instance to the scene. This will open the **Create Object: ParticleEmitterNode** dialog box as shown in the following screenshot.

20. In the **Object Name** field of dialog box enter `TriggerEffect2`.

21. Click on the `datablock` drop-down menu of dialog box and select the `DefaultEmitterNodeData Datablock` instance.

22. Click on the **Particle data** drop-down menu of dialog box and select the `GLWaterExpSparkEmitter Datablock` instance.

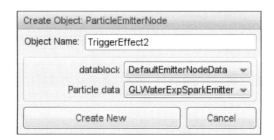

23. Click on the **Create New** button of dialog box to create the new **ParticleEmitterNode** object instance and add it to the scene under the **TriggerEffectGroup** group.

24. Use the axis gizmo to place this particle emitter just below the streetlamp that is beside the yellow car. Rotate the emitter so it faces down towards the street as shown in the next screenshot:

25. From the *property inspector* find the emitter's `class` property, enter a value of `TriggerEffectClass` and press *Enter*.

26. We don't want the emitter to be on right now, so find the emitter's `active` property in the *property inspector* and make sure it is unchecked.

27. Save the level from the **File** menu and close Torque 3D. We will now move on to the TorqueScript changes. We will come back to Torque 3D and the *World Editor* later on.

28. Open `scripts/server/game.cs` in a text editor, such as Torsion, and add the following TorqueScript code to the bottom of the file:

```
// This function is called from //GameCore::onMissionLoaded() to
// set everything up.
function createMessageQueues()
{
    // Create the event manager we will use for
    // our messages.
    new EventManager(MissionEvents)
    {
```

```
            queue = "MissionEventQueue";
        };

        // Add the event manager to the MissionCleanup group
        // so it will automatically be deleted when the
        //mission is unloaded.
        MissionCleanup.add(MissionEvents);

        // Register the events related to the player trigger
        //area
        MissionEvents.registerEvent("PlayerEnterEvent");
        MissionEvents.registerEvent("PlayerLeaveEvent");

        // Set up our particle emitters from the mission here.
        // Normally we would want to do this in an object's
        //onAdd() callback or something similar.
        //Unfortunately, ParticleEmitterNodes don't support
        //any callbacks //when they are created. That is why
        //we have them under a SimGroup in the mission for
        //easy access without needing to know their names.
        %count = TriggerEffectGroup.getCount();
        for(%i=0; %i<%count; %i++)
        {
            %obj = TriggerEffectGroup.getObject(%i);
            MissionEvents.subscribe(%obj, "PlayerEnterEvent");
            MissionEvents.subscribe(%obj, "PlayerLeaveEvent");
        }
}

// Event message callback when a player enters the //trigger area
function TriggerEffectClass::onPlayerEnterEvent(%this, %data)
{
    // Activate the particle effect
    %this.setActive(true);

    // Reset the particle emitter node's datablock.  This
    // ensures that any one-time particle effects start //over.
    %this.setEmitterDataBlock(%this.emitter);
}

// Event message callback when a player leaves the //trigger area
function TriggerEffectClass::onPlayerLeaveEvent(%this, %data)
{
    // Disable the particle effect
    %this.setActive(false);
}
```

29. Save the file.

30. Open `scripts/server/gameCore.cs` in a text editor. Make the following changes to the `GameCore::onMissionLoaded()` method:

```
function GameCore::onMissionLoaded(%game)
{
    //echo (%game @"\c4 -> "@ %game.class @" ->
    //GameCore::onMissionLoaded");

    //set up the game and game variables
    %game.initGameVars(%game);

    $Game::Duration = %game.duration;
    $Game::EndGameScore = %game.endgameScore;
    $Game::EndGamePause = %game.endgamePause;

    physicsStartSimulation( "server" );

    // Set up the event messaging
    createMessageQueues();

    if($Pref::Server::MinPlayers <= 1)
        %game.startGame();

}
```

31. Save the file.

32. Start our `FPS Tutorial` game again and load the `China Town Day` level.

33. Press *F11* to open the *World Editor*. Make sure the *Object Editor* is active (*F1* or by using the **Editors** menu).

34. Scroll down the **Scene Tree** window under the **Scene** tab until you find the `PlayerTrigger` object and click on it to select it.

35. Using the *property inspector* find the `enterCommand` property of the trigger. Click on the text field beside this property to open the **Text Pad** dialog box.

36. Enter the following into the **Text Pad** dialog box:

```
MissionEvents.postEvent("PlayerEnterEvent");
```

37. Click on the **OK** button of the **Text Pad** dialog box.

38. Now find the trigger's `leaveCommand` property. Click on the text field beside it to open the **Text Pad** dialog box and enter the following text:

```
MissionEvents.postEvent("PlayerLeaveEvent");
```

39. Click on the **OK** button of the **Text Pad** dialog box.

40. Save the level from the **File** menu.

41. Press *F11* to close the *World Editor*.

42. Run the soldier into the trigger area to see the sparks fly from the streetlamp and smoke come from the manhole cover. So long as the player is within the trigger volume, the particle effects will continue.

43. Run the soldier out of the trigger volume to stop the particle effects. Re-enter the volume to start the particle effects again.

How it works...

Using Torque 3D's event messaging system allows us to separate cause from effect. In our previous example, the cause is a player entering a trigger volume. When this event occurs, a message is broadcast to any object that is listening. In our example, the listeners are a couple of particle effect objects that activate themselves. When the player leaves the trigger's volume, a second message is broadcast that the particle effects respond to by deactivating themselves.

By decoupling cause from effect, it makes it very easy to modify what happens in response to the broadcast messages. We could, for example, add a sound emitter to the level that also listens for the trigger's messages and sounds an alarm. Adding effects like these doesn't require any modification to the trigger itself, whose sole job is to watch for the player.

The messaging system begins by creating an instance of the `EventManager` class. When creating an `EventManager` instance you give it the name of a message queue. Our example `EventManager` instance named `MissionEvents` defines its queue as `MissionEventQueue`. This name may be used by other objects that wish to work with the message queue.

Now that the manager has been created, we may define the events that other objects may subscribe to. We use the `registerEvent()` method to define events, which has the following form:

```
result = EventManager.registerEvent( event );
```

In the previous code, the `event` parameter is a text string with the name of the event. The `registerEvent()` method returns `true` if the event name hasn't already been registered. Our previous example registers two events named `PlayerEnterEvent` and `PlayerLeaveEvent`.

We may also unregister an event at any time with the following method:

```
EventManager.unregisterEvent( event );
```

In the previous code, the `event` parameter is the name of the event to unregister. Registered events are automatically unregistered when the `EventManager` instance is destroyed. Manually removing an event also unsubscribes all listeners from the event.

We may also discover if an event has already been registered with the following method:

```
result = EventManager.isRegisteredEvent( event );
```

In the previous code, the `event` parameter is the name of the event to search for. This method returns `true` if the event has been registered with this `EventManager` instance.

A game could have multiple `EventManager` instances defined to organize the events by some appropriate categories. We could create one manager to handle player generated events, one that handles time-based events, and another that handles AI generated events, for example. It all depends on what makes sense for our game.

With one or more event registered with an `EventManager` instance we may now add listeners to the event. We use the `subscribe()` method to attach listeners to an event, which has a form of:

```
result = EventManager.subscribe( listener, event,
                                 [callback] );
```

In the previous code, the `listener` parameter is a `SimObject` instance that will receive a callback when the event message is broadcast, the `event` parameter is the name of the event to listen for, and the optional `callback` parameter is the name of the callback to use with this listener. The `subscribe()` method returns `true` if the listener `SimObject` is successfully subscribed to the event. If the `callback` parameter is not provided, the name of the callback method used is the event's name with the word "on" added as a prefix. For example, our registered `PlayerEnterEvent` will have a default callback name of `onPlayerEnterEvent()`. Defining a custom listener callback for an event allows for the same callback method to be used by multiple events.

We may also unsubscribe from an event with the following method:

```
EventManager.remove( listener, event );
```

In the previous code, the `listener` parameter is the `SimObject` instance to remove from the event, and the `event` parameter is the name of the event.

Any time after an event has been registered with an `EventManager` instance, we may trigger the event with the following method:

```
result = EventManager.postEvent( event, [data] );
```

In the previous code, the `event` parameter is the name of the event, and the optional `data` parameter is a text string that will be passed along to all listeners. This method returns `true` if the event was successfully triggered.

When an event message is triggered all listeners of the event will receive a callback. The callback method will either be the name of the event with the word "on" added as a prefix, or the optional listener-specific callback name passed through the `EventManager` `subscribe()` method. Using the `PlayerEnterEvent` instance from our previous example, and assuming a listener has not passed-in a custom callback name when subscribing, the callback method would be as follows:

```
Function SimObject::onPlayerEnterEvent(%this, %data)
{
    // Work with the event message here
    ...
}
```

If no data was passed along to the `postEvent()` method that generated the event message, the `%data` parameter above will be an empty string.

There's more...

Let's continue our discussion of working with event messages.

Removing a listener from all event messages

We may want to remove a listener from all of its subscribed events, such as just before deleting a listener object. We could call `EventManager.remove()` for each subscribed event, but then we would have to manually keep track of each event the listener has subscribed to. An alternative is the following method:

```
EventManager.removeAll( listener );
```

In the previous code, the `listener` parameter is the `SimObject` instance to remove from all events. Now we only need to call this method on each `EventManager` a listener object may have subscribed to any time we wish to clean ourselves up.

Peeking into an EventManager instance

While working on a game, it can be handy to be able to see what events are currently registered on an `EventManager` instance, and what `SimObject` instances are listening to each event. Torque 3D provides the following method that will output a list of all events to the console for the given `EventManager` instance:

```
EventManager.dumpEvents();
```

Now with the name of each event, the following method will output a list of all listeners for a given event and `EventManager` instance to the console:

```
EventManager.dumpSubscribers( event );
```

In the previous code, the `event` parameter is the name of the event to retrieve.

Index

DragonAlarm sound emitter 213
dropAnimateMS property 248
drops and splashes
  sprite sheet for 247, 248
dropSize property 247
dynamic property 35

E

EchoService::onLine() method 305
elevation parameter 262
Empty Terrain level 28, 208, 236, 295, 326
enterCommand property 345
eventID parameter 62
EventManager instance 349
EventManager.remove() 348
event messages
  listener, removing 348
event parameter 347, 348
events
  generating, TimeOfDay object used 255-260
  ScatterSky class for night, setting up 260
  time of day, modifying 261, 262
event, trigerring
  on sound playback 230-232
exclude parameter 153
Explosion class 232
expression parameter 104
eyeMat, constant 185
eyePos, constant 185
eyePosWorld, constant 185, 203

F

F10 key 95
fadeColor property 254
filePath parameter 205
File Select button 127
findObjectByInternalName() 29
fire spread, weapon
  adjusting 329, 330
fog
  about 69
  adding, to level 69-71
  and ScatterSky class 71
fogAtmosphereHeight property 69-71
fogColor, constant 185, 203

fogColor property 70
fogData, constant 185, 203
fogDensityOffset property 69, 70
fogDensity property 69, 70
followCam property 250
foreach$() function 15, 17, 23
foreach$() method 17
foreach() function 23, 287
foreach() method 24
foreach() operator 287
Forest Editor 68
forest metric 105
found object
  distance, obtaining to 337
  to closet point, distance obtaining to 337
fps 102
FPS (Frame Per Second) camera control 140
fps gfx string 104
fps metric 105
FPS Tutorial game 102, 231
FPS Tutorial template 211
frames per second. *See* fps
Full template 258
functionName parameter 52, 152
function parameter 62
functions
  scheduling 61, 63

G

GameConnection::initialControlSet()
        method 219, 220, 226
GameConnection object 277
GameConnection::onConnect() method 276
GameCore::onMissionLoaded()
        method 257, 259
game objects
  game objectslist, displaying 110, 111
gameplay 321
game-specific metrics
  game-specific metricscreating 109
GameTSCtrl class 113, 124
getBlogsFeed() method 316
getBlogTitles() method 316
getInternalName() method 36
getLevelInfo() function 122

Thank you for buying
Torque 3D Game Development Cookbook

About Packt Publishing

Packt, pronounced 'packed', published its first book "*Mastering phpMyAdmin for Effective MySQL Management*" in April 2004 and subsequently continued to specialize in publishing highly focused books on specific technologies and solutions.

Our books and publications share the experiences of your fellow IT professionals in adapting and customizing today's systems, applications, and frameworks. Our solution based books give you the knowledge and power to customize the software and technologies you're using to get the job done. Packt books are more specific and less general than the IT books you have seen in the past. Our unique business model allows us to bring you more focused information, giving you more of what you need to know, and less of what you don't.

Packt is a modern, yet unique publishing company, which focuses on producing quality, cutting-edge books for communities of developers, administrators, and newbies alike. For more information, please visit our website: www.packtpub.com.

Writing for Packt

We welcome all inquiries from people who are interested in authoring. Book proposals should be sent to author@packtpub.com. If your book idea is still at an early stage and you would like to discuss it first before writing a formal book proposal, contact us; one of our commissioning editors will get in touch with you.

We're not just looking for published authors; if you have strong technical skills but no writing experience, our experienced editors can help you develop a writing career, or simply get some additional reward for your expertise.

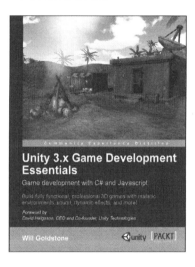

Unreal Development Kit Game Programming with UnrealScript: Beginner's Guide

ISBN: 978-1-849691-92-5   Paperback: 466 pages

Create games beyond your imagination with the Unreal Development Kit

1. Dive into game programming with UnrealScript by creating a working example game

2. Learn how the Unreal Development Kit is organized and how to quickly set up your own projects

3. Recognize and fix crashes and other errors that come up during a game's development

Unreal Development Kit Game Design Cookbook

ISBN: 978-1-849691-80-2   Paperback: 544 pages

Over 100 recepies to accelerate the process of learning game design with UDK

1. An intermediate, fast-paced UDK guide for game artists

2. The quickest way to face the challenges of game design with UDK

3. All the necessary steps to get your artwork up and running in game

Please check **www.PacktPub.com** for information on our titles